W9-BHM-934

# The
# Rocky Mountain Wonderland

A WILD GARDEN IN THE WONDERLAND
On the Eastern Boundary-Line of the Rocky Mountain National Park

# The Rocky Mountain Wonderland

By
Enos A. Mills

With Illustrations from Photographs

Introduction and notes
by James H. Pickering

University of Nebraska Press
Lincoln and London

Introduction and notes copyright © 1991 by
the University of Nebraska Press
All rights reserved
Manufactured in the United States of America

First Bison Book printing: 1991
Most recent printing indicated by the last digit below:
10    9    8    7    6    5    4    3    2    1

Library of Congress Cataloging-in-Publication Data
Mills, Enos Abijah, 1870–1922.
The Rocky Mountain wonderland / by Enos A. Mills: with illustrations
from photographs; introduction and notes by James H. Pickering.
p.   cm.
Reprint, with new introd. Originally published: Boston: Houghton Mif-
flin, 1915.
Includes index.
ISBN 0-8032-8173-0 (pa only)
1. Rocky Mountain National Park (Colo.)—History.    2. Mills, Enos
Abijah, 1870–1922.    I. Pickering, James H.    II. Title.
F782.R59M52    1991
917.88'69—dc20
90-21151 CIP

This Bison Book reproduces the original 1915 edition published by
Houghton Mifflin Company. To this edition an introduction with two
photographs and notes for the entire volume have been added.

♾

To
George Horace Lorimer

# Contents

# Illustrations

# Illustrations

Except as otherwise noted the illustrations are
from photographs by the author.

# Introduction
## By James H. Pickering

"My chief aim in life is to arouse interest in the
outdoors."
— Enos A. Mills (ca. 1917)

The afternoon of September 4, 1915, was a festive holiday
throughout the Estes Park region. All that morning a steady
stream of cars, carriages, wagons, and horses made their way
through Estes Park village and out along Fall River Road to the
western end of Horseshoe Park. There, near the Lawn Lake trail-
head, a banner strung between two pines, flanked by Colorado
flags, announced the spot where the formal ceremonies dedicating Rocky Mountain National Park were to take place. The crowd
of visitors—estimated at between two and three thousand—came
from Denver, Loveland, Greeley, Boulder, Fort Collins, and other
towns along the Front Range, as well as from Estes Park and its
surrounding cottages and hotels. Early arrivers were treated to
music by a band from Fort Collins and to hot coffee provided by
the Estes Park Women's Club. At 2:00 P.M. the formal ceremonies
began with a chorus of "America the Beautiful" sung by school-
children. Then Enos Mills, in his role as master of ceremonies, approached the impromptu rostrum to read congratulatory mes-
sages from President Woodrow Wilson and Secretary of the
Interior Franklin K. Lane and introduce the attending dignitaries
and speakers.[1] As he did so clouds, thunder, and a light rain descended upon Horseshoe Park. Fortunately, by the time the third
speaker, Governor George Carlson, had concluded his remarks,
"the clouds parted . . . and the sun of Colorado broke forth in
rain-tinged splendor from across the newly laid snow on Longs
Peak and made a new fairyland of the dazzling land of bewilder-
ment."[2]

No amount of unpredictable weather, however, could detract from the significance of the occasion or dampen the spirits of Enos Mills and his fellow participants. "This was," as Frank Lundy Webster of the *Denver Post* reminded his readers, "Enos Mills day in Estes Park . . . his dream of years finally brought to reality." Mills, cheered by the crowd as the "Father of Rocky Mountain National Park,"[3] responded in kind. "This is," he told his audience, "the proudest moment of my life. I have lived to see the realization of a great dream come true. It means great things for Colorado and for the nation."[4] He continued: "In years to come when I am asleep forever beneath the pines, thousands of families will find rest and hope in this park, and on through the years others will come and be happy in the splendid scenes that I helped to save for them."[5] On this day and in this place Enos Mills stood at the very pinnacle of his public career. Success, however, had not been without its costs. If, as he wrote later, the six-year campaign for the establishment of Rocky Mountain National Park was "the achievement of my life," it was also "the most strenuous and growth-compelling occupation that I have ever followed."[6]

What made this achievement all the more remarkable was the unpromising nature of Mills's own beginnings. Though associated throughout most of his adult life with the mountain wilderness of Colorado, Enos Abijah Mills (1870–1922) was born and raised on a farm in Kansas, some five miles south of the Linn County town of Pleasanton. Mills speaks very little in his writings about the details of his early life,[7] perhaps because his sick and weakly constitution (the result of a digestive problem that took years to overcome) rendered the memories of those years far from pleasant. Unsuited to the tasks and responsibilities of farm life, Mills remained in Kansas only until 1884. That year, at the age of fourteen, after the family doctor announced that he would probably not live if he stayed at home,[8] Enos Mills made his way alone via Kansas City and Denver to Estes Park, a small, relatively unknown summer resort community northwest of Denver, nestled among the scenery of Colorado's Front Range.

Though he tended to exaggerate the extent of his isolation during the early years in Colorado,[9] the fact is that from age fourteen on Enos Mills was left pretty much on his own. Whatever he could achieve in the way of health, education, and career would be largely up to him. That, in time, he achieved all three—and became in the process one of the better known men of his generation—speaks directly to the energetic determination, the active and acquisitive intelligence, the uncompromising individualism, and the Protestant discipline and work ethic that formed the bedrock of Enos Mills's character.

Having landed in Colorado, Enos Mills set out at once to make the most of his new opportunities. His whereabouts during the winter of 1884–85 are not entirely clear, but by the following spring he was back in Estes Park, working for Elkanah Lamb and his son Carlyle at Longs Peak House, a small ranch-resort some nine miles south of the hamlet of Estes Park. To a teenage boy, particularly one with an active imagination, the world in which the Lambs lived no doubt seemed close to idyllic. Flanked by Longs Peak and its lofty neighbors Mount Meeker and Mount Lady Washington to the southeast and northeast and Twin Sisters Mountain to the east, this high, flower-filled upland valley, teeming with wildlife, was a virtually unspoiled and unexplored wilderness of closely gathered lodgepole pine forests intermixed with stands of aspen and willow. Here were to be found lodges of active beaver, as well as deer, mountain lions, big-horn sheep, bears, martens, foxes, chipmunks, rabbits, and chattering pine squirrels, together with every known variety of mountain bird. It was a spot ready-made for pioneers and adventuring.

Late that summer, on a parcel of land directly to the east of the Lamb's house on the lower slope of the Twin Sisters, Mills staked his claim to a share of the region by beginning work on a log-cabin homestead measuring twelve-by-fourteen feet. He also made his first successful climb to the top of 14,256 foot-high Longs Peak, under the careful tutelage of Carlyle Lamb (1862–1958), who had inherited his father's role as premier guide to the peak. In the years that followed, Mills himself would repeat this feat often, in every season and at every hour, some forty times alone and two hundred and fifty-seven times while serving as a guide for others.[10]

Although it was easy enough to find gainful employment in Estes Park during the short and busy summer season, locating a steady winter job that offered decent wages and the possibility for advancement posed a definite problem. Most residents of Estes Park, the Lambs included, moved back to towns on the plains once the tourists departed in the fall. By 1887 Mills had decided that he, too, must cast a wider net. That fall, he traveled north to the sprawling mining town of Butte, Montana, where he secured a job at the Anaconda Copper Company as a tool boy, with the responsibility of making sure that the miners had at their disposal a ready supply of sharp drills. In a potentially dangerous occupation, in which new miners received little or no supervised training and the inexperienced were left to learn as they could, Mills proved to be a quick study. He was soon promoted to miner and then, in turn, to machine driller, compressor operator, night foreman, and plant engineer. In 1890 Mills was offered a front office secretarial position by Butte bank and mining magnate William A. Clark (1839–1925)[11] at a salary of $120 a month, the preparation for which led him to enroll that September in Heald's Business College in San Francisco.

In addition to good wages (some five dollars a day), Butte offered the other thing that the teenage Mills needed most: the opportunity for a good education, or, to put it more accurately in Mills's case, the opportunity for self-education. Mills could learn a great deal about human nature in the masculine mining community of Butte, a raw, wide-open town that boasted dozens of flourishing saloons and brothels as well as (by July 1885) a gas-lit 764-seat Grand Opera House. As preparation for the rest of the world, there were books, and Mills took full advantage of Butte's excellent free public library. Though Mills borrowed and read eclectically, he read well: classical writers like Cervantes, Shakespeare, Scott, Dickens, Macaulay, Thackeray, Byron, Stevenson, Eliot, Tennyson, Hugo, Irving, Emerson, and Whitman; nature writers like Henry David Thoreau, John Burroughs, and (especially after 1889 and their meeting near San Francisco) John Muir; modern progressive thinkers like Darwin, Huxley, Tyndall, Spencer, and Ingersoll. Mills credited his "love of good books" to the influence of his mother, but whatever its source his appetite for reading was insatiable, becoming increasingly more specialized as he focused his attention on the world of nature and the out-of-doors. Eventually, Mills himself would amass a substantial personal library that lined the walls of his cabin study behind Longs Peak Inn. Not surprisingly, this reading influenced both the style and the content of his own subsequent published work, in ways that can be inferred both by the allusions and references he makes and by the steadily improving quality of his prose and literary technique.

Winters spent mining underground in Butte seemed but a small price to pay for the freedom to pursue the summer months largely as he saw fit. Mills initially used this leisure time to explore thoroughly the mountain areas adjacent to his cabin below Longs Peak. Then he began to range more widely: so widely, in fact, that he would eventually claim that "in Alaska, Canada, Mexico, and in every state in the union I have sat by a camp-fire alone."[12] One such journey—a trip to California in the fall of 1889, undertaken at a time when a fire had closed the mines at Butte—proved to be the turning point of his life. There, in December, on a wind-swept beach in San Francisco's Golden Gate Park, Enos Mills "came upon a number of people around a small gray bearded little man who had a hand full of plants which he was explaining. . . ." The man was John Muir (1838–1914), already well known in scientific and naturalist circles, who at the time was doing everything in his power to expose the destruction taking place throughout the Sierras, especially in the Yosemite Valley. Mills waited until the group about Muir dispersed, and then asked him a question "concerning a long-rooted plant that someone had dug from a sand dune."[13] A conversation began, and before long Mills and Muir were walking together through Golden Gate Park. Muir was apparently struck by the freshness and accuracy of the younger man's observations, but he also immediately put his finger on Mills's limitations. "He asked if Mills had systematized his knowledge, if he could write of what he had seen in a manner to make other people believe they had seen it." Mills confessed that he could not, "that his information was in a chaotic state, and that his facility at writing was very slight."[14] In addition, Muir used the occasion to query Mills about his vocation.

The effect of that brief interlude on the beach upon Mills's subsequent career was dramatic. Not only did Muir awaken Mills to the need to remedy his deficiencies as a writer, but, by giving him "a glimpse of a larger field of usefulness,"[15] Muir served as the catalyst for transforming Mills's real, yet largely undirected, appreciation and understanding of nature into a commitment to follow the Scotchman's own emerging program of wilderness preservation. "You have helped me more than all the others," he would write Muir in 1913; "but for you I might never have done anything for scenery."[16] "I owe everything to Muir," Mills added four years later. "If it hadn't been for him I would have been a mere gypsy."[17] Once made, Enos Mills never wavered in his commitment, though it would be another fifteen years before he would begin to devote anything like full attention to the task.

Mills returned to Montana in January 1891 to take up his post with Clark, his future apparently assured. But within weeks Mills had quit his job and left Butte. The decade that followed was a full and varied one. Mills spent time in Yellowstone with a U.S. Geological Survey party; visited Alaska twice; traveled to the Chicago World's Fair in 1893; worked in the mining towns of Ward, Victor, and Cripple Creek, Colorado; and climaxed the decade in June 1900 by setting sail from New York, bound for Southampton in the company of Elkanah Lamb to visit the Paris Exposition, Switzerland, Venice, Florence, Rome, Geneva, London, Scotland, and the English Lake District. This period also saw Mills deliver his first public address, a speech on forestry delivered at Kansas City in the fall of 1895, and make his debut as a paid journalist for the *Denver Times and Republican,* reporting the news of summer visitors to Estes Park. Mills gathered his news (which he sold for a third of a cent per word) by riding among the scattered hotels and guest ranches of the region, talking to anyone willing to talk to him. In the process he also gathered and stored away much of the history and lore of early Estes Park that, combined with information of interest to current tourists, would form the basis for his first published book, *The Story of Estes Park and a Guide Book* (1905).[18]

Writing did not come easily for Mills. His surviving papers contain several labored drafts of early essays on such topics as "Lewis and Clark," "A View of Greece and Turkey," and "Peru When the Incas Ruled." In later years Mills on occasion admitted the difficulties he faced in trying to get his ideas and observations down on paper. "You can't imagine how mentally stupid I was," he told a reporter for the *Kansas City Star*, "and what little idea I had of order and arrangement." As late as 1917, at a time when he had long since become an established author, able to place articles and essays in such big-circulation magazines as *Saturday Evening Post, Atlantic, World's Work, Colliers*, and *Harper's* and in more specialized country, outdoor, and juvenile magazines such as *Craftsman, Country Gentleman, Sunset, Country Life, American Boy*, and *Youth's Companion*, Mills confessed that "writing . . . even now . . . is the hardest sort of work for me." To illustrate the point he told about his early association with George Horace Lorimer, editor of the prestigious *Saturday Evening Post*: "One story that I wrote he sent back with a note, saying he would pay me a certain amount for the story as it was, but if I would cut it in two he would pay just twice the amount."[19] Such remarks and anecdotes, coming as they do from a writer whose literary production was enormous—some sixteen books and several hundred articles and essays, in a span of little more than two decades—serve to underscore the fact that as a writer, as in everything else he achieved, Mills owed his success less to native talent than to determination and hard work.

The winter of 1901–1902, in which he returned once more to the mines of Butte, marked the end of Mills's mining career. That spring, in fulfillment of a long-standing dream, Mills purchased Longs Peak House from the Lambs and embarked on a new career as mountain innkeeper. It was a shrewd investment. Not only was the setting, with its full view of the three-thousand-foot face of Longs Peak, a spectacular one, but the Lamb ranch—which Mills immediately renamed Longs Peak Inn—enjoyed a long-standing reputation as a convenient base of operations for mountaineers on their way to the summit. It was from here, for example, in October 1873 that the redoubtable Englishwoman Isabella Bird (1831–1904), accompanied by the legendary "Rocky Mountain Jim" Nugent, made the journey up the peak that she later recounted with so much gusto in her travel adventure *A Lady's Life in the Rockies* (London, 1879). Some fourteen years later, Lamb's ranch was also the point of departure for Frederick H. Chapin (1852–1900) of Connecticut, a member of the Appalachian Mountain Club, who made his climb with Carlyle Lamb the central episode of the first published mountain guide to the Estes

Park region, *Mountaineering in Colorado: The Peaks about Estes Park* (Boston, 1889).

Under Mills's very personal supervision, Longs Peak Inn soon became one of the better known mountain hostelries in the nation. Though a fire (against which Mills was uninsured) destroyed the sixteen-room main lodge and its recently enlarged fifty-foot dining room on June 4, 1906, while he was off lecturing in St. Paul, Mills lost little time in rebuilding. Employing, wherever possible, wind- or fire-killed trees, gnarled roots and tree stumps, Mills gave the "new" Longs Peak Inn the unusual and distinctive appearance for which it became famous.

"Such a lovely place I have never seen before," wrote a young collegian who visited in August 1907:

> I believe it must be the most beautiful spot in God's whole garden. Mr. Enos Mills met us at the park [Estes Park village] & we were transferred from autos to a stage. When we were all packed & ready to start[,] Mr. Mills came up with a sack of warm popcorn for each one. He is certainly an eccentric fellow. After a nine mile ride we reached Longs Peak Inn. As soon as I saw it I fell head over heels in love with the place. All the buildings are log ones & when we entered the central one there a great fire in an open fireplace welcomed us. There were cosy seats filled with pillows scattered around the room & the bookcases & table were filled with books & magazines. Our crowd was given a 2 roomed log cabin with a fireplace in it. . . .
>
> The dining room is just as unique as the rest of the place. The tables are round with the natural pine boards for a top and no table cloths are used. Supper was delicious.
>
> As we were sitting about the fire in our cabin we heard steps on the porch and when we opened the door a pan was pushed in from the darkness and not a word was said. In the pan we found hot roasted peanuts & some maple sugar. Well[,] we think that Longs Peak Inn is the nicest and homiest spot in the world.[20]

The dominant mood at the Inn was one of rustic austerity. Mills ran his "non-tip house" with a firm set of rules that were as fastidious as its proprietor. Activities such as drinking, dancing, music, cardplaying, and flower gathering were strictly prohibited. Guests with cats and dogs in tow were promptly asked to leave in deference to the local wildlife (Mills's famous collie Scotch, of course, being an exception). "Slow time" was similarly frowned upon, for Mills wanted his guests to be out and about the world of nature, whether hiking, climbing, horseback riding, or simply rambling through the adjacent fields and woods. Until the summer of 1906, when he permanently turned guiding over to others, Mills made himself available to parties bound for Longs Peak (at a fee of twenty-five dollars). Thereafter he was content to play the role of host, available for less strenuous trips to nearby beaver ponds and for his famous weekly nature talks delivered by firelight in the Inn's main lobby.[21] Guests who expressed an interest in Enos Mills's world not infrequently found themselves singled out for special attention. "Mr. Mills and I sat up so many evenings after all the guests and help had retired," one visitor recalled, "sometimes till nearly 2 a.m. . . . These evenings were treats to me—more than that, they were inspirations."[22]

Mills employed a staff of about thirty-five. With the exception of the dining-room supervisors and one or two others, all the Inn's employees were college students and school teachers (because, it was said, Mills wanted everyone to know that his staff was not made up of "professionals"). Though these young people received only thirty-five dollars a month plus room and board for their three months of work, exemplary behavior was demanded. When three staff members, a schoolteacher from Denver and two young men, decided to climb Longs Peak by moonlight and returned by 5:00 A.M., they had the misfortune to encounter an early-rising Enos Mills "prowling around." By nine or ten that morning, all three had been fired and were on their way to town.[23]

Over the years Mills built up a large clientele, many of whom loyally returned year after year to partake of Enos Mills's brand of hospitality in which education and recreation existed comfortably side by side. Though his visitors came from every walk of life, they also included the rich and famous: among them, Jane Addams, Frank Chapman, Clarence Darrow, Eugene Debs, Russell Doubleday, the senior Douglas Fairbanks, Edna Ferber, Charles Evans Hughes, David Starr Jordan, Vernon Kellogg, George Horace

Lorimer, Will and Charles Mayo, Gene Stratton Porter, Otis Skinner and Cornelia Otis Skinner, and William Allen White.

For all his success and growing popularity as an innkeeper, it is likely that Enos Mills would have remained little more than a local celebrity had it not been for two events during the first decade of the twentieth century that, together with his growing authority as a magazine writer, provided him with the audience, reputation, and influence he needed to achieve his larger goals. The first of these came in late 1902 with his appointment as Colorado's official State Snow Observer, a career he followed for three successive seasons. In this role it was Mills's assignment to traverse the length of Colorado's high country, recording the depth of the snowpack at the head of streams together with data on wind, weather, and timber conditions in anticipation of the annual spring runoff—a matter of major concern for the ranchers and farmers along the parched Front Range. Though basically utilitarian in purpose (as suggested by the highly detailed reports that Mills filed with the Denver office of State Engineer L. G. Carpenter, head of Colorado's Irrigation Department), the position of Snow Observer was clearly a romantic, and sometimes dangerous, calling. "Snow observers," he told a reporter for the *Denver Times* in January 1904, "must go beyond the trails, climb the heights and traverse the wilds through all kinds of weather. They experience an amusing variety of conveyances, eat strange food and lodge in the best and in the worst of quarters. The work has roughness and its dangers, but there is abundance of life and fun in it."[24] Mills traveled alone and light, clad in woolen flannels, canvas coat, high-cut overshoes and slouch hat, carrying only matches, barometer, thermometer, compass, a small ax, a spare candle or two, and the most meager supply of food. "I rarely take anything but raisins for food," he wrote in 1905. "A pound of these will sustain me for a week."[25] Upon occasion, his activities and whereabouts became cause for concern. "Do you know Enos Mills got horse here Sept. 28 not heard from since [?]," [26] A. G. Wood telegraphed the State Engineers Office in Denver from Lake City in the San Juans on October 4, 1904. But Mills always turned up, with his report for Carpenter complete, and not infrequently with a hair-raising tale to tell. It was from precisely such incidents and stories, along with the disarming and engaging persona that Mills so carefully managed to project in the role, that the stuff of reputation was made.

Enos Mills's second reputation-enhancing assignment of the decade followed quickly upon the first. When he traveled to Washington in January 1907 to attend a meeting of the American Forestry Association, he carried with him a letter to President Theodore Roosevelt from fellow Coloradan Irving Hale (1861–1930), introducing him as "an enthusiast on Nature and especially Forestry, [who] has done splendid work in lecturing on this important subject throughout the country."[27] As a consequence of their meeting, Mills was offered the position of an independent lecturer on forestry at an annual salary of $2,400 plus expenses in Gifford Pinchot's new Forest Service.[28]

From the perspective of Roosevelt and his chief forester, the appointment of someone like Enos Mills made a great deal of sense. Only two years old, and struggling to consolidate and expand its role at the cutting edge of the administration's conservation policy, the Forest Service under Pinchot's able and aggressive leadership had embarked on a nationwide campaign to publicize the need for conservation and to win over, or at least neutralize, its opponents. Much of the controversy over the "new" conservation policies involved, of course, the undeveloped lands beyond the hundredth meridian. In western states like Colorado, where the unfettered exploitation of the environment had become for many a way of life, lumber, grazing, water, and mining interests were solidly entrenched. Such interests had the most to lose from policies of preservation and controlled use and, not surprisingly, they constituted serious opposition to Pinchot's management of the nation's forest system. Between July 26, 1906, and January 1, 1908, alone, the Roosevelt administration withdrew from use 13,246,480 acres of Colorado's public domain,[29] and in the aftermath no state was more critical of Pinchot and his regulations. As a means of countering charges that such conservation measures were nothing more than an attempt by the wealthy, urbanized eastern establishment to curtail traditional pioneering freedom, to "lock up" resources and thereby restrict economic development, the prospect of employing the services of a fully credentialled westerner like Enos Mills to carry and spread the Roosevelt-Pinchot message must have seemed almost ideal.

In retrospect, given the fact that he would shortly become one of the Forest Service's most vigorous and outspoken critics, Mills's decision to cast his lot with Pinchot, even temporarily, is somewhat difficult to understand. From the very beginning of his official career, Pinchot had charted a decidedly utilitarian approach to conservation: "The object of our forest party," he told the Society of American Forests in March of 1903, "is not to preserve the forests because they are beautiful . . . or because they are refuges for the wild creatures of the wilderness . . . but [it is] . . . the making of prosperous homes. . . . Every other consideration comes as secondary."[30] With the publication in 1906 of the Forest Service's new *Use Book*, there could be little doubt of just how radically Pinchot's views of the wilderness differed from those of John Muir and his fellow scenic preservationists.

Yet for better than two years Mills chose to minimize or overlook those differences. There is nothing in the surviving record to suggest that the message he delivered from the lecture platform departed in any significant way from Pinchot's own scientific approach to wilderness use. In fact, just the opposite seems to have been true. As a reporter for the *Idaho Daily Statesman* noted in November 1907, "Mr. Mills prefers the term 'national forest' to forest reserves, as the policy of the government is not simply to reserve but to cut and use the trees just as fast as they grow large enough, but no faster, and to plant trees in the place of those cut."[31] Such remarks, coming as they do from a man who was already engaged in correspondence with strict preservationists like John Muir and J. Horace McFarland,[32] can only be explained in terms of Mills's own personal growth and development and the evolution of his thinking on issues having to do with the environment. Naïveté, together with misplaced idealism of the sort that often results from being caught up in an all-consuming cause, no doubt played a role, as did the flattery that came from being courted by the press, the conservation establishment, and men like Pinchot and the president. It was only later, when he could view the situation from a totally different context, that Mills became convinced just how much he—and the nation—had been betrayed.

As an enthusiast for forestry and the need for conservation,

Mills proved to be worth his salary many times over, and his career as lecturer assumed a life and momentum of its own. The de-
mand for his instruction, it has been said, came from every part of
the United States,[33] and the schedule he set for himself in comply-
ing was as peripatetic as the man himself. Just who made the careful advance arrangements for Mills's tightly packed schedule of
appearances is unclear, but one surviving set of itineraries, for the
period from October 6, 1908, to May 14, 1909, suggests that Mills
was very much a part of the well-oiled and well-financed publicity
machine for which Pinchot's Forest Service became famous.[34]
Those itineraries list more than one hundred and forty separate
speaking engagements in thirty-two states plus the District of Columbia (on six occasions Mills made three separate appearances
in a single day). Though the majority of these talks were apparently given under the aegis of the State Federation of Women's
Clubs, Mills was clearly prepared to take his message on forestry
to virtually any group willing to offer an invitation: lecture soci-
eties; social, cultural, and civic clubs; schools and colleges; forestry and scientific associations; YMCAs and church organizations. So active was his agency that by August 1910 Mills himself
could write, by way of summary, that "I made, or tried to make,
my first forestry address in 1895, and since that time have made
2,118 forestry addresses. Besides these forestry addresses have
been scores of short talks concerning trees, birds, and nature."[35]
    Though he sometimes modified his remarks to fit a given local
audience, Mills's message (delivered without notes, most often
under the title "Our Friends the Trees") was pretty much the
same wherever he went. What he offered was an appealing combination of personal experience and adventure, information on
American forest history and the "importance of forestry conducted on scientific principles," boosterism and the need "to see
America first," and his own program of nature study that explic-
itly linked exposure to the out-of-doors with health and moral improvement. Mills and his message struck a responsive chord. Ha-
bitually clad in a brown sack suit, the medium-sized athletically-
built Mills assumed the plain and unpretentious pose of the simple, down-to-earth man of the West. Audiences found him, by
turns, "epigrammatic, original, happy in simile and illustration,

eloquent, a master of his speciality," "entertaining and witty;" his
remarks delivered with a "sincerity and conviction" that "made
the people listen and believe." "The lecture," one reporter wrote
in 1907, "was an odd but effective mixture of sentiment and
sense: an illumination of both the practicality and poetry of forestry." "Moreover," commented another newspaper, "his talk is
flavored with a subtle western humor which enhances the effective mission which he has been commissioned to fulfill in spreading the doctrine of tree planting and preservation of forests."[36]

No one could have long sustained the pace that Mills set for
himself. In May 1909, shortly after completing the impressive lecture tour noted above, Mills left the Forest Service with little in the
way of fanfare or public explanation. Though his original agreement with the Forest Service apparently could be broken by either
party at any time,[37] a number of factors made that decision inevitable. One of them surely had to do with Roosevelt's departure
from the presidency that January, leaving the nation's future conservation policy uncertain, as well as Mills's own position as government lecturer. The key factor, however, surely had to do with
Enos Mills himself. By the spring of 1909, when the upcoming
tourist season called him once again home to Estes Park, Mills had
no doubt decided to move on to new and different challenges. His
tenure as government lecturer, however brief, had clearly been a
success. He had taken his message on forestry to virtually every
part of the country, including the conservation establishment of
the East. He had created a reputation and an audience for himself
that was national in scope. It was now time for Enos Mills to campaign for the most important undertaking of his career, a project
even then underway: the establishment of Rocky Mountain National Park.

The germ of the proposal calling for a new national park in the
Estes Park region apparently grew out of a suggestion made by
Herbert N. Wheeler, head of the Medicine Bow National Forest,[38]
at a spring 1908 meeting of the Estes Park Protection and Improvement Association, an organization made up of local busi-
nessmen.[39] "If you want to draw tourists," Wheeler recalls having
told his audience, "you should establish a game refuge where
tourists can see the wild life."[40] By way of illustration, he then pro-

duced a map covering four townships that he believed the Forest
Service could secure as a game preserve. It showed an area of over
a thousand square miles extending from the Poudre River along
the foothills through Estes Park and west toward North Park.
Enos Mills did not attend that meeting, but Wheeler's proposition
struck a resonant chord.[41] Accordingly, he wrote Wheeler, now
headquartered at Fort Collins, to inquire about where the actual
boundaries for such a preserve might be located.

Mills, preoccupied elsewhere with his career as government
lecturer, waited a year. But within days of the September 4, 1909,
annual meeting of the Association, at which the town fathers of
Estes Park voted unanimously to seek government cooperation to
create the Estes National Park and Game Preserve along the lines
of Wheeler's original suggestion, Mills issued for publication a
proposal of his own:

> Around Estes Park, Colorado, are mountain scenes of exceptional
> beauty and grandeur. In this territory is Longs Peak and one of the
> most rugged sections of the Continental Divide of the Rockies. The
> region is almost entirely above the altitude of 7,500 feet, and in it
> are forests, streams, waterfalls, snowy peaks, great canons, gla-
> ciers, scores of species of wild birds, and more than a thousand va-
> rieties of wild flowers.
>
> In many respects this section is losing its wild charms. Extensive
> areas of primeval forests have been misused and ruined; saw-mills
> are humming and cattle are in the wild gardens! The once nu-
> merous big game has been hunted out of existence and the pictur-
> esque beaver are almost gone.
>
> These scenes are already extensively used as places of recre-
> ation. If they are to be permanently and more extensively used and
> preserved it will be necessary to hold them as public property and
> protect them within a national park.[42]

Mills went to work at once to enlist support for his project,
using not only the lecture platform but his own expanding reputation as a writer.[43] These efforts were aided considerably in January 1913 by the release of the enthusiastic report and endorse-
ment of Chief Geographer Robert Marshall of the United States

Geological Survey, who had been dispatched to the area the preceding fall by Secretary of the Interior Walter L. Fisher with ver-
bal instructions to "Go out and see what you can and come back
and tell me about it."[44] Mills's major problem was a tactical and political one. It required, above all, the establishment of an effective
coalition of interest groups that would lobby hard for a park bill.
J. Horace McFarland and his powerful American Civic Association came into the fold early. So did the ever-dependable John
Muir, who wrote Mills on February 21, 1910, that "I'm heartily
with you in your plan for a National Park in Colorado. . . . Will
call attention of the Sierra Club to the proposed new park."[45]

As finally assembled, the coalition was a broad one: the American Civic Association, the Sierra Club, the National Federation of
Women's Clubs, the Daughters of the American Revolution, the
Colorado Legislature, Colorado's Democratic and Republican
party organizations, the Colorado Mountain Club, the Denver
Chamber of Commerce, the Denver Real Estate Exchange, Colorado's major newspapers, and local business and civic organizations throughout Boulder, Larimer, and Grand counties and up
and down the Front Range. Mills's role was pivotal in building and
sustaining momentum, particularly during the many months of
frustrating delay when nothing seemed to be forwarding the
project an inch. Nowhere was his role more critical than with the
Colorado Mountain Club and the General Federation of Women's
Clubs. Without Enos Mills's personal involvement, the former
would not have been founded[46] nor would the latter have become
so vigorously engaged in support of the new Colorado park.[47]

During the six years of the park campaign Mills, it is said, made
more than three hundred appearances,[48] using a variety of argu-
ments, including the economic self-interest of keeping American
tourist dollars at home. For five months during the winter and
spring of 1911–12, Mills took Colorado's case to the nation in a series of lectures arranged around his appearance at McFarland's
annual convention of the American Civic Association and meet-
ings with Secretary of the Interior Fisher and President Taft in
Washington. He returned again to Washington in December 1914
to speak on behalf of the pending park bill before a hearing of the
House Committee on Public Lands—taking time, in the process,

to make appearances in Omaha, Peoria, St. Louis, Indianapolis, Columbus and elsewhere. "Had a very pleasant though strenuous five weeks enroute home and did as much good work as I know how," he wrote McFarland on April 24, 1912. "This campaigning annihilates me and on arrival home I felt so aged."[49]

Though there was, as might be expected, opposition in some quarters from grazing, timber, and water interests who argued against restricting still further the amount of land available for commercial use, the only open local objections came from a group of Estes Park residents who called themselves the Front Range Settlers League.[50] On the other hand, as Mills was quick to point out to McFarland and others, just where the Forest Service stood on the issue of the park was far from clear.

Like any bureaucracy, the Forest Service guarded its prerogatives closely. Having labored hard to enlarge the nation's forest reserves, it was understandably less than enthusiastic about any effort to remove land from its jurisdiction.[51] This, in turn, led to objections and requests for clarification and delay that inevitably slowed down the park-creation process. Mills, however, sensed more sinister designs. As a former employee, he became convinced that the well-organized, well-financed Forest Service, now under the leadership of Pinchot's long-time friend and protégé Henry Graves, had become an active opponent that was out to sabotage, delay, and, if possible, kill the Estes Park project.[52] "Colorado Forest Service is active in opposing park," he wired McFarland in January of 1911. "Methods not the best. Will you protest vigorously and at once?" Once his suspicions were aroused, Mills remained adamant. "Scratch any old Forest Service man," he wrote McFarland that March," and you will find a Tartar who is opposed to all National Parks."[53] Protestations of innocence and good intentions—including Graves's insistence that he only wanted a moratorium on parks until "the question of the permanent administration of all the national parks is definitely settled"[54]—might mollify men like McFarland. They did not mollify Enos Mills. In the end, however, it was the give and take of political compromise that carried the day. Between the date when the first park bill was introduced into the House by Congressman Atterson Walden Rucker of Aspen on February 6, 1913, and the

This editorial cartoon appeared in the *Denver Post* on January 20, 1915.

The principal speakers at the dedication of Rocky Mountain National Park on September 5, 1915, were left to right: Enos A. Mills, Freelan O. Stanley, Edward T. Taylor, Mary Belle King Sherman.
Courtesy of the Colorado Historical Society.

date of its final passage on January 18, 1915, it took three separate park bills and five major revisions to get the measure through the Congress and onto the desk of President Woodrow Wilson.

The celebration dedicating Rocky Mountain National Park was clearly the high point of Enos Mills's public career. Never again would he enjoy so much good will, influence, and wide acclaim as a major figure in America's preservationist movement. The next four years were relatively quiet and productive ones. Though he continued his advocacy of parks and returned often to the lecture circuit, for the most part Mills was content to do what he did best and loved most: pursue his rapidly expanding career as a literary naturalist and preside over Longs Peak Inn, whose facilities he doubled in 1916 in response to an increase in summer visitors lured by the new park. That same summer, Mills entertained as a guest an auburn-haired young woman from Cleveland named Esther Burnell (1889–1964).[55] Two years later, on August 12, 1918, she became his wife in a civil ceremony at

Mills's homestead cabin, and the following year, on April 27, 1919, the mother of their only child.

Viewed with the hindsight of the park campaign, Mills's subsequent collision with the administration of Rocky Mountain National Park in the summer of 1919 was almost inevitable. Though Mills had worked hard to secure the establishment of an independent park bureau, he quickly came to believe that the National Park Service, created by law in August 1916 as an agency within the Department of the Interior, was simply another version of his old nemesis, the Forest Service. The management of the nation's growing system of parks, as Mills readily admitted, required the implementation and enforcement of new rules and policies, and not all of these were likely to be popular with local residents. But when in May 1919 Park Superintendent L. C. Way, without public discussion or competitive bidding, awarded Roe Emery's Rocky Mountain Parks Transportation Company an exclusive long-term franchise agreement to operate in the park, effectively banning rent-car drivers who operated either on their own or in the employ of local hotel and resort owners, Enos Mills and the Park Service came to an irremediable parting of the ways.

For all his outward geniality and public high-mindedness, Mills was a difficult man to get along with. When aroused, he became a formidable and tenacious foe. Fastidious and exacting in establishing standards for himself, Mills placed similar demands on those around him. But where other men might compromise when expectation clashed with reality, Enos Mills would not. He was, for all his apparent self-confidence, surprisingly thin-skinned. Challenges to his authority were rejected aggressively out of hand, and disagreements on ideas or approaches, even with close friends and family members, were all too often converted into personal disputes, ending in severed relationships and self-imposed isolation.[56]

As the years went by, these quarrels multiplied in number and increased in ferocity, until many came to believe that Enos Mills had fallen victim to his own sense of grandiosity and self-importance. Would-be friends tried to counsel him against the extremism of his positions. "Mr. Mills, you are dead wrong in your attitude," McFarland bluntly told him at the height of the transportation controversy. You "are losing not only the opportunity to extend the great work you have already done but to be regarded seriously by worth-while people. . . . You cannot possibly maintain as one single American that you are always right and everyone you criticize always wrong, nor can you possibly sustain an attitude of continuous objurgation and scolding with any expectation that you will be taken seriously."[57] Where principle was presumed to be at stake, Mills simply refused to listen to his old comrade McFarland or to anyone else. James Grafton Rogers, the founding president of the Colorado Mountain Club, summarized the problem that many had with Mills when he observed in December 1914 that "in spite of his very real merits as an author, an innkeeper, and outdoor enthusiast, [Enos Mills] has a genios [sic] for making enemies."[58] He also had the unfortunate ability of alienating at critical times the very individuals whose help he needed most to attain his goals. And nowhere were these disturbing tendencies more apparent than in the furor Mills created over Way's new concessions policy.[59]

The fact of the matter was that except for F. O. Stanley and Clem Yore, both of them local hotel owners, and one or two others, Mills stood pretty much alone.[60] In support of his position against the transportation monopoly, Mills was at first content to use his not inconsiderable ability and reputation as a writer to unleash a barrage of letters to congressmen and conservation organizations and a series of equally strident articles to the local, regional, and national press. Mills's argument was couched in the populist language that westerners had traditionally used in declaring their rights as individuals, his complaints numerous and, at least at first glance, seemingly plausible and specific. The Transportation Company "doubled prices and reduced services to outlying hotels." It conspired with the Lewiston Hotel, one of Mills's competitors, to intercept visitors while simultaneously "acting as a political machine for the director of the National Park Service." "The park officials are used as servants of this monopoly, used to give public protection to a company that is overcharging travelers for poor service and neglecting the repair and improvement of roads and trails, even fire protection, to do this."[61]

Way and other Park Service officials developed a standard line of rebuttal: controlled access to the park was necessary to sound and efficient management; the creation of the Rocky Mountain Parks Transportation Company concession was accomplished fully within the law; Emery utilized first-rate drivers and excellent machines, at fair and competitive prices; the Company substation at Longs Peak Inn assured that the needs of Mills's guests would be taken care of; care had been taken to canvass other hotel owners for complaints and only Mills, whose professed altruism masked the vested interests of a shrewd innkeeper, had any objections and his were so vague, generalized, and unsubstantiated as to lack credibility.[62] Moreover, the Park Service argued that, since it was not within its charge to utilize public funds to operate resorts and transportation facilities, but rather to induce others to do so with their own capital, long-term concession arrangements were necessary, given the short tourist season.

The Estes Park transportation controversy would probably have remained largely a war of words, conducted by letters and in the press, had it not been for Mills's deliberate decision to provoke a crisis in order to establish a test case. On August 16, 1919, having telephoned Way of his intention in advance, Mills dispatched a car, driver, and three passengers into the Park, which Way promptly intercepted on Fall River Road and ejected. Despite the clear provocation, and Mills's rejoinder "that he would notify me as to his next move," Way tried to compromise the issue (as his superiors in Washington urged him to do), for the fact was that, despite the formal creation of Rocky Mountain National Park, the question of just who held legal jurisdiction over the roads within the park was anything but a clear and settled issue. Mills's response was a lawsuit, filed with the U.S. District Court of Colorado, claiming that the Park Service had interfered with "his common rights as a citizen of the State of Colorado in traveling over the Park roads." The case was called in Denver on September 4th before Judge Robert Lewis, who turned down Mills's motion for a temporary injunction against the Park Service, stating, in Way's words, "that it was ridiculous for any person to set up litigation that the United States Government did not have power to regulate traffic and business for the benefit of the people, within the Rocky Mountain National Park."[63] Mills was not convinced, even though, as Way tried to remind him, the success of his suit would have the chilling effect of calling into question all park regulations and reopen the door to the very interests that he had worked so hard to exclude. McFarland tried a similar argument. "Now at this time," he wrote Mills in September 1920, "the National Parks, all of them, are in greater danger than they ever have been since their creation. . . . It is about the worst time that ever has occurred for a sane man who loves the parks as you do, to slam them because of some incidental inequity you have discovered in their management."[64]

Despite the Park Service's victory, the issue did not die.[65] Thanks, in part at least to Mills's agitation, the question of the right of private citizens to use park roads in pursuit of commercial interests became subsumed in a much larger issue, the so-called "Cede Jurisdiction" controversy, in which the State of Colorado formally challenged in court the right of the federal government to regulate traffic over roads built with state funds that had never, formally, been ceded to the jurisdiction of the United States. By the time this issue was finally resolved in February 1929, Enos Mills had been dead for seven years.[66]

Death came suddenly and without warning in the early hours of September 22, 1922. Mills had not been well all summer. Earlier that year, while visiting New York, he suffered two broken ribs and a punctured lung in a freak subway accident. Returning home, the usually robust Mills did not recover, and by August he was still too sick to accompany into the field a biologist from Syracuse University who had sought his help in making a detailed study of the beaver population in the vicinity of Longs Peak Inn. There was a brief secular funeral service at the Inn, the coffin resting on two great logs at the foot of the stairway and in front of the huge stone fireplace where Mills customarily stood as he delivered his evening lectures. Then a small party escorted Enos Mills's remains across the road to a burial place near the homestead cabin he had erected in 1885–86, "in a spot," it was noted, "where the light of the setting sun, dropping below the crest of the bleak and massive peak, would strike it daily."[67]

Fortunately for Mills's reputation as a naturalist and writer, both in his own time and in our own, his quarrels and disputes were for the most part carried on behind the scenes or in arenas with which few besides the immediate participants were likely to be familiar. The Enos Mills that most Americans came to know was the Mills whose articles of adventuring in the world of nature appeared with some regularity in big-circulation magazines like *Saturday Evening Post*, or whose series of attractively illustrated collections of essays were published by Houghton Mifflin and later by Doubleday. Mills's books sold well for their day, and reached thousands of readers.[68] His magazine articles, on the other hand, quite literally, reached millions.[69]

Mills's career as a nature essayist began during the late 1890s and accelerated throughout the first decade of the twentieth century.[70] A writer of essays and articles rather than books, a fact that undoubtedly reflected both his temperament and busy schedule, Mills did not attempt a full-length publication until 1909, when he persuaded Houghton Mifflin, already the publisher of both John Muir and John Burroughs, to bring out the collection he titled *Wild Life on the Rockies*. It was followed by *Spell of the Rockies* (1911), and *In Beaver World* (1913), both cut from essentially the same cloth.

No small part of Mills's popularity was attributable to the fact that he was an all-purpose naturalist, to an approach which he first put to use and then matured during the early years as a Longs Peak guide. "I can't say that I have any particular system in nature study," he told Colorado journalist Arthur Chapman late in life. "It's just trying to make the most of what offers."[71] And for Mills, whose powers of close observation were extraordinary, that was precisely the point. While guiding others up the peak, Mills developed what he afterwards referred to as "the poetic interpretation of the facts of nature." Nature, he insisted, was not to be discussed in the "dead language" of scientific information, but rather in terms "of its manners and customs, its neighbors and its biography." Such attitudes found their human embodiment in the wilderness avatar that Mills called the "nature guide." "A nature guide," Mills explained in *The Adventures of a Nature Guide* (1920), is

> a naturalist who can guide others to the secrets of nature. Every
> plant and animal, every stream and stone, has a number of fas-

cinating facts associated with it and about each there are number-
less stories. Beavers build houses, bears play, birds have a summer
and a winter home thousands of miles apart, flowers have colour
and perfume—every species of life is fitted for a peculiar life zone.
The why of these things, how all came about, are of interest. Touched
by a nature guide the wilderness of the outdoors becomes a wonderland. Then, ever after, wherever one goes afield he enjoys the poetry
of nature.

This simple and commonsensical approach to the wilderness and
"its big principles"—which Mills said he hoped to see "become a
nation-wide and distinct profession" that would "rank with the
occupations of authors and lecturers"[72]—summarized his approach to nature writing as well. Stripped to their essentials, his
essays and articles, with their mixture of scientific information,
field observations, and personal anecdote, were only nature guiding in a more refined, better organized, and more compact form.

Mills's approach to his subject matter is only part of the story of
his success. Much of the rest had to do with the persona through
which he spoke to the reader. The youthful and attractive figure
who parades through Mills's writings is, of course, not the "real"
Enos Mills. Rather, he is an idealized and softened version of the
man (is perhaps even the man he saw himself as being)—the
imaginatively created embodiment of the values and beliefs that
defined the nature guide at his best. Sometimes this persona
moves to center stage to tell an action-packed, hair-raising story of
his adventure on some isolated mountain height. Usually, however, he is more disingenuous, content to retire to the sidelines
and allow nature and its creatures to occupy the full focus of attention. It was easy to like Mills's narrator, with his wide-eyed, boy-
ish sense of wonder and astonishment, his good and genial spirits,
his tight nerve in tough places, his penchant for adventure and
fun, and his ability to summarize the important bond or "spell"
linking man to the natural world that gave the pursuit of nature
its final (and moral) meaning.[73]

Mills's readers and reviewers invariably greeted this persona
with a mixture of pleasure and incredulity, but always in positive
and fully engaged terms. The book's "chief charm," noted Chicago's *Dial* in its review of *Wild Life on the Rockies*,

is in the revelation of the author's personality. A man who refuses
to carry fire-arms in a country where mountain lions and timber
wolves are plenty, and who always manages in some way when he
encounters them to justify his hardihood, who sleeps out of doors
on mountain peaks in the dead of winter without blankets or over-
coat and often without a camp-fire, who carries only raisins for
food and is not disturbed if even these give out for a day or two,
who passes through an electric storm which pulls his hair, binds his
muscles, and shakes his heart—literally—with no other emotion
than that of enjoyment,—this is the genuine sort of man whose
name may worthily be added to the number of our Nature
teachers.[74]

Mills's fourth book, *Rocky Mountain Wonderland*, published in
1915, carries on the established tradition. What distinguished this
miscellany from its predecessors, however, is the special occasion
that called it into being. While eleven of the eighteen essays had
appeared earlier, the majority in Lorimer's *Post*, five of the seven
new essays are plainly connected to the author's ongoing campaign to establish Rocky Mountain National Park. In fact, the final essay, as the note on page 315 intimates, was no doubt deliberately written in celebration of the successful completion of that
event.

   Though a number of the previously published essays, most no-
tably "Wild Mountain Sheep," "Associating with Snow-Slides,"
"The Grizzly Bear," "Bringing Back the Forest," and "My Chipmunk Callers" are quintessential Mills and may be compared with
his best efforts, most of the late additions are of a decidedly different character. They are, in a very real sense, set promotional
pieces, designed to provide readers with a sense of the majesty, variety, and immensity of the natural beauties of Colorado, at a time
when, Mills was fully persuaded, the fate of forest preservation
and the national park movement very much hung in the balance.
However calculated, these essays often struck the desired response. "Whoever reads of this park," a reviewer for the *New York
Times* noted, "will want to go there; those who cannot go will at
least be glad they can read of it, and see glimpses of its noble peaks
and solitary lakes, its wild forests and wild flowers in the very
beautiful photographs taken by the author.[75]

Most reviewers of *Rocky Mountain Wonderland* seemed to understand what Mills was up to in celebrating "his first and enduring love, the high ranges of the Continental Divide; the pines, the lakes, the grizzlies, the mountain sheep, the snowslides." Moreover, in praising the book these reviewers paused to take note of the role that Mills had played in bringing about the new Rocky Mountain National Park. One review, in particular, no doubt caught Enos Mills's eye, for it paid him what was unquestionably the highest compliment that he would ever receive as a nature writer. "He is of the brotherhood of John Muir," commented the *Springfield Republican* on August 18, 1915: "larger, freer, simpler, than our eastern states naturalists,—for wide as Thoreau's thoughts swept, we must allow that not all the phenomenon of earth can be found in Concord, and joyously as Burroughs or Torrey or Dr. Abbott noted things, they were all parochial in comparison. Mills is to the Rockies as Muir to the Sierras; and there are no more interesting books than theirs in respect to Nature in the large."[76] One can only imagine the intense pleasure and sense of achievement (perhaps even of vindication) that Enos Mills must have felt in reading those lines. It was a compliment of the sort that any man would be content to hang a career on.

# Notes

1. They included Stephen T. Mather (1867–1930), the assistant secretary of the interior, who would a year later become the first director of the new National Park Service; George A. Carlson (1876–1926), governor of Colorado; Mary Belle King (Mrs. John D.) Sherman (1863–1935), chairman of the Conservation Department of the General Federation of Women's Clubs, whose advocacy of preservation soon earned her the title of "the Natural Park Lady"; Representative Edward T. Taylor (1858–1941) of Colorado, who had helped to shepherd the park bill through Congress; Freelan O. Stanley (1849–1940), inventor of the Stanley Steamer, builder-owner of Estes Park's luxurious Stanley Hotel, and a regional booster known affectionately as "the grand old man of Estes Park."

2. Morris Legg, *Rocky Mountain News,* September 5, 1915, p. 1.

3. Frank Lundy Webster, *Denver Post,* September 5, 1915, p. 1.

4. Ibid.

5. Enos Mills File, Rocky Mountain National Park Library.

6. Enos A. Mills, "Who's Who—and Why: Enos A. Mills Himself, By Himself," *Saturday Evening Post* (September 1, 1917): 9.

7. Though Mills was a public figure for much of his adult life, the biographical record is a surprisingly meager one. Other than several small collections of letters retained by those with whom Mills corresponded (Horace J. McFarland, James Grafton Rogers, and John Muir), the major repository of Mills materials, hereafter cited as the Enos Mills papers, is housed in the Western History Department of the Denver Public Library. This heterogeneous collection, presented to the Library by Mills's widow, consists of manuscripts, correspondence, speeches, biographical data, and clippings and articles by and about Enos Mills. An additional collection of materials remains in the possession of Mills's heirs and has not, to date, been made available to scholars. The only existing full-length study, *Enos Mills of the Rockies* (New York: Junior Literary Guild and Houghton Mifflin, 1935), an appreciative biography written by Mills's widow Esther Burnell Mills (1889–1946) in collaboration with Hildegarde Hawthorne (the granddaughter of Nathaniel Hawthorne) is flawed as much by the lack of solid biographical information as by its authors' very evident biases.

8. "The Friend of the Rocky Mountains," *Literary Digest* 55 (July 14, 1917): 44–45.

9. He had, in fact, been preceded to Colorado by the Reverend Elkanah J. Lamb (1832–1915), who was related to Mills on both his mother's and father's side. Lamb, a minister of the Church of the United Brethren, had been living in Longs Peak valley (now the Tahosa Valley) since 1875, where he augmented his preacher's salary by guiding parties of visitors to the summit for five dollars a trip. The Lambs also operated the small resort they called "Longs Peak House," where those bound for the peak could obtain a night's lodging and a good meal.

Years earlier, in the summer of 1860, Elkanah Lamb had accompanied Enos Mills's parents, Enos A. Mills, Sr. (1834–1910) and Ann Lamb Mills (1837–1923) to the gold fields of Tarryall and Breckenridge. Though the adventure yielded more stories than gold, the memories of that Colorado summer, passed on by Ann Mills to her son, constituted Mills's single most vivid recollection of his childhood. Elkanah Lamb recorded his early adventures in Colorado in his autobiography, *Memories of the Past and Thoughts of the Future* (United Brethren Publishing House, 1906), to which Enos Mills contributed a foreword. The best published account of Lamb's career to date, title notwithstanding, is Nedra C. Jenkins's two-part "Adventures of a Pistol-Packing Parson," published in *The West* in May and June of 1968: 24–27, 44–45; 22–25, 50–54.

During his first summer in Colorado, Mills worked at the Elkhorn

Lodge just west of the village of Estes Park. In an oral interview of November 14, 1940, Dr. Homer James, son of the Elkhorn's founders, told Park Naturalist Howard Gregg that "Enos Mills' sister May was working at the Elkhorn Lodge back in the 80s. The next summer she brought Enos with her and he worked at the Elkhorn washing dishes." Oral interview, Estes Park Public Library. Though I have been unable to corroborate James's story, it cannot be dismissed out of hand.

10. Mills remained surprisingly reticent about his mountaineering accomplishments. Emerson Lynn, who at one time managed Longs Peak Inn for Mills, is doubtless correct in his statement that "Enos Mills, so far as I know, didn't claim to be an extraordinary mountaineer. Time and again he said publicly that he had done nothing which others could not do; his objective was to lure others to the mountains, believing they would be won as he had been, by the beauty and joys found in nature." Emerson E. Lynn, "The Minister's Son" (1959), in *The Scottage*, typescript copies in both the Rocky Mountain National Park Library and Estes Park Public Library.

11. William Andrews Clark (1839–1925) rose by dint of shrewdness, hard dealing, and grit to become, in Michael Malone's words, "the ultimate example of the grasping and garish western mining king." By the end of the 1880s, Clark and his brothers controlled more than a dozen Butte mines, though not the Anaconda, which was managed and co-owned by Clark's hated enemy and archrival Marcus Daly. Clark's reputation as being "tight, starched, ruthless" and "an uncompromising individualist," coupled with the fact that by 1890 he was well into his bitter twenty-year feud with Daly, may have encouraged Mills not to link his own career with Clark's and hastened his departure from Butte. Michael P. Malone, "Midas of the West: The Incredible Career of William Andrews Clark," *Montana: The Magazine of Western History* 33 (Autumn 1983): 2; Isaac F. Marcosson, *Anaconda* (New York: Dodd, Mead and Company, 1957), p. 82.

The source of the Clark identification is the Mills-Hawthorne biography (p. 83). The Enos Mills Papers, on the other hand, contain an undated and unattributed biographical sketch of Mills that identifies Marcus Daly (who in character and reputation was Clark's antithesis) as the individual who offered Mills "rapid advancement if he would only stay with it," a suggestion that fits far better with what little we know of Mills's Butte mining career.

12. Enos A. Mills, *Waiting in the Wilderness* (Garden City, N.Y.: Doubleday, Page and Co., 1921), p. 93.

13. Undated and untitled autobiographical essays, Enos Mills Papers, Denver Public Library.

14. "A Friend of the Rocky Mountains," pp. 46–47.

15. Ibid.

16. Muir to Mills, January 31, 1913. Muir-Mills Correspondence, Pacific Center for Western Historical Studies, University of the Pacific, Stockton, California. Hereafter cited as Muir Papers.

17. "A Friend of the Rocky Mountains," p. 44.

18. Privately published in 1905, this small guidebook was updated during Mills's lifetime in editions of 1911, 1914, and 1917. After his death in 1922, it was enlarged to become *The Rocky Mountain National Park* (1924).

19. See "A Friend of the Rocky Mountains," p. 47.

20. Nellie Stevenson, unpublished diary of 1907, Colorado Historical Society. Nellie Stevenson was a college student studying botany in North Dakota, who came to Colorado with members of her family for a three-month visit in 1907, which included almost three weeks at Longs Peak Inn. For a more detailed description of Longs Peak Inn, see M. Kennedy Bailey, "A Forest House," *Craftsman* 20 (May 1911): 205–7.

21. Letter of Robert P. Gookins to Rocky Mountain Park Ranger Ferrel Atkins, August 19, 1975. Gookins, who spent the summer of 1913 working at Longs Peak Inn, recalled that Enos Mills was "a good speaker" who "entertained the guests with stories of his experiences in roaming the hills for nearly 30 years at that time. . . . Many times when a lecture was going on several of us sat at the head of this stairs [leading from the lobby] and listened to his tales. We were young and more or less inexperienced in the folklore of the mountains and we really thought he was 'taking in the green Easterners' with his 'tall tales' and sometimes we had a hard time trying to keep from laughing out loud. Looking back after 61 or 62 years I think he was giving some good talks and knew more than we thought."

22. Letter of Frank N. Harrison to Esther Mills, July 11, 1934, Enos Mills Papers.

23. Gookins to Atkins, Enos Mills Papers.

24. Quoted in unsigned article, *Denver Times*, January 16, 1904, Enos Mills Papers.

25. Enos A. Mills, "Some Experiences of Colorado's Snow Observer," *Physical Culture* (c. 1905): 97–98. This five-page published account, illustrated by Mills's own photographs, is in the Enos Mills Papers.

26. Telegram from A. G. Wood to C. W. Wells, October 4, 1904, Enos Mills Papers.

27. Quoted in Patricia M. Fazio, "Cragged Crusade: The Fight for Rocky Mountain National Park, 1909–1915," unpublished master's thesis, University of Wyoming, 1982, p. 64.

28. Under the administration of Theodore Roosevelt (1901–1909), the nation's forest reserves were greatly expanded. When he became president, there were some 41 reserves totalling 46,410,209 acres. Before he left office in 1909, Roosevelt had increased the nation's total number of reserves to 159 and the number of acres to 150,832,665. Behind Roosevelt's every conservationist move was the capable and self-confident Gifford Pinchot (1865–1946), America's first professionally trained forester, whose zeal on behalf of the scientific use of forests irremediably left its imprint on the history of the progressive period. Pinchot had surveyed America's forest reserves as early as 1897, and by the time, a year later, he became head of the Division of Forestry within the Department of Agriculture he had established a very clear action agenda. It was not until 1905, four years into Roosevelt's presidency, however, that Pinchot's seven years of forest advocacy reached fruition. On February 1 of that year, Roosevelt signed a bill consolidating the forestry administration in the Bureau of Forestry which, transferred from the Department of the Interior to the Department of Agriculture, became the Forest Service. At the same time, the nation's forest reserves were renamed "national forests" to reflect better Pinchot's doctrine of wise use.

29. For a study of the dispute over the imposition of the federal government's new conservation policies in Colorado, see G. Michael McCarthy, *Hour of Trial: The Conservation Conflict in Colorado and the West, 1891–1907* (Norman: University of Oklahoma Press, 1977), pp. 75–93, 170.

30. Quoted in Samuel P. Hays, *Conservation and the Gospel of Efficiency: The Progressive Conservation Movement, 1890–1920* (Cambridge, Mass.: Harvard University Press, 1959), pp. 41–42.

31. Unsigned review, *Idaho Daily Statesman*, November 27, 1907, Enos Mills Papers.

32. McFarland told Pinchot exactly what he thought. "I want to say," he wrote on November 26, 1909, "that somehow we must get you to see that . . . the preservation of forests, water powers, minerals and other items of national prosperity in a sane way must be associated with the pleasure to the eye and the mind and the regeneration of the spirit of man." Papers of J. Horace McFarland, Division of Public Records, Pennsylvania Historical Museum Commission, Harrisburg, Pennsylvania. Hereafter cited as McFarland Papers.

33. Harold T. Pinkett, *Gifford Pinchot: Private and Public Forester* (Urbana: University of Illinois Press, 1970), p. 85.

34. See, for example, Chapter 11 of Pinkett's book, "Publicist and Educator," pp. 81–88. "In advance of other officials of his day," Pinkett writes (p. 81), "Pinchot clearly understood how closely related were propaganda, control of public opinion, political lobbies, law-making, and ap-

propriations. Hence, as head of the Forest Service he conducted an extensive and varied publicity program designed to acquaint the populace with the need for forest conservation and development and, thereby, to enlist support of the Service by the American people and their representatives in Congress." These several detailed schedules of dates, neatly typed and labeled "Itinerary of Enos A. Mills," are clearly the work of someone familiar with the demands of the lecture circuit. They are included in the Enos Mills Papers.

35. Quoted in Fazio, p. 61.

36. Miscellaneous newspaper reviews, Enos Mills Papers.

37. Unsigned article, Enos Mills Papers.

38. In May 1905, as part of his program to increase the size of the nation's forest reserves, Roosevelt extended Wyoming's Medicine Bow Forest Preserve southward to include the wilderness area now embraced by Rocky Mountain National Park, a decision that led in 1907 to the establishment of a local Forest Service headquarters at Estes Park under the direction of Herbert N. Wheeler. His office was moved in June 1908 to Fort Collins. (In 1910 the section of the Medicine Bow Forest Reserve in Colorado was renamed the Colorado National Forest, a name that lasted until 1932 when it was changed to the Roosevelt National Forest.)

39. The single most detailed account of the campaign to create the Rocky Mountain National Park is Patricia Fazio's "Cragged Crusade" (see note 27). For other accounts, see C. W. Bucholtz, *Rocky Mountain National Park: A History* (Boulder: Colorado Associated University Press, 1983), pp. 126–37, and Lloyd K. Musselman, *Rocky Mountain National Park: Administrative History, 1915–1965* (Washington: U.S. Department of the Interior, National Park Service, 1971), pp. 17–27.

40. Memoirs of Herbert N. Wheeler. Quoted in Louisa Ward Arps and Elinor Eppich Kingery, *High Country Names: Rocky Mountain National Park* (Estes Park, Co.: Rocky Mountain Nature Association, 1972), p. 156.

41. There are indications that Mills's plan for a park dated back to at least 1906. In a letter of February 15, 1915, to J. Horace McFarland, Mills noted: "Thank you for your warm congratulations concerning the Rocky Mountain National Park. This project was started in the Mount Pleasant press room [the Mount Pleasant Press was located in Harrisburg, where McFarland made his living as a successful printer and publisher] about midnight some nine years ago. You cannot realize how terrific the fight at times has been. It has added a few gray hairs to my head but I think a few convulsions to my brain." See McFarland Papers.

42. Enos A. Mills, *The Rocky Mountain National Park* (Garden City, N.Y.: Doubleday, Page and Co., 1924), p. 86. Elk had, in fact, all but disappeared from Estes Park and had to be reintroduced by importing new

herds from Montana in 1913 and 1915. There were, on the other hand, sufficient beaver in Mills's own Longs Peak Valley to allow him to produce a book on the subject, *In Beaver World* (1913).

43. See, for example, the following articles by Mills touting national parks in general and a new park for the Estes Park region in particular: "A New National Park," *Saturday Evening Post* (March 5, 1910); "The Proposed Estes National Park," *Sierra Club Bulletin* (June 1910); "Park for the Nation," *Collier's* (June 8, 1912); "Rocky Mountain Region," *Country Life* (August 1, 1912); "Touring in our National Parks," *Country Life in America* (January 1913); "A New National Park," *New York Evening Post,* July 16, 1914.

44. Quoted in Fazio, p. 136. Marshall's report of January 9, 1913, recommended the establishment of a park of some seven hundred square miles (450,450 acres): "Taking all things into consideration, it is my opinion that the creation and maintenance of a national park in this section of the Rocky Mountains is not only feasible but highly desirable and that every effort should be made to secure the establishment of such a park at the earliest possible date." Robert B. Marshall, "Report on an Examination of the Area of the Proposed Rocky Mountain (Estes) National Park, Colorado," January 9, 1913, Records of the Office of the Secretary of the Interior, R.G. 79, National Archives. It is worth noting that the name for the new park originated in the title of Marshall's report.

45. Muir to Mills, Feb 21, 1910, Muir Papers.

46. The surviving correspondence of the young Denver lawyer James Grafton Rogers (1883–1971), now in the collections of the Colorado Historical Society, reveals that as early as the summer of 1911 Mills was urging Rogers to take the lead in establishing "a Mountain Climbing Club" along the lines of the Sierra Club and the Appalachian Mountain Club. From the start, it is clear, Mills keenly appreciated the potential value of such an organization as a lobbying force on preservationist issues. Mills himself declined to stand for office, and despite Rogers's plea ("We cannot form a mountain club without you. If it really is impossible to be present . . . please send us a good letter or something of the sort to show your interest and participation.") he absented himself from the founding meeting of April 26, 1912. It was hardly accidental, however, that the new organization announced as one of its goals: "to encourage the preservation of forests, flowers, and natural scenery; and to render readily accessible the alpine attractions of this region . . . to make the best of Colorado's most striking resource—its mountains." Quoted in Fazio, pp. 126, 131.

Rogers became, perhaps by default, the first president of the Colorado Mountain Club. His subsequent involvement in the campaign for

Rocky Mountain National Park proved as critical as Mills's, for it was Rogers who actually drafted the initial park bill (and its two amended versions) and then lobbied hard on their behalf.

Ironically, it was over lobbying activities on behalf of the park—a goal that they shared—that Mills and Rogers came to a parting of the ways. Unlike Mills, Rogers was willing to make compromises during the course of what he referred to in February 1915 as "the most strenuous and unpleasant struggle that I was ever connected with." (Rogers to William E. Colby, February 9, 1915, James Grafton Rogers Papers, Colorado Historical Society. Hereafter referred to as Rogers Papers.) "In order to unite all these various interests," Rogers tried to explain to Mills in a letter of February 6, 1913, "we had to make a number of concessions in the way of mining rights, water rights, and so on, but I think that these are all details which can be overlooked in the general success of the project" (Rogers to Mills, February 6, 1913, Rogers Papers). Mills, a noncompromiser whose frustration intensified with delay, would not listen. He became convinced that Rogers was "conniving with the Forest Service" to the point of being "the greatest opponent that the Park has" (McFarland Papers). "As a loyal member of the Colorado Mountain Club," Mills wrote Rogers in May 1914, "and as one who is trying to help the making of the Rocky Mountain and other National Parks, . . . I can no longer remain silent while the President of the Colorado Mountain Club exhibits the Forest Service on one shoulder and the Park on the other." (Mills to Rogers, May 3, 1914, Rogers Papers.) Their split proved irreparable.

47. Mary Belle King Sherman (1863–1935), whose efforts on behalf of scenic preservation as chair of the Conservation Department of the General Federation of Women's Clubs earned her the title of "The National Park Lady," had fallen under Mills's influence in 1913 when she sought refuge in Estes Park for reasons of health. At first she and her husband, John Dickinson Sherman, editor of the Chicago *Inter-Ocean,* stayed at Longs Peak Inn; later they built a summer home of their own nearby on eighty acres purchased from Mills. The fact that Mrs. Sherman and Mills became close friends just before and during the critical period when the park bill was in the Congress (she became Conservation Department chair during 1914 when, in fact, the fate of the bill hung in the balance) was extremely fortuitous for the cause in which Mills had already invested so much. The General Federation was made up of some two million, mostly middle-class and married, women, and as such constituted a powerful lobby for issues they supported.

48. Fazio, p. 177.

49. Mills to McFarland, April 24, 1912, McFarland Papers.

50. The Front Range Settlers League was made up entirely of Enos

Mills's own near neighbors and enemies. Their protest of June 1910, containing exactly ten names, including those of Elkanah J. Lamb and his wife, voiced "apprehension" that "the prominent part he [Mills] is taking in said movement may be thought to entitle him to a place in the administration of said park, if created, and we feel that any authority he may acquire over our property or the surrounding region will be used to our detriment." Quoted in Fazio, p. 116.

51. For example, Colorado congressman Atterson W. Rucker openly complained in an article of January 3, 1912 in the *Denver Republican* that the Forest Service opposed the park because it was afraid of a loss of revenue from timber sales.

52. Mills's suspicions and his deteriorating relationship with the Forest Service during the park campaign can be traced in the McFarland Papers. On April 9, 1911, Mills complained to McFarland that during the preceding summer of 1910 the local Forest Service had deliberately allowed cattle to graze on his property "to force me to quit my National Park activities." In June, Mills took the issue directly to Graves in Washington, who promptly investigated, and in a long, detailed, and clearly patient letter tried to assure Mills that there was "no evidence of overgrazing." Mills was not satisfied. "That this vicious work was planned by the District Forester at Denver, by the Forest Supervisor, by the local Forest Rangers and by the stockman," he told McFarland on August 19, "there isn't in my mind the slightest doubt, and that it may have been with the knowledge of Graves is easily possible." By way of an epitaph on his career as government lecturer, Mills concluded that "a number of Western people who are, like myself, heartily in favor of conservation, have come to realize that in the West the real hindrance to Forest Conservation is the Forest Service." By late 1914 his insistence that an "aggressive" conspiratorial Forest Service was using every means "to suppress and blackmail into silence any opposition to its methods" had become so strident that McFarland warned him in a letter of December 28 that "your splendid work is being discounted because of the hostility toward the Forest Service. . . . I do not trust the Forest Service any more than you do, but I do not want to let my feelings in that direction handicap the possibility of doing something for the National parks."

53. Mills to McFarland, January 31, 1911, and March 20, 1911, McFarland Papers.

54. Quoted in Fazio, p. 100.

55. Esther Burnell Mills, a native of Kansas, was the daughter of the Reverend Arthur Burnell. She was educated at Lake Erie College and at Pratt Institute, after which she began a career as an interior decorator for Sherman-Williams in Cleveland. It was a nervous breakdown that

brought her to Longs Peak Inn during the summer of 1916, together
with her sister Elizabeth. (She had apparently attended a Mills lecture in
Cleveland the preceding year, and like so many others followed the lec-
turer home to his mountains.) That summer she did part-time secretarial
work for Mills, but rather than return east in the fall elected to remain in
Estes Park and take up a homestead near Castle Mountain just west of
Estes Park village. Under Mills's tutelage, both Esther and Elizabeth became nature guides. Mills wrote appreciatively of Esther in a chapter in
*The Adventures of a Nature Guide* (Garden City, N.Y.: Doubleday, Page and
Co., 1920), which he titled "The Development of a Woman Guide" (pp.
259–71).

56. The story of Mills's quarrel with his brother Enoch Josiah ("Joe")
Mills (1880–1935) is found in the introduction to my edition of Joe Mills's
*A Mountain Boyhood* (1926), reprinted by the University of Nebraska
Press in 1988. For the equally unfortunate story of his relationship with
the Reverend Elkanah J. Lamb, see my reprint edition of Mills's 1909 collection, *Wild Life on the Rockies* (Lincoln: University of Nebraska Press,
1988), pp. xxxviii–xl.

57. McFarland to Mills, October 11, 1920, McFarland Papers.

58. Rogers to Edmund Seymour, December 18, 1914, Rogers Papers.

59. For the transportation concessions controversy from Enos Mills's
point of view, see Esther Mills and Hildegarde Hawthorne's *Enos Mills of
the Rockies*, pp. 223–51. For another account, which is not without its Park
Service biases, see Musselman's *Rocky Mountain National Park,* pp. 29–76.
Though Way's concessions policy provided the occasion for a full-scale
battle with the National Park Service, relations between Mills and the new
agency were already strained and Mills, on his part, had decided as early
as the summer of 1917 that administrators like Park Secretary Stephen
Mather and his assistant Horace Albright were not being aggressive
enough in their support of Rocky Mountain National Park and in fact
were guilty of using their official positions "to screen the insidious work
of the Forest Service." Albright, in particular, he denounced as a "menace
to the entire cause of the National Parks" (quoted in Donald C. Swain,
*Wilderness Defender: Horace M. Albright and Conservation* [Chicago: University of Chicago Press, 1970], pp. 86, 94). See also Horace M. Albright, *The
Birth of the National Park Service: The Founding Years, 1913–1933* (Salt Lake
City: Howe Brothers, 1985), p. 62.

60. Way attributed Stanley's opposition to "the failure of the Rocky
Mountain Parks Transportation Company to continue the use of the
Stanley steamers, Mr. Stanley being one of the original promoters of the
old stage line, where Stanley steamers were entirely used. They were
junked by the Rocky Mountain Parks Transportation Company, after

Mr. Emery took charge of the management of the Company, and White automobiles substituted in their place. . . ." L. C. Way, Superintendent's Monthly Report, February 20, 1920, Rocky Mountain National Park Library. Clement Yore (1875–1936), proprietor of the Big Thompson Hotel, was the former city editor of the *Chicago American* who arrived on the Estes Park scene in June 1915 and quickly intruded himself into local affairs. Like Mills, Yore was an author, who would eventually claim some twenty novels, two books of verse, and more than six hundred short stories.

61. Enos A. Mills, "The Kingdom of National Parks," *Trail Talk* 1 (August 27, 1920): 5. Although *Trail Talk* was a small local weekly publication, designed mainly "to give the social news to the people of Estes Park and surrounding regions," Mills carried virtually the same argument to the pages of the *New York Times* and the *New Republic,* obtaining in return editorial support from papers as geographically separated as Boston, Des Moines, and Houston.

62. Mills's hard, unyielding attitudes and intemperate, even outrageous, behavior make it easy to take the side of the Park Service. Yet, as Carl Abbott helpfully reminds us, "Implicit in the response of park bureaucrats—Way, Albright, Mather, Arno Cammerer [Mather's deputy in Washington]—was the assumption that Mills's obsession was a product of personal pique. As historian Donald Swain has interpreted their attitudes in his biography of Horace Albright, Mills seemed simply another of the 'old-time park boosters, usually with vested interests' who interfered with the evolution of uniform and rational policies." Carl Abbott, "The Active Force: Enos A. Mills and the National Park Movement," *Colorado Magazine,* 56 (1979): 69.

63. Arno Cammerer, acting as director in Mather's absence, was sufficiently worried that Mills might, in fact, win his case that he telegrammed Way on August 26, 1919, instructing him to find out what Mills "wants" and negotiate a compromise of some sort to get them through the current season. The best example of Mills's failure to reciprocate such attempts at conciliation came later that fall. When Park Director Mather paid a visit to Estes Park to investigate the situation, Mills was personally invited to attend the special meeting in Way's office and offered a special car and chauffeur service to get him there. Mills not only chose not to attend, but, Way reported, told him that "he did not have time for such trivial matters." Way to Director of the National Park Service, December 13, 1919, and September 9, 1919. See Mills vs. L. C. Way File, Rocky Mountain National Park Library.

64. McFarland to Mills, September 25, 1920, McFarland Papers.

65. Mills, however, was ultimately no more successful in pressing his argument in other arenas. On May 27, 1921, for example, he took his

case against the Park Service before a noon luncheon meeting of the
Denver Civic and Commercial Association and delivered a series of
charges "that fairly sizzled" ("Enos Mills Touches Off Fire Works By
Charges of Coercion and Graft," *Denver Express*, May 27, 1921). Because
of the seriousness of his accusations and the danger they potentially
posed to the Colorado tourist industry, the Board of Directors appointed
a special committee to look into Mills's allegations. Although Mills declined to substantiate his charges, the committee mounted an exhaustive
investigation: it "examined the original records at Washington, D.C.; . . .
corresponded with all parties who . . . possessed any knowledge as to the
facts of the case; . . . read many resolutions, letters, and published articles bearing on the subject and in every way . . . [went] into the matter
thoroughly and impartially with the intention of enabling the members
of the Association to reach a just conclusion and a business-like determination."

Though the committee was doubtless aided in their determination by
materials supplied by the Park Service, their report, which was unanimously adopted by the Board on November 21, 1921, was devastating.
The committee took no position on the legality of the franchise agreement, an issue then in the courts. But as far as Mills's other assertions
were concerned, the report minced few words: "Every one of the specific
charges made by Enos Mills has not only been disproven but no facts have
been found that would tend to furnish a foundation for any one of the
charges." Mills's conduct was "decidedly reprehensible," his speech filled
with "vituperation, vindictiveness, fabrication, [and] deliberately mis-
leading statements and untruths." Particularly damaging to Mills's credibility was the statement, "It is illuminating when considering the present
opposition of Mills to the granting of franchises in National Parks to note
that on November 7, 1919, he made application for the granting of such
a franchise to himself: 'over all the roads within Rocky Mountain National Park.'" A copy of the Association's report is included in the McFarland Papers.

Mills continued to push his case despite McFarland's counsel, which,
he warned Mills, was counterproductive. "I think your course tends toward the belief that you are somewhat unbalanced," he bluntly told Mills
on September 25, 1920, apparently with reference to one of Mills's articles in which he had compared Emery's transportation company to "a
Prussian invader . . . [which] has its iron heel upon resident people and
the power of blackmail over privately owned hotels and places of business" (undated article, Rocky Mountain National Park Library). "Cer-
tainly," McFarland continued, "you are losing influence, which is unfortunate. All this slop about Prussian invaders, transportation monopolies,

and other things you do not like, does nothing for you and only discredits the parks you really love. Can't you cut it out Mr. Mills?" Mills at once lashed back, effectively bringing to a close still one more personal relationship: "I learned years ago that the President of the American Civic Association was no fighter; was not likely to campaign against the powers that be." See McFarland Papers.

66. A series of inconclusive legal cases reached their climax in January 1926, when the State of Colorado, threatened with the loss of major federal appropriations for road maintenance and construction within the park, dropped the litigation. This placed the issue squarely in the hands of the Colorado legislature, which was called upon to debate a bill ceding to the federal government final jurisdiction over all state roads within the park. The high drama that ensued, which fully engaged the attention of the state press and brought forth a variety of lobbying efforts on both sides of the issue, was filled with heated accusations of government intimidation and federal "encroachment on the rights and property of States." The issue continued to be contested until February 1929, when political fervor gave way to economic realities—in the form of some $500,000 in federal road appropriations—and the cede bill was passed by both legislative houses and signed into law. The purely legal aspects of the cede jurisdiction dispute are found in William Sherman Bell, "The Legal Phases of Cession of Rocky Mountain National Park," *Rocky Mountain Law Review* 1 (1928): 35–46. The public controversy is well documented in two scrapbooks containing clippings on the cede jurisdiction bill that are part of the permanent collection of the Rocky Mountain National Park Library.

67. *Denver Post* (June 1, 1923), p. 16. That year, apparently fearing that Mills's grave might be desecrated by vandals, Esther Mills had her husband's remains cremated. Esther Mills continued to operate Longs Peak Inn until 1945, when she sold it. A year later, in 1946, it burned to the ground.

68. According to Houghton Mifflin Company, in a letter of October 27, 1988, to the author, from Wendy R. Withington, manager, Trade and Reference Contracts, the sales of Mills's early book sales ran as follows: *Wild Life on the Rockies* (1909), 21,941 copies; *Spell of the Rockies* (1911), 12,597 copies; *In Beaver World* (1913), 7,381 copies; *The Story of a Thousand-Year Pine* (1914), 12,472 copies; *Rocky Mountain Wonderland* (1915), 7,333 copies; *The Story of Scotch* (1916), 11,555 copies; and *Your National Parks* (1917), 6,428 copies.

69. The circulation of the *Saturday Evening Post* had reached 1,000,000 copies per week on December 12, 1908; 1,250,000 copies by October 9, 1909; 1,500,000 copies by March 26, 1910; and 2,000,000 copies by Jan-

uary 15, 1913.

70. For accounts of Mills's developing career as a writer, see Carl Abbott, "The Literary Career of Enos Mills," *Montana: The Magazine of Western History*, 31 (April 1981): 2–15; and Peter Wild, *Enos Mills* (Boise, Idaho: Boise State University, 1979).

71. Arthur H. Chapman, "Enos Mills, The First Nature Guide," *Country Life* (1921), 14. Estes Park Public Library Pamphlet File.

72. Enos A. Mills, *The Adventures of a Nature Guide*, pp. 158, 245.

73. Though Enos Mills could be lyrical and expansive in embracing nature, and dwell upon its "wild reveries" and "occult eloquence" with the best of romantic writers, the final significance he places on nature is moral, not religious as it is with Muir.

74. Unsigned review, *Dial,* June 1, 1909, Enos Mill Papers.

75. Unsigned review, *New York Times*, August 8, 1915, Enos Mills Papers.

76. Unsigned reviews, *Chicago Journal,* April 24, 1915, and *Springfield Republican*, August 18, 1915, Enos Mills Papers. The allusions in the latter review are to Bradford Torrey (1843–1912), a well-known New England essayist and ornithologist, and author of such works of natural history as *Birds in the Bush* (1885), *A Rambler's Lease* (1889), *A Florida Sketchbook* (1894), *Spring Notes from Tennessee* (1896), *Nature's Invitation* (1904), and *Field Days in California* (1913); and Charles Conrad Abbott (1843–1919), a naturalist and archaeologist associated for many years with Harvard's Peabody Museum, and the author of *Upland and Meadow* (1886), *Cyclopaedia of Natural History* (1886), *Days Out of Doors* (1889), *The Birds about Us* (1894), and *In Nature's Realm* (1900).

# Preface

COLORADO has one thousand peaks that rise more than two miles into the sky. About one hundred and fifty of these reach up beyond thirteen thousand feet in altitude. There are more than twice as many peaks of fourteen thousand feet in Colorado as in all the other States of the Union. An enormous area is entirely above the limits of tree-growth; but these heights above the timber-line are far from being barren and lifeless. Covering these mountains with robes of beauty are forests, lakes, meadows, brilliant flowers, moorlands, and vine-like streams that cling to the very summits. This entire mountain realm is delightfully rich in plant and animal life, from the lowest meadows to the summits of the highest peaks.

Each year the State is colored with more than three thousand varieties of wild flowers, cheered by more than four hundred species of birds, and enlivened with a numerous array of other wild life. Well has it been called the "Playground of America." It is an enormous and splendid hanging wild garden.

This mountain State of the Union has always appealed to the imagination and has called forth many graphic expressions. Thus Colorado sought statehood from Congress under the name of Tahosa, — "Dwellers of the Mountain-Tops." Even more of poetic suggestiveness has the name given by an invading Indian tribe to the Arapahoes of the Continental Divide, —"Men of the Blue Sky."

I have visited on foot every part of Colorado and have made scores of happy excursions through these mountains. These outings were in every season of the year and they brought me into contact with the wild life of the heights in every kind of weather. High peaks by the score have been climbed and hundreds of miles covered on snowshoes. I have even followed the trail by night, and by moonlight have enjoyed the solemn forests, the silent lakes, the white cascades, and the summits of the high peaks.

The greater part of this book deals with na-

# Preface

ture and with my own experiences in the Rocky Mountains of Colorado. Some of the chapters in slightly different form have been printed in various publications. The *Saturday Evening Post* published "The Grizzly Bear," "Wild Folk of the Mountain-Summits," "Wild Mountain Sheep," "Associating with Snow-Slides," "The Forest Frontier," "Bringing back the Forest," and "Going to the Top." *Country Life in America* published "A Mountain Pony"; *The Youth's Companion*, "Some Forest History"; *Recreation*, "Drought in Beaver World"; and *Our Dumb Animals*, "My Chipmunk Callers." The editors of these publications have kindly consented to the publishing of these papers in this volume.

E. A. M.

LONG'S PEAK, ESTES PARK, COLORADO,
January, 1915.

# Going to the Top

# Going to the Top

THE seven football-players who engaged me to guide them to the top of Long's Peak did not reveal their identity until we were on the way. Long's Peak, high, massive, and wildly rugged, is the king of the Rocky Mountains, and there were five thousand feet of altitude and seven steeply inclined miles between our starting-point and the granite-piled summit.

We set out on foot. The climbers yelled, threw stones, and wrestled. They were so occupied with themselves during the first mile that I managed to keep them from running over me. Presently they discovered me and gave a cheer, and then proceeded energetically with the evident intention of killing me off.

It was fortunate for me that the experience of more than a hundred guiding trips to the summit was a part of my equipment. In addition to the valuable lessons that had been dearly learned in guiding, I had made dozens of trips to the summit before offering my services as guide. I had made climbs in every kind of weather to familiarize myself thoroughly with the way to the top. These trips — always alone — were first made on clear days, then on stormy ones, and finally at night. When I was satisfied that I could find the trail under the worst conditions, endurance tests were made. One of these consisted in making a quick round trip, then, after only a few minutes' rest, shouldering thirty or forty pounds of supplies and hastening to the rescue of an imaginary climber ill on the summit.

Besides two seasons of this preliminary experience, the rocks, glacial records, birds, trees, and flowers along the trail were studied, other peaks climbed, and books concerning mountain-climbing diligently read. But long before my two hundred and fifty-seven guiding trips were completed, I found myself ignorant of one of the most important factors in guiding, and perhaps, too, in life, — and that is human nature.

Several climbs had been made simply to learn

4

the swiftest pace I could maintain from bottom to summit without a rest. Thus ably coached by experience, I steadied to the work when my noisy football-players started to run away from me. Each player in turn briefly set a hot pace, and in a short time they were ahead of me. Even though they guyed me unmercifully, I refused to be hurried and held to the swiftest pace that I knew could be maintained. Two hours raised us through thirty-five hundred feet of altitude and advanced us five miles. We were above the timber-line, and, though some distance behind the boys, I could tell they were tiring. Presently the guide was again in the lead!

By-and-by one of the boys began to pale, and presently he turned green around the mouth. He tried desperately to bluff it off, but ill he was. In a few minutes he had to quit, overcome with nausea. A moment later another long-haired brave tumbled down. On the others went, but three more were dropped along the trail, and only two of those husky, well-trained athletes reached the summit! That evening, when those sad fellows saw me start off to guide another party up by moonlight, they concluded that I must be a wonder; but as a matter of fact, being an invalid, I had learned something of conservation. This experience fixed in my mind the importance of climbing slowly.

Hurriedly climbing a rugged peak is a dangerous pastime. Trail hurry frequently produces sickness. A brief dash may keep a climber agitated for an hour. During this time he will waste his strength doing things the wrong way,—often, too, annoying or endangering the others.

Finding a way to get climbers to go slowly was a problem that took me time to solve. Early in the guiding game the solution was made impossible by trying to guide large parties and by not knowing human nature. Once accomplished, slow going on the trail noticeably decreased the cases of mountain-sickness, greatly reduced the number of quarrels, and enabled almost all starters to gain the height desired. Slow climbing added pleasure to the trip and enabled every one to return in good form and with splendid pictures in his mind.

# Going to the Top

To keep the party together, — for the tendency of climbers is to scatter, some traveling rapidly and others slowly, — it became my practice to stop occasionally and tell a story, comment on a bit of scenery, or relate an incident that had occurred near by. As I spoke in a low tone, the climbers ahead shouting "Hurry up!" and the ones behind calling "Wait!" could not hear me. This method kept down friction and usually held the party together. With a large party, however, confusion sometimes arose despite my efforts to anticipate it.

Hoping to get valuable climbing suggestions, I told my experiences one day to a gentleman who I thought might help me; but he simply repeated the remark of Trampas that in every party of six there is a fool! It is almost impossible for a numerous party, even though every one of them may be well-meaning, to travel along a steep trail without friction.

My most unpleasant climb was with a fateful six, — three loving young couples. Two college professors about to be married formed one of the

7

couples. He, the son of wealthy parents, had been sent West to mend his health and manners; he met a young school-ma'am who reformed him. They attended the same college and became professors in a State school. They were to be married at the end of this outing; but on this climb they quarreled. Each married another! Sweethearts for years was the story of the second couple. They, too, quarreled on the trail, but made up again. The story of the third couple is interestingly complicated. He was rich, young, and impetuous; she, handsome and musical. For years she had received his ardent attentions indifferently. As we approached the top of the peak, he became extremely impatient with her. As though to make confusion worse confounded, after years of indifference the young lady became infatuated with her escort. He tried to avoid her, but she feigned a sprained ankle to insure his comforting closeness. They are both single to this day. Meantime the six had a general row among themselves, and at the close of it united to "roast" me! Whether imp or altitude was to blame for this deviltry matters not; the guide had to suffer for it.

Early in guiding I conceived it to be my duty to start for the top with any one who cared to try it, and I felt bound also to get the climber to the top if possible. This was poor theory and bad practice. After a few exasperating and exhausting experiences I learned the folly of dragging people to the top who were likely to be too weak to come back. One day a party of four went up. Not one of them was accustomed to walking, and all had apparently lived to eat. After eight hard hours we reached the summit, where all four collapsed. A storm came on, and we were just leaving the top when daylight faded. It rained at intervals all night long, with the temperature a trifle below freezing. We would climb down a short distance, then huddle shivering together for a while. At times every one was suffering from nausea. We got down to timber-line at one o'clock in the morning. Here a rest by a rousing camp-fire enabled all to go on down. We arrived at the starting-place just twenty-four hours after we had left it!

# Rocky Mountain Wonderland

Mountain-climbing is not a good line of activity for an invalid or for one who shies at the edge of a precipice, or for any one, either, who worries over the possible fate of his family while he is on a narrow ledge. Altitude, the great bugbear to many, is the scapegoat for a multitude of sins. "Feeling the altitude" would often be more correctly expressed as feeling the effects of high living! The ill effects of altitude are mostly imaginary. True, climbing high into a brighter, finer atmosphere diminishes the elastic clasp — the pressure of the air — and causes physiological changes. These usually are beneficial. Climbers who become ill through mountain-climbing would also become ill in hill-climbing. In the overwhelming number of cases the lowland visitor is permanently benefited by a visit to the mountains and especially by a climb in the heights.

Mountain-sickness, with its nausea, first comes to those who are bilious, or to those who are hurrying or exerting themselves more than usual. A slight stomach disorder invites this nausea, and on the heights those who have not been careful of diet, or those who celebrated the climb the evening before it was made, are pretty certain to find out just how mountain-sickness afflicts. Altitude has, I think, but little to do with bringing on so-called mountain-sickness. It is almost identical with sea-sickness, and just as quickly forces the conclusion that life is not worth living! Usually a hot drink, rest, and warmth will cure it in a short time.

Clarence King in his "Mountaineering in the Sierra Nevada" says concerning the effects of altitude, "All the while I made my instrumental observations the fascination of the view so held me that I felt no surprise at seeing water boiling over our little faggot blaze at a temperature of one hundred and ninety-two degrees F., nor in observing the barometrical column stand at 17.99 inches; and it was not till a week or so after that I realized we had felt none of the conventional sensations of nausea, headache, and I don't know what all, that people are supposed to suffer at extreme altitudes; but these things go with guides and porters, I believe."

Altitude commonly stimulates the slow tongue,

and in the heights many reserved people become talkative and even confiding. This, along with the natural sociability of such a trip, the scenery,. and the many excitements, usually ripens acquaintances with amazing rapidity. Lifelong friendships have commenced on the trail, and many a lovely romance, too. One day two young people met for the first time in one of my climbing parties. Thirty days afterward they were married, and they have lived happily to date.

In one climb a chaperon gave out and promptly demanded that two young sweethearts turn back. As we moved on without the chaperon, she called down upon my head the curses of all the gods at once! In order to save the day it is sometimes necessary for the guide to become an autocrat. Occasionally a climber is not susceptible to suggestion and will obey only the imperative mood. A guide is sometimes compelled to stop rock-rolling, or to say "No!" to a plucky but sick climber who is eager to go on. A terrible tongue-lashing came to me one day from a young lady because of my refusal to go farther after she had fainted. She went forward alone for half an hour while I sat watching from a commanding crag. Presently she came to a narrow unbanistered ledge that overhung eternity. She at once retreated and came back with a smile, saying that the spot where she had turned back would enable any one to comprehend the laws of falling bodies.

Occasionally a climber became hysterical and I had my hands full keeping the afflicted within bounds. Mountain ledges are not good places for hysterical performances. One day, when a reverend gentleman and his two daughters were nearing the top, the young ladies and myself came out upon the Narrows a few lengths ahead of their father. The ladies were almost exhausted and were climbing on sheer nerve. The stupendous view revealed from the Narrows overwhelmed them, and both became hysterical at once. It was no place for ceremony; and as it was rather cramped for two performances at once, I pushed the feet from beneath one young lady, tripped the other on top of her, — and sat down on both! They struggled, laughed, and

13

cried, and had just calmed down when the father came round the rocks upon us. His face vividly and swiftly expressed three or four kinds of anger before he grasped the situation. Fearing that he might jump on me in turn, or that he might "get them" too, I watched him without a word. Finally he took in the entire situation, and said with a smile, "Well, I don't know whether it's my move or not!"

Twice, while guiding, I broke my lifelong rule never to take a tip. One tip had with it a surprise to redeem the taking. It came from the gentleman who had organized the party. On the way up he begged leave to set the pace and to lead the party to the top. He appeared sensible, but I made a blunder by consenting to the arrangement, for his pace was too rapid, and at Keyhole he was attacked by nausea. He pluckily insisted that we go on to the summit and leave him behind. It was five hours before we returned to him. For two hours he had lain helpless in a cold rain and was badly chilled. He was so limp and loose-jointed that it was difficult to carry him across the moraine called

14

THE NARROWS, LONG'S PEAK TRAIL
(Figures of climbers can be made out on the trail)

# Going to the Top

Boulderfield. At the Inn the following morning he was completely restored. I was still so exhausted from getting him down that when he insisted that he be allowed to give me a tip in addition to the guiding fee I agreed to accept it. The instant I had consented it occurred to me that a tip from a millionaire for the saving of his life would be worth while. I was startled when, with a satisfied expression, he handed me twenty-five cents!

Early one season, before the ice had melted, one of my five climbers met with an accident in one of the most dangerous places along the way. We were descending, and I was in front, watching each one closely as he crossed a narrow and extremely steep tongue of ice. The gentleman who brought up the rear was a good climber when not talking; but this time he was chattering away and failed to notice me when I signaled him for silence while each climber, in turn, carefully crossed the steep ice in the footholds chopped for that purpose. Still talking, he stepped out on the ice without looking and missed the foothold! Both feet shot from beneath him, and down the smooth, deadly steep he plunged.

Early in guiding I had considered the dangerous places and planned just where to stand while the climbers passed them and just what to do in case of accident. When an accident actually occurred, it was a simple matter to go through a ticklish grand-stand performance that had been practiced dozens of times, and which for years I had been ready to put into effect. The instant he slipped, I made a quick leap for a point of rock that barely pierced the steep ice-tongue. This ice was steeper than half pitch. He shot down, clawing desperately and helplessly, with momentum sufficient to knock over half a dozen men. There was just time to grab him by the coat as he shot by the rock. Bracing with all my might to hold him for a fraction of a second so as to divert him and point him at an angle off the ice, I jumped upward as the violent jerk came. We went off as it were on a tangent, and landed in a heap upon the stones, several yards below the spot from which I had leaped to the rescue. His life was saved.

# Going to the Top

The last season of my guiding career was a full one. Thirty-two ascents were made during the thirty-one days of August. Half a dozen of these were by moonlight. In addition to these climbs a daily round trip was made to Estes Park, eight miles distant and fifteen hundred feet down the mountain. These Estes Park trips commonly were made on horseback, though a few were by wagon. My busiest day was crowded with two wagon trips and one horseback trip to Estes Park, then a moonlight climb to the summit. In a sixty-hour stretch I did not have any sleep or take any food. Being in condition for the work and doing it easily, I was in excellent shape when the guiding ended.

The happiest one of my two hundred and fifty-seven guiding experiences on the rugged granite trail of this peak was with Harriet Peters, a little eight-year-old girl, the youngest child who has made the climb. She was alert and obedient, enjoyed the experience, and reached the top without a slip or a stumble, and with but little assistance from me. It was pleasant to be with her on the summit, listening to her comments and hearing her childlike questions. I have told the whole story of this climb in "Wild Life on the Rockies."

Thoughtfulness and deliberation are essentials of mountain-climbing. Climb slowly. Look before stepping. Ease down off boulders; a jump may jar or sprain. Enjoy the scenery and do most of your talking while at rest. Think of the fellow lower down. A careful diet and training beforehand will make the climb easier and far more enjoyable.

Tyndall has said that a few days of mountain-climbing will burn all the effete matter out of the system. In climbing, the stagnant blood is circulated and refined, the lungs are exercised, every cell is cleansed, and all parts are disinfected by the pure air. Climbing a high peak occasionally will not only postpone death but will give continuous intensity to the joy of living. Every one might well climb at least one high peak, and for those leaving high school or college, the post-graduate work of climbing a rugged peak might be a more informative ex-

# Going to the Top

perience or a more helpful test for living than any examination or the writing of a thesis.

Scenery, like music, is thought-compelling and gives one a rare combination of practical and poetical inspiration. Along with mountain-climbing, scenery shakes us free from ourselves and the world. From new grand heights one often has the strange feeling that he has looked upon these wondrous scenes before; and on the crest one realizes the full meaning of John Muir's exhortation to "climb the mountains and get their good tidings!"

# Wild Mountain Sheep

# Wild Mountain Sheep

ONE day in Glacier Gorge, Colorado, I was astonished to see a number of sheep start to descend the precipitous eastern face of Thatch-Top Mountain. This glaciated wall, only a few degrees off the perpendicular, rises comparatively smooth for several hundred feet. Down they came, slowly, with absolute composure, over places I dared not even try to descend. The nearness of the sheep and the use of field-glasses gave me excellent views of the many ways in which they actually seemed to court danger.

It is intensely thrilling to watch a leaping exhibition of one of these heavy, agile, alert, and athletic animals. Down precipitous places he plunges head foremost, turning and checking himself as he descends by striking his feet against walls and projections — perhaps a dozen times — before alighting on a ledge for a full stop. From this he walks overboard and repeats the wild performance!

Wild mountain sheep are perhaps the most accomplished and dare-devil acrobats in the animal world. They are indifferent to the depths beneath as they go merrily along cañon-walls. The chamois and the wild mountain goat may equal them in climbing among the crags and peaks, but in descending dizzy precipices and sheer walls the bighorn sheep are unrivaled. When sheep hurriedly descend a precipice, the laws of falling bodies are given a most spectacular display, and the possibilities of friction and adhesion are tested to the utmost.

A heavily horned ram led the way down Thatch-Top. He was followed by two young rams and a number of ewes, with two small lambs in the rear. They were in single file, each well separated from the others. Down this frightful wall the lambs appeared to be going to certain death. At times they all followed the contour round small spurs or in niches. In places, from my point of view they appeared to be flattened against the wall and descending head foremost.

# Wild Mountain Sheep

There was one long pitch that offered nothing on which to stand and no place on which to stop. Down this the old ram plunged with a series of bouncing drops and jumps, — falling under control, with his fall broken, checked, and directed, without stopping, by striking with the feet as frequently as was necessary. First came three or four straightforward bouncing dives, followed by a number of swift zigzag jumps, striking alternately right and left, then three or four darts to the right before again flying off to the left. At last he struck on a wide ledge, where he pulled up and stopped with masterly resistance and stiff-legged jumps! Mind controlled matter! This specialty of the sheep requires keen eyesight, instant decision, excellent judgment, a marvelous nicety in measuring distances, and a complete forgetfulness of peril. Each ewe in turn gave a similar and equally striking exhibition; while the lambs, instead of breaking their necks in the play of drop and bounce, did not appear to be even cautious. They showed off by dropping farther and going faster than the old ones!

This was sheer frolic for these children of the crags.

Down a vertical gulley — a giant chimney with one side out — they went hippety-hop from side to side, and at the bottom, without a stop, dropped fifteen feet to a wide bench below. The ram simply dived off, with front feet thrust forward and with hind feet drawn up and forward, and apparently struck with all four feet at once. A number of others followed in such rapid succession that they appeared to be falling out of the air. Each, however, made it a point to land to the right or the left of the one it was following. Two ewes turned broadside to the wall as they went over and dropped vertically, — stiff-legged, back horizontal, and with head held well up. The lambs leaped overboard simultaneously only a second behind the rear ewe, each lamb coming to a stop with the elastic bounce of youth.

Beneath this bench where all had paused, the wall was perilously steep for perhaps one hundred feet. A moment after the lambs landed, the ram followed the bench round the wall for

several yards, then began to descend the steep
wall by tacking back and forth on broken and
extremely narrow ledges, with many footholds
barely two inches wide. He was well down,
when he missed his footing and fell. He tumbled
outward, turned completely over, and, after a
fall of about twenty feet, struck the wall glan-
cingly, at the same time thrusting his feet against
it as though trying to right himself. A patch of
hair — and perhaps skin — was left clinging to
the wall. A few yards below this, while falling
almost head first, he struck a slope with all four
feet and bounded wildly outward, but with
checked speed. He dropped on a ledge, where
with the utmost effort he regained control of himself and stopped, with three or four stiff plunges
and a slide. From there he trotted over easy
ways and moderate slopes to the bottom, where
he stood a while trembling, then lay down.

One by one his flock came down in good
order. The leaps of flying squirrels and the
clever gymnastic pranks of monkeys are tame
shows compared with the wild feats of these
masters of the crags.

# Rocky Mountain Wonderland

The flock, after playing and feeding about for an hour or more, started to return. The injured leader lay quietly on the grass, but with head held bravely erect. The two lambs raced ahead and started to climb the precipice over the route they had come down. One ewe went to the bottom of the wall, then turned to look at the big-horned leader who lay still upon the grass. She waited. The lambs, plainly eager to go on up, also waited. Presently the ram rose with an effort and limped heavily away. There was blood on his side. He turned aside from the precipice and led the way back toward the top by long easy slopes. The flock slowly followed. The lambs looked at each other and hesitated for some time. Finally they leaped down and raced rompingly after the others.

The massive horns of the rams, along with the audacious dives that sheep sometimes make on precipices, probably suggested the story that sheep jump off a cliff and effectively break the shock of the fall by landing on their horns at the bottom! John Charles Frémont appears to have started this story in print. Though sheep do not alight on their horns, this story is still in circulation and is too widely believed. Every one with whom I have talked who has seen sheep land after a leap says that the sheep land upon their feet. I have seen this performance a number of times, and on a few occasions there were several sheep; and each and all came down feet first. Incidentally I have seen two rams come down a precipice and strike on their horns; but they did not rise again! The small horns of the ewes would offer no shock-breaking resistance if alighted upon; yet the ewes rival the rams in making precipitous plunges.

The sheep is the only animal that has circling horns. In rams these rise from the top of the head and grow upward, outward, and backward, then curve downward and forward. Commonly the circle is complete in four or five years. This circular tendency varies with locality. In mature rams the horns are from twenty to forty inches long, measured round the curve, and have a basic circumference of twelve to eighteen inches. The largest horn I ever measured was at the base nineteen and a half inches in circumference. This was of the Colorado bighorn species, and at the time of measurement the owner had been dead about two months. The horns of the ewes are small, and extend upward, pointing slightly outward and backward.

The wildest leap I ever saw a sheep take was made in the Rocky Mountains a few miles northwest of Long's Peak. In climbing down a precipice I rounded a point near the bottom and came upon a ram at the end of the ledge I was following. Evidently he had been lying down, looking upon the scenes below. The ledge was narrow and it ended just behind the ram, who faced me only five or six feet away. He stamped angrily, struck an attitude of fight, and shook his head as if to say, "I've half a mind to butt you overboard!" He could have butted an ox overboard. My plan was to fling myself beneath a slight overhang of wall on the narrow ledge between us if he made a move.

While retreating backward along almost nothing of a ledge and considering the wisdom of keeping my eyes on the ram, he moved, and

# Wild Mountain Sheep

I flung myself beneath the few inches of projecting wall. The ram simply made a wild leap off the ledge.

This looked like a leap to death. He plunged down at an angle to the wall, head forward and a trifle lower than the rump, with feet drawn upward and thrust forward. I looked over the edge, hoping he was making a record jump. The first place he struck was more than twenty feet below me. When the fore feet struck, his shoulder blades jammed upward as though they would burst through the skin. A fraction of a second later his hind feet also struck and his back sagged violently; his belly must have scraped the slope. He bounded upward and outward like a heavy chunk of rubber. This contact had checked his deadly drop and his second striking-place was on a steeply inclined buttress; apparently in his momentary contact with this he altered his course with a kicking action of the feet.

There was lightning-like foot action, and from this striking-place he veered off and came down violently, feet first, upon a shelf of granite. With a splendid show of physical power, and with desperate effort, he got himself to a stand with stiff-legged, sliding bounds along the shelf. Here he paused for a second, then stepped out of sight behind a rock point. Feeling that he must be crippled, I hurriedly scrambled up and out on a promontory from which to look down upon him. He was trotting down a slope without even the sign of a limp!

Sheep do sometimes slip, misjudge a distance, and fall. Usually a bad bruise, a wrenched joint, or a split hoof is the worst injury, though now and then one receives broken legs or ribs, or even a broken neck. Most accidents appear to befall them while they are fleeing through territory with which they are unacquainted. In strange places they are likely to have trouble with loose stones, or they may be compelled to leap without knowing the nature of the landing-place.

A sheep, like a rabbit or a fox, does his greatest work in evading pursuers in territory with which he is intimately acquainted. If closely pursued in his own territory, he will flee at high speed up or down a precipice, perform seemingly impossible feats, and triumphantly escape. But no matter how skillful, if he goes his utmost in a new territory, he is as likely to come to grief as an orator who attempts to talk on a subject with which he is not well acquainted. It is probable that most of the accidents to these masters of the crags occur when they are making a desperate retreat through strange precipitous territory.

In the Elk Mountains a flock of sheep were driven far from their stamping-ground and while in a strange country were fired upon and pursued by hunters. They fled up a peak they had not before climbed. The leader leaped upon a rock that gave way. He tumbled off with the rock on top. He fell upon his back — to rise no more. A ewe missed her footing and in her fall knocked two others over to their death, though she regained her footing and escaped.

One day a ram appeared on a near-by skyline and crossed along the top of a shattered knife-edge of granite. The gale had driven me to shelter, but along he went, unmindful of the gale that was ripping along the crags and knocking things right and left. Occasionally he made a long leap from point to point. Now and then he paused to look into the cañon far below. On the top of the highest pinnacle he stopped and became a splendid statue. Presently he rounded a spur within fifty feet of me and commenced climbing diagonally up a wall that appeared almost vertical and smooth. My glass showed that he was walking along a mere crack in the rock, where footholds existed mostly in imagination. On this place he would stop and scratch with one hind foot and then rub the end of a horn against the wall!

As he went on up, the appearance was like a stage effect, as though he were sustained by wires. At the end of the crack he reared, hooked his fore feet over a rough point, and drew himself up like an athlete, with utter indifference to the two hundred feet of drop beneath him. From this point he tacked back and forth until he had ascended to the bottom of a vertical gully, which he easily mastered with a series of zigzag jumps. In some of these he leaped several feet almost horizontally to gain a few inches vertically. Occasionally he leaped up and struck with his feet in a place where he could not stand, but from which he leaped to a place more roomy. His feet slipped as he landed from one high jump; instantly he pushed himself off backward and came down feet foremost on the narrow place from which he had just leaped. He tried again and succeeded.

The edges of sheep's hoofs are hard, while the back part of the bottom is a rubbery, gristly pad, which holds well on smooth, steep surfaces. Coöperating with these excellent feet are strong muscles, good eyes, and keen wits.

Wild sheep are much larger than tame ones. They are alert, resourceful, and full of energy. Among the Colorado bighorns the rams are from thirty-eight to forty-two inches high, and weigh from two hundred to three hundred and fifty pounds. The ewes are a third smaller. The common color is grayish brown, with under parts and inside of the legs white. In the north there is one pure-white species, while on neighboring ranges there is a black species. Though wild sheep usually follow a leader, each one is capable of independent action. Tame sheep are stupid and silly; wild sheep are wide-awake and courageous. Tame sheep are dirty and smelly, while wild sheep are as well-groomed and clean as the cliffs among which they live.

In discussing wild life many people fail to discriminate between the wild sheep and the wild goats. The goat has back-curving spike horns and a beard that makes the face every inch a goat's. Though of unshapely body and awkward gait, his ungainliness intensified by his long hair, the goat is a most skillful climber. The sheep excel him for speed, grace, and, perhaps, alertness.

It is believed that the three or four species of sheep found in the wilds of America had their origin in Asia. In appearance and habits they bear a striking resemblance to the sheep which now inhabit the Asiatic mountains.

Wild sheep are found in Alaska, western Canada, and the United States west of the Plains, and extend a short distance down into

Mexico. Most flocks in the Sierra and the Rocky Mountains live above the timber-line and at an altitude of twelve thousand feet. Winter quarters in these high stamping-grounds appear to be chosen in localities where the high winds prevent a deep accumulation of snow. This snow-removal decreases the danger of becoming snowbound and usually enables the sheep to obtain food.

Their warm, thick under covering of fine wool protects them from the coldest blasts. During storms the sheep commonly huddle together to the leeward of a cliff. Sometimes they stand thus for days and are completely drifted over. At the close of the storm the stronger ones lead and buck their way out through the snow. Occasionally a few weak ones perish, and occasionally, too, a mountain lion appears while the flock is almost helpless in the snow.

Excursions from their mountain-top homes are occasionally made into the lowlands. In the spring they go down early for green stuff, which comes first to the lowlands. They go to salt licks, for a ramble, for a change of food, and for the fun of it. The duration of these excursions may be a few hours or several days.

Most of the time the full-grown rams form one flock; the ewes and youngsters flock by themselves. Severe storms or harassing enemies may briefly unite these flocks. One hundred and forty is the largest flock I ever counted. This was in June, on Specimen Mountain, Colorado; and the sheep had apparently assembled for the purpose of licking salty, alkaline earth near the top of this mountain. Wild sheep appear to have an insatiable craving for salt and will travel a day's journey to obtain it. Occasionally they will cross a high, broken mountain-range and repeatedly expose themselves to danger, in order to visit a salt lick.

The young lambs, one or two at a birth, are usually born about the first of May in the alpine heights above timber-line. What a wildly royal and romantic birthplace! The strange world spreading far below and far away; crags, snowdrifts, brilliant flowers, — a hanging wild garden, with the ptarmigan and the rosy finches for companions! The mother has sole care of the young; for several weeks she must guard them from hungry foxes, eagles, and lions. Once I saw an eagle swoop and strike a lamb. Though the lamb was knocked heels over head, the blow was not fatal. The eagle wheeled to strike again, but the mother leaped up and shielded the wounded lamb. Eaglets are occasionally fed on young lambs, as skulls near eagle's nests in the cliffs bear evidence.

A number of ewes and lambs one day came close to my hiding-place. One mother had two children; four others had one each. An active lamb had a merry time with his mother, butting her from every angle, rearing up on his hind legs and striking with his head, and occasionally leaping entirely over her. While she lay in dreamy indifference, he practiced long jumps over her, occasionally stopping to have a fierce fight with an imaginary rival. Later he was joined by another lamb, and they proceeded to race and romp all over a cliff, while the mothers looked on with satisfaction. Presently they all lay down, and a number of magpies, apparently hunting insects, walked over them.

# Rocky Mountain Wonderland

In one of the side cañons on the Colorado in Arizona, I was for a number of days close to a flock of wild sheep which evidently had never before seen man. On their first view of me they showed marked curiosity, which they satisfied by approaching closely, two or three touching me with their noses. Several times I walked among the flock with no excitement on their part. I was without either camera or gun. The day I broke camp and moved on, one of the ewes followed me for more than an hour.

They become intensely alert and wild when hunted; but in localities where they are not shot at they quickly become semi-domestic, often feeding near homes of friendly people. During the winter sheep frequently come from the heights to feed near my cabin. One day, after a number had licked salt with my pony, a ram which appeared as old as the hills walked boldly by my cabin within a few feet of it, head proudly up. After long acquaintance and many attempts I took his photograph at five feet and finally was allowed to feel of his great horns!

A few years ago near my cabin a ram lost his

40

A WILD MOUNTAIN SHEEP

Copyright, 1913, by Enos A. Mills

life in a barbed-wire fence. He and a number of other rams had fed, then climbed to the top of a small crag by the roadside. While they were there, a man on horseback came along. Indifferently they watched him approach; but when he stopped to take a picture all but one fled in alarm, easily leaping a shoulder-high fence. After a minute the remaining ram became excited, dashed off to follow the others, and ran into the fence. He was hurled backward and one of his curved horns hooked over a wire. Finding himself caught, he surged desperately to tear himself free. In doing this a barb severed the jugular vein. He fell and freed his horn from the wire in falling. Rising, he ran for the crag from which he had just fled, with his blood escaping in great gushes. As he was gaining the top of the crag he rolled over dead.

A flock which is often divided into two, one of ewes and one of rams, lives on the summit of Battle Mountain, at an altitude of twelve thousand feet, about four miles from my cabin. I have sometimes followed them when they were rambling. About the middle of one September this flock united and moved off to the south. I made haste to climb to the top of Mt. Meeker so as to command most of their movements. I had been watching for several hours without even a glimpse of them. Rising to move away, I surprised them as they lay at rest near-by, a little below the summit; and I also surprised a lion that evidently was sneaking up on them. This was close to the altitude of fourteen thousand feet. The mountain lion is the game-hog of the heights and is a persistent and insidious foe of sheep. He kills both old and young, and usually makes a capture by sneaking up on his victim. Sometimes for hours he lies in wait by a sheep trail.

The day following the surprise on Mt. Meeker, this flock appeared at timber-line about three miles to the southeast. Here some hunters fired on it. As it fled past me, I counted, and one of the twenty-eight was missing. The flock spent most of the next day about Chasm Lake, just under the northern crags of Meeker. Before night it was back at its old stamping-ground on Battle Mountain. Early the following morning the big ram led the way slowly to the west on the northern slope of Long's Peak, a little above timber-line.

During the morning a grizzly came lumbering up the slope, and as I thought he would probably intercept the sheep, I awaited the next scene with intense interest. The bear showed no interest in the sheep, which, in turn, were not alarmed by his approach. Within a few yards of the flock he concluded to dig out a fat woodchuck. The sheep, full of curiosity, crowded near to watch this performance, — evidently too near to suit Mr. Grizzly, who presently caused a lively scattering with a *Woof!* and a charge. The bear returned to his digging, and the sheep proceeded quietly on their way.

The flock went down into Glacier Gorge, then out on the opposite side, climbing to the summit of the Continental Divide. The following day another flock united with it; and just at nightfall another, composed entirely of ewes and lambs, was seen approaching. At daylight the following morning the Battle Mountain flock was by itself and the other flocks nowhere in sight. During the day my flock traveled four or five miles to the north, then, doubling back, descended Flat-Top Mountain, and at sundown, after a day's trip of about twenty miles and a descent from twelve thousand feet to eight thousand, arrived at the Mary Lake salt lick in Estes Park. Before noon the following day this flock was on the Crags, about three miles south of the lake and at an altitude of eleven thousand feet.

Near the Crags I saw a fight between one of the rams of this flock and one that ranged about the Crags. The start of this was a lively pushing contest, head to head. At each break there was a quick attempt to strike each other with their horns, which was followed by goat-like rearing and sparring. As they reared and struck, or struck while on their hind legs, the aim was to hit the other's nose with head or horn. Both flocks paused, and most of the sheep intently watched the contest.

Suddenly the contestants broke away, and each rushed back a few yards, then wheeled with a fine cutting angle and came at the other full tilt. There was a smashing head-on collision, and each was thrown upward and almost back on his haunches by the force of the impact. Instantly they wheeled and came together in a flying butt. A number of times both walked back over the stretch over which they rushed together. It was a contest between battering rams on legs. Occasionally one was knocked to his knees or was flung headlong. The circular arena over which they fought was not more than twenty-five feet in diameter. In the final head-on butt the ram of the Crags was knocked end over end; then he arose and trotted away down the slope, while the victor, erect and motionless as a statue, stared after him. Both were covered with blood and dirt. During the day the flock returned to Battle Mountain.

The following day this flock separated into two flocks, the youngsters and ewes in one and the old rams in the other. At mating-time, early in October, the flocks united, and the rams had it out among themselves. There were repeated fights; sometimes two contests were in progress at once. In the end a few rams were driven off without mates, while three or four rams each led off from one to five ewes.

Over the greater part of their range the wild mountain sheep are threatened with extermination. They are shot for sport and for their flesh, and are relentlessly hunted for their horns. But the mountain sheep are a valuable asset to our country. They are picturesque and an interesting part of the scenery, an inspiration to every one who sees them.

Says Mary Austin: —

> " But the wild sheep from the battered rocks,
> Sure foot and fleet of limb,
> Gets up to see the stars go by
> Along the mountain rim."

Fortunate is the locality that perpetuates its mountain sheep. These courageous climbers add much to the ancient mountains and snowy peaks; the arctic wild gardens and the crags would not be the same for us if these mountaineers were to vanish forever from the heights.

# The Forest Frontier

# The Forest Frontier

TIMBER-LINE in the high mountains of the West wakes up the most indifferent visitor. The uppermost limit of tree-growth shows nature in strange, picturesque forms, and is so graphic and impressive that all classes of visitors pause to look in silent wonder. This is the forest frontier.

It appears as old as the hills and as fixed and unchanging as they; but, like every frontier, that of the forest is aggressive, is ever struggling to advance. To-day this bold and definite line is the forest's Far North, its farthest reach up the heights; but this simply marks where the forest is, and not where it was or where it is striving to be. Here is the line of battle between the woods and the weather. The elements are insistent with "thus far and no farther," but the trees do not heed, and the relentless elements batter and defy them in a never-ending battle along the timber-line.

# Rocky Mountain Wonderland

From a commanding promontory the forest-edge appears like a great shore-line, as it sweeps away for miles along the steep and uneven sides of the mountains. For the most part it follows the contour line; here it goes far out round a peninsula-like headland, there it sweeps away to fold back into cove or cañon and form a forested bay. In Colorado and California this forest-line on the mountains is at an altitude of between eleven and twelve thousand feet. Downward from this line a heavy robe of dark forest drapes the mountains; above it the treeless heights rise cool and apparently barren, piled with old and eroded snowdrifts amid silent moorlands and rocky terraces.

The trees of timber-line are stunted by cold, crushed by snow, and distorted by prolonged and terrific winds. Many stretches appear like growths of coarse bushes and uncouth vines. They maintain a perpetual battle, and, though crippled, bent, dwarfed, and deformed, they are stocky and strong old warriors, determined, no weaklings, no cowards. They are crowded together and tangled, presenting a united front.

# The Forest Frontier

Few trees in this forest-front rise to a greater height than twelve feet. The average height is about eight feet, but the length of some of the prostrate ones is not far from the normal height. Wind and other hard conditions give a few trees the uncouth shapes of prehistoric animals. I measured a vine-like ichthyosaurus that was crawling to leeward, flat upon the earth. It was sixty-seven feet long, and close to the roots its body was thirty-eight inches in diameter. One cone-shaped spruce had a base diameter of four feet and came to a point a few inches less than four feet above the earth. Here and there a tough, tall tree manages to stand erect. The high wind either prevents growing or trims off all limbs that do not point to leeward. Some appear as though molded and pressed into shape. A profile of others, with long, streaming-bannered limbs, gives a hopeful view, for they present an unconquerable and conscious appearance, like tattered pennants or torn, triumphant battle-flags of the victorious forest!

The forest is incessantly aggressive and

eternally vigilant to hold its territory and to advance. Winds are its most terrible and effective foe. To them is due its weird and picturesque front. Occasionally they rage for days without cessation, blowing constantly from the same quarter and at times with the rending and crushing velocity of more than one hundred miles an hour. These terrific winds frequently flay the trees with cutting blasts of sand. At times the wind rolls down the steeps with the crushing, flattening force of a tidal wave. Many places have the appearance of having been gone over by a terrible harrow or an enormous roller. In some localities all the trees, except the few protected by rocky ledges or closely braced by their encircling fellows, are crippled or overthrown.

Although I have visited timber-line in a number of States, most of my studies have been made on the eastern slope of the Continental Divide in Colorado. This ragged edge, with its ups and downs and curves, I have eagerly followed for hundreds of miles. Exploring this during every month of the year, I have had

THE WAY OF THE WIND AT TIMBER-LINE

great days and nights along the timber-line. It was ever good to be with these trees in the clear air, up close to the wide and silent sky. Adventurers they appeared, strangely wrapped and enveloped in the shifting fog of low-drifting clouds. In the twilight they were always groups and forms of friendly figures, while by moonlight they were just a romantic camp of fraternal explorers.

Many a camp-fire I have had in the alpine outskirts of the forest. I remember especially one night, when I camped alone where pioneer trees, rusty cliffs, a wild lake-shore, and a subdued, far-off waterfall furnished sights and sounds as wild as though man had not yet appeared on earth. This night, for a time, a cave man directed my imagination, and it ran riot in primeval fields. After indulging these prehistoric visions, I made a great camp-fire with a monumental pile of tree-trunks and limbs on the shore of the lake, close to the cliff. These slow-grown woods were full of pitch, and the fire was of such blazing proportions that it would have caused consternation anywhere in

Europe. The leaping, eager flames threw wavering lights across the lake on the steeply rising heights beyond. These brought the alarm cry of a coyote, with many an answer and echo, and the mocking laughter of a fox.

Even these wild voices in the primeval night were neither so strange nor so eloquent as the storm-made and resolute tree-forms that rose, peered, and vanished where my firelight fell and changed.

At most timber-lines the high winds always blow from one direction. On the eastern slope of the Colorado divide they are westerly, down the mountain. Many of the trees possess a long vertical fringe of limbs to leeward, being limbless and barkless to stormward. Each might serve as an impressive symbolic statue of a windstorm. Permanently their limbs stream to leeward together, with fixed bends and distortions as though changed to metal in the height of a storm.

Whenever a tree dies and remains standing, the sand-blasts speedily erode and carve its unevenly resistant wood into a totem pole which bears many strange embossed pictographs. In time these trees are entirely worn away by the violence of wind-blown ice-pellets and the gnawings of the sand-toothed gales.

Novel effects are here and there seen in long hedges of wind-trimmed trees. These are aligned by the wind. They precisely parallel the wind-current and have grown to leeward from the shelter of a boulder or other wind-break. Apparently an adventurous tree makes a successful stand behind the boulder; then its seeds or those of other trees proceed to form a crowding line to the leeward in the shelter thus afforded. Some of these hedges are a few hundred feet in length; rarely are they more than a few feet high or wide. At the front the sand-blasts trim this hedge to the height and width of the wind-break. Though there may be in some a slight, gradual increase in height from the front toward the rear, the wind trims off adventurous twigs on the side-lines and keeps the width almost uniform throughout.

During the wildest of winds I sometimes deliberately spent a day or a night in the most exposed places at timber-line, protected in an elkskin sleeping-bag. Wildly, grandly, the surging gusts boomed, ripped, roared, and exploded, as they struck or swept on. The experience was somewhat like lying in a diver's dress on a beach during a storm. At times I was struck almost breathless by an airy breaker, or tumbled and kicked indifferently about by the unbelievable violence of the wind. At other times I was dashed with sand and vigorously pelted with sticks and gravel.

This was always at some distance from tree, boulder, or ledge, for I took no risks of being tossed against trees or rocks. Many times, however, I have lain securely anchored and shielded beneath matted tree-growths, where in safety I heard the tempestuous booms and the wildest of rocket-like swishes of the impassioned and invisible ocean of air. The general sound-effect was a prolonged roar, with an interplay of rippings and tumultuous cheerings. There were explosions and silences. There were hours of Niagara. In the midst of these distant roarings the fearful approach of an advancing gale could be heard before the unseen breaker rolled down on me from the heights.

The most marked result of cold and snow is the extreme shortness of the growing-season which they allow the trees. Many inclined trees are broken off by snow, while others are prostrated. Though the trees are flattened upon the earth with a heavy load for months, the snow cover affords the trees much protection, from both the wracking violence of the winds and their devitalizing dryness. I know of a few instances of the winter snows piling so deeply that the covered trees were not uncovered by the warmth of the following summer. The trees suspended in this enforced hibernating sleep lost a summer's fun and failed to envelop themselves in the telltale ring of annual growth.

Snow and wind combined produce acres of closely matted growth that nowhere rises more than three feet above the earth. This growth is kept well groomed by the gale-flung sand, which clips persistent twigs and keeps it closely trimmed into an enormous bristle brush. In places the surface of this will support a pedestrian, but commonly it is too weak for this; and, as John Muir says, in getting through, over, under, or across growths of this kind, one loses all of his temper and most of his clothing!

Timber-line is largely determined by climatic limitations, by temperature and moisture. In the Rocky Mountains the dry winds are more deadly, and therefore more determining, than the high winds. During droughty winters these dry winds absorb the vital juices of hundreds of timber-line trees, whose withered standing skeletons frequently testify to the widespread depredations of this dry blight. A permanent advance, too, is made from time to time. Here and there is a grove, a permanent settlement ahead of and above the main ranks. In advance of these are a few lone trees, heroes scouting in the lead. In moist, sheltered places are seedlings and promising young trees growing up in front of the battle-scarred old guard. Advances on dry, wind-swept ridges are more difficult and much less frequent; on a few dry ridges these trees have met with a repulse and

58

in some places have lost a little territory, but along most of its front the timber-line is slowly advancing into the heights.

With this environment it would be natural for these trees to evolve more hardiness than the present trees have. This would mean trees better fitted to contend with, and more likely to triumph over, the harsh conditions. Evolutionary development is the triumphing factor at the timber-line.

The highest timber-line in the world is probably on Mount Orizaba, Mexico. Frank M. Chapman says that there are short-leaved pines (*Pinus Montezumæ*) from thirty to forty feet high, on the southern exposure of this peak at an altitude of about 13,800 feet. In Switzerland, along the steep and snowy Alps, it is sixty-four hundred; on Mt. Washington, about forty-five hundred feet. In the mountains of Colorado and California it is of approximately equal altitude, between eleven and twelve thousand feet. Advancing northward from California along the timber-line, one enters regions of heavy snowfall as well as of restricting latitude. Combined, these speedily lower the altitude of timber-line, until on Mt. Rainier it is below eight thousand feet. There is a noticeable dwarfing of the forest as one approaches the Land of the Midnight Sun, and in its more northerly reaches it comes down to sea-level to form the Land of Little Sticks. It frays out at its Farthest North just within the Arctic Circle. Most of the Arctic Ocean's icy waves break on treeless shores.

Everywhere at timber-line the temperature is low, and on Long's Peak the daily average is two degrees below the freezing-point. At timber-line snow may fall any day of the year, and wintry conditions annually prevail from nine to ten months. The hardy trees which maintain this line have adjusted themselves to the extremely short growing-season, and now and then mature and scatter fertile seeds. The trees that do heroic service on all latitudinal and altitudinal timber-lines of the earth are members of the pine, spruce, fir, birch, willow, and aspen families. At timber-line on the Rocky Mountains there are three members each from the deciduous trees and the evergreens. These are the Engelmann spruce, limber pine, alpine fir, arctic willow, black birch, and quaking aspen.

A few timber-line trees live a thousand years, but half this time is a ripe old age for most timber-line veterans. The age of these trees cannot be judged by their size, nor by general appearance. There may be centuries of difference in the ages of two arm-in-arm trees of similar size. I examined two trees that were growing within a few yards of each other in the shelter of a crag. One was fourteen feet high and sixteen inches in diameter, and had three hundred and thirty-seven annual rings. The other was seven feet high and five inches in diameter, and had lived four hundred and ninety-two years!

One autumn a grizzly I was following — to learn his bill-of-fare — tore up a number of dwarfed trees at timber-line while digging out a woodchuck and some chipmunks. A number of the smaller trees I carried home for careful examination. One of these was a black birch with a trunk nine-tenths of an inch in diameter, a height of fifteen inches, and a limb-spread of twenty-two. It had thirty-four annual rings. Another was truly a veteran pine, though his trunk was but six-tenths of an inch in diameter, his height twenty-three inches, and his limb-spread thirty-one. His age was sixty-seven years. A midget that I carried home in my vest pocket was two inches high, had a limb-spread of about four inches, and was twenty-eight years of age.

A limber pine I examined was full of annual rings and experiences. A number of its rings were less than one hundredth of an inch in thickness. At the height of four feet its trunk took on an acute angle and extended nine feet to leeward, then rose vertically for three feet. Its top and limbs merged into a tangled mass about one foot thick, which spread out eight feet horizontally. It was four hundred and nine years old. It grew rapidly during its first thirty-eight years; then followed eighteen years during which it almost ceased growing; after this it grew evenly though slowly.

One day by the sunny and sheltered side of a boulder I found a tiny seed-bearer at an altitude of eleven thousand eight hundred feet. How splendidly unconscious it was of its size and its utterly wild surroundings! This brave pine bore a dainty cone, yet a drinking-glass would have completely housed both the tree and its fruit.

Many kinds of life are found at timber-line. One April I put on snowshoes and went up to watch the trees emerge from their months-old covering of snow. While standing upon a matted, snow-covered thicket, I saw a swelling of the snow produced by something moving beneath. "Plainly this is not a tree pulling itself free!" I thought, and stood still in astonishment. A moment later a bear burst up through the snow within a few yards of me and paused, blinking in the glare of light. No plan for immediate action occurred to me; so I froze. Presently the bear scented me and turned back for a look. After winking a few times as though half blinded, he galloped off easily across the compacted snow. The black bear and the grizzly occasionally hibernate beneath these low, matted tree-growths.

# Rocky Mountain Wonderland

The mountain lion may prowl here during any month. Deer frequent the region in summer. Mountain sheep often take refuge beneath the clustered growths during the autumn storms. Of course the audacious pine squirrel comes to claim the very forest-edge and from a point of safety to scold all trespassers; and here, too, lives the cheery chipmunk.

This is the nursery, or summer residence, of many kinds of birds. The "camp-bird," the Rocky Mountain jay, is a resident. Here in spring the white-crowned sparrow sings and sings. During early summer the solitaire, the most eloquent songster I have ever heard, comes up from his nest just down the slope to pay a tribute of divine melody to the listening, time-worn trees. In autumn the Clarke crow appears and, with wild and half-weird calls of merriment, devours the fat nuts in the cones of the limber pine. During this nutting, magpies are present with less business than at any other time and apparently without a plan for deviltry. Possibly they are attracted and entertained by the boisterousness of the crows.

A TIMBER-LINE LAKE IN NORTHWESTERN COLORADO

# The Forest Frontier

Lovely wild-flower gardens occupy many of the openings in this torn and bristling edge of the forest. In places acres are crowded so closely with thrifty, brilliant bloom that one hesitates to walk through and trample the flowers. Here the columbine, the paintbrush, the monument-plant, and scores of other bright blossoms cheer the wild frontier.

Rarely are strangers in the mountains thoroughly aroused. They need time or explanation in order to comprehend or appreciate the larger scenes, though they do, of course, have periodic outbursts in adjectives. But at timber-line the monumental scene at once has the attention, and no explanation is needed. Timber-line tells its own stirring story of frontier experience by a forest of powerful and eloquent tree statues and bold, battered, and far-extending figures in relief.

Only a few of the many young people whom I have guided to timber-line have failed to feel the significance of the scene, but upon one party fresh from college the eloquent pioneer spirit of the place made no impression, and they talked glibly and cynically of these faithful trees with such expressions as "A Doré garden!" "Ill-shapen fiends!" "How foolish to live here!" and "Criminal classes!" More appreciative was the little eight-year-old girl whose ascent of Long's Peak I have told of in "Wild Life on the Rockies." She paid the trees at timber-line as simple and as worthy a tribute as I have ever heard them receive: "What brave little trees to stay up here where they have to stand all the time with their feet in the snow!"

The powerful impressions received at timber-line lead many visitors to return for a better acquaintance, and from each visit the visitor goes away more deeply impressed: for timber-line is not only novel and strange, it is touched with pathos and poetry and has a life-story that is heroic. Its scenes are among the most primeval, interesting, and thought-compelling to be found upon the globe.

# The Chinook Wind

# The Chinook Wind

COLD and snow took possession of the ranges on one occasion while I was making a stay in the winter quarters of a Montana cattle company. There was a quiet, heavy snow, a blizzard, and at last a sleet storm. At first the cattle collected with drooping heads and waited for the storm to end, but long before the sky cleared, they milled and trampled confusedly about. With the clearing sky came still and extreme cold. Stock water changed to ice, and the short, crisp grass of the plains was hopelessly cemented over with ice and snow. The suffering of the cattle was beyond description. For a time they wandered about, apparently without an aim. There were thousands of other herds in this appalling condition. At last, widely scattered, they stood humped up, awaiting death. But one morning the foreman burst in excitedly with the news, "The Chinook is coming!" Out in the snow the herds were aroused, and each "critter" was looking westward as though good news had been scented afar. Across the mountain-tops toward which the stock were looking, great wind-blown clouds were flying toward the plains. In less than an hour the rescuing Chinook rushed upon the scene. The temperature rose forty degrees in less than half as many minutes; then it steadied and rose more slowly. The warm, dry wind quickly increased to a gale. By noon both the sleet and the snow were gone, and thousands of cattle were eagerly feeding in the brown and curly grass of the wide, bleached plain.

This experience enabled me to understand the "Waiting for a Chinook" picture of the "Cowboy Artist." This picture was originally intended to be the spring report, after a stormy Montana winter, to the eastern stockholders of a big cattle company. It showed a spotted solitary cow standing humped in a snowy plain. One horn is broken and her tail is frozen off. Near are three hungry coyotes in different waiting attitudes. The picture bore the legend "The Last of Five Thousand, Waiting for a Chinook."

70

# The Chinook Wind

It is "Presto! Change!" when the warm Chinook wind appears. Wintry landscapes vanish in the balmy, spring-like breath of this strange, hospitable, though inconstant Gulf Stream of the air. This wind is extra dry and warm; occasionally it is almost hot. Many times in Montana I have experienced the forcing, transforming effectiveness of this hale, eccentric wind.

The completion of the big copper refinery at Great Falls was celebrated with a banquet. One of the larger rooms in the new building was used for the banquet-hall. Out to this, a mile or so from the city, the banqueters were taken in a sleigh. That evening the roads were snow-and-ice-covered, and the temperature was several degrees below zero. A Chinook wind arrived while the banquet was in session, and although the feast was drawn out no longer than usual, the banqueters, on adjourning, found the snow and ice entirely gone, the earth dry, and the air as balmy as though just off an Arizona desert in June.

The Chinook blows occasionally over the

Northwest during the five colder months of the year. Though of brief duration, these winds are very efficacious in softening the asperities of winter with their moderating warmth, and they are of great assistance to the stock and other interests. Apparently the Chinook starts from the Pacific, in the extreme Northwest, warm and heavily moisture-laden. Sweeping eastward, it is chilled in crossing the mountains, on which it speedily releases its moisture in heavy snowfalls. Warmed through releasing moisture, it is still further warmed through compression while descending the Cascades, and it goes forward extremely feverish and thirsty. It now feels like a hot desert wind, and, like air off the desert's dusty face, it is insatiably dry and absorbs moisture with astounding rapidity.

It may come from the west, the southwest, or the northwest. Its eastward sweep sometimes carries it into Wisconsin, Iowa, and Kansas, but it most frequently floods and favors the Canadian plains, Oregon, Washington, Montana, Idaho, Wyoming, and Colorado. It may come gently and remain as a moderate breeze or it may appear violently and blow a gale. Its duration is from a few hours to several days.

There are numerous instances on record of a Chinook greatly raising the temperature, removing several inches of snow, and drying the earth in an unbelievably short time. An extreme case of this kind took place in northern Montana in December, 1896. Thirty inches of snow lay over everything; and the quicksilver-tip in thermometers was many lines below zero. In this polar scene the Chinook appeared. Twelve hours later the snow had entirely vanished! The Blackfoot Indians have a graphic term for this wind, — "the snow-eater."

In most respects this wind is climatically beneficial. A thorough warming and drying a few times each winter renders many localities comfortably habitable that otherwise scarcely would be usable. The occasional removal of snow-excesses has its advantages to all users of roads, both wagon and rail, as well as being helpful to stock interests. There are times when this wind leaves the plains too dry, but far more frequently it prevents terrible floods by reducing the heavy snow covering over the sources of the Columbia and the Missouri before the swift spring thaw appears. The Chinook is not likely to create floods through the rapidity of its action, for it changes snow and water to vapor and carries this away through the air.

The Chinook is nothing if not eccentric. Sometimes it warms the mountain-tops and ignores the cold lowlands. Often in snowy time it assists the railroad men to clear the tracks on the summit before it goes down the slope a few miles to warm the muffled and discouraged snow-shovelers in the valley. Now and then a wind tempers the clime for a sheepman, while in an adjoining valley only a few miles away the stockman and his herd wait in vain for the Chinook.

The Chinook may appear at any hour of the day or night. Occasionally with a rush it chases winter. Frequently and fortunately it follows a blizzard. Often it dramatically saves the suffering herds, both wild and tame, and at the eleventh hour it brings the balm of the south-land to the waiting, starving birds.

# The Chinook Wind

The Chinook wind is a Westerner. Similar though less far-reaching winds blow in the mountains of Europe and Asia. In the West, and especially the Northwest, it has a happy and important place, and the climate of this region cannot be comprehended without understanding the influence of the Chinook wind.

# Associating with Snow-Slides

# Associating with Snow-Slides

EVERY snow-fall caused a snow-slide to rush down Bobtail Gulch. This run-off of snow was as regular as the run-off of storm-water. The snow which accumulated at the head of this gulch was a danger to the trail below, and if the snow showed the slightest hesitation to "run" when the storm had ended, a miner from a neighboring mine started it by rolling a few stones into it or by exploding a stick of dynamite near by.

During my stay at a miners' boarding-house in the San Juan Mountains a heavy snow-fall came to a close. "Has the Greagory run yet?" inquired the foreman of one of the miners. "No." "Better start it, then." Ten minutes later fifty thousand tons of snow went plunging down Greagory Gulch.

"This cabin will never be caught by a snow-slide!" said the prospector with whom I was having supper. "A slide hit my cabin in the Sawtooth Mountains. No more sleeping for me in the possible right-of-way of a slide! I sized up the territory before building this cabin and I've put it out of the range of slides."

All this was encouraging, as I was to spend the night in the cabin and had arrived after the surrounding mountains were hidden in darkness. A record-breaking snow of eight days and nights had just ended a few hours before. During the afternoon, as I came down from Alpine Pass on snowshoes, the visible peaks and slopes loomed white and were threateningly overladen with snow. Avalanches would run riot during the next few hours, and the sliding might begin at any minute. Gorges and old slide-ways would hold most of these in the beaten slide-tracks, but there was the possibility of an overladen mountain sending off a shooting star of a slide which might raise havoc by smashing open a new orbit.

The large spruces around the cabin showed that if ever a slide had swept this site it was longer ago than a century. As no steep slope came down upon the few acres of flat surrounding the cabin, we appeared to be in a slide-proof situation. However, to the north was a high snow-piled peak that did not look assuring, even though between it and the cabin was a gorge and near by a rocky ridge. Somewhat acquainted with the ways of slides, I lay awake in the cabin, waiting to hear the muffled thunder-storm of sound which would proclaim that slides were "running."

Snow-slides may be said to have habits. Like water, they are governed by gravity. Both in gulches and on mountain-sides, they start most readily on steep and comparatively smooth slopes. If a snow-drift is upon a thirty-degree incline, it may almost be pushed into sliding with a feather. A slope more steeply inclined than thirty degrees does not offer a snow-drift any visible means of support. Unless this slope be broken or rough, a snow-drift may slide off at any moment.

In the course of a winter, as many as half a dozen slides may start from the same place and each shoot down through the same gorge or over the same slope as its predecessor. Only so much snow can cling to a slope; therefore the number of slides during each winter is determined by the quantity of snow and the character of the slope. As soon as snow is piled beyond the holding-limit, away starts the slide. A slide may have slipped from this spot only a few days before, and here another may slip away a few days later; or a year may elapse before another runs. Thus local topography and local weather conditions determine local slide habits, — when a slide will start and the course over which it will run.

The prospector was snoring before the first far-off thunder was heard. Things were moving. Seashore storm sounds could be heard in the background of heavy rumbling. This thunder swelled louder until there was a heavy rumble everywhere. Then came an earthquake jar, closely followed by a violently explosive crash. A slide was upon us! A few seconds later tons of snow fell about us, crushing the trees and wrecking the cabin. Though we escaped without a scratch, a heavy spruce pole, a harpoon flung by the slide, struck the cabin at an angle, piercing the roof and one of the walls.

The prospector was not frightened, but he was mad! Outwitted by a snow-slide! That we were alive was no consolation to him. "Where on earth did the thing come from?" he kept repeating until daylight. Next morning we saw that to the depth of several feet about the cabin and on top of it were snow-masses, mixed with rock-fragments, broken tree-trunks, and huge wood-splinters, — the fragment remains of a snow-slide.

This slide had started from a high peak-top a mile to the north of the cabin. For three quarters of a mile it had coasted down a slope at the bottom of which a gorge curved away toward the west; but so vast was the quantity of snow that this slide filled and blocked the gorge with less than half of its mass. Over the snowy bridge thus formed, the momentum carried the remainder straight across the gulch. Landing, it swept up a steep slope for three hundred feet and rammed the rocky ridge back of the cabin. The greater part came to a stop and lay scattered about the ridge. Not one tenth of the original bulk went over and up to wreck the cabin! The prospector stood on this ridge, surveying the scene and thinking, when I last looked back.

Heavy slides sometimes rush so swiftly down steep slopes that their momentum carries their entire mass destructively several hundred feet up the slope of the mountain opposite.

Desiring fuller knowledge of the birth and behavior of avalanches, or snow-slides, I invaded the slide zone on snowshoes at the close of a winter which had the "deepest snow-fall on record." Several days were spent watching the snow-slide action in the San Juan Mountains. It was a wild, adventurous, dramatic experience, which closed with an avalanche that took me from the heights on a thrilling, spectacular coast down a steep mountain-side.

A thick, snowy, marble stratum overlay the slopes and summits. Appearing on the scene at the time when, on the steeps, spring was melting the icy cement that held winter's wind-

LIZARD HEAD PEAK IN THE SAN JUAN MOUNTAINS

piled snows, I saw many a snowy hill and embankment released. Some of these, as slides, made meteoric plunges from summit crags to gentler places far below.

A snow-storm prevailed during my first night in the slide region, and this made a deposit of five or six inches of new snow on top of the old. On the steeper places this promptly slipped off in dry, small slides, but most of it was still in place when I started to climb higher.

While I was tacking up a comparatively smooth slope, one of my snowshoes slipped, and, in scraping across the old, crusted snow, started a sheaf of the fluffy new snow to slipping. Hesitatingly at first, the new snow skinned off. Suddenly the fresh snow to right and left concluded to go along, and the full width of the slope below my level was moving and creaking; slowly the whole slid into swifter movement and the mass deepened with the advance. Now and then parts of the sliding snow slid forward over the slower-moving, crumpling, friction-resisted front and bottom.

With advance it grew steadily deeper from

constantly acquired material and from the influence of converging water-channels which it followed. A quarter of a mile from its birthplace it was about fifty feet deep and twice as wide, with a length of three hundred feet. Composed of new snow and coasting as swiftly as a gale, it trailed a white streamer of snow-dust behind. A steeper or a rougher channel added to the volume of snow-dust or increased the agitation of the pace-keeping pennant. The morning was clear, and, by watching the wig-wagging snow flag, I followed easily the fortunes of the slide to the bottom of the slope. After a swift mile of shooting and plunging, the slide, greatly compressed, sprawled and spread out over a level glacier meadow, where its last remnant lingered for the warmth of July.

Dismissing this slide, I watched along the range to the north and south, and from time to time saw the white scudding plumes of other slides, which, hidden in the cañons, were merrily coasting down from the steep-sloping crest.

These slides, unless they had run down an animal, did no damage. They were composed of freshly fallen snow and in their flight had moved in old channels that had been followed and perhaps formed by hundreds of slides in years gone by. Slides of this kind — those which accompany or follow each storm and which promptly make away with new-fallen snow by carrying it down through stream-channels — may be called Storm, or Flood, slides. These usually are formed in smooth gulches or on steep slopes.

The other kinds of slides may be called the Annual and the Century. In places of rough surface or moderate slope there must be a large accumulation of snow before a slide will start. Weeks or even months may pass before storm and wind assemble sufficient snow for a slide. Places of this kind commonly furnish but one slide a year, and this one in the springtime. At last the snow-drifts reach their maximum; warmth assists starting by melting snow-cornices that have held on through the winter; these drop, and by dropping often start things going. Crags wedged off by winter ice are also re-'eased in spring; and these, in going recklessly

87

down, often knock hesitating snow-drifts into action. A fitting name for those slides that regularly run at the close of winter would be Spring, or Annual. These are composed of the winter's local accumulation of snow and slide rock, and carry a much heavier percentage of rock-débris than the Storm slide carries. They transport from the starting-place much of the annual crumbling and the weatherings of air and water, along with the tribute pried off by winter's ice levers; with this material from the heights also goes the year's channel accumulation of débris. The Annual slide does man but little damage and, like the Flood slide, it follows the gulches and the water-courses.

In snowy zones the avalanche is commonly called a snow-slide, or simply a slide. A slide, with its comet tail of powdered snow, makes an intense impression on all who see one. It appears out of order with the scheme of things; but, as a matter of fact, it is one of gravity's working ways, a demonstration of the laws of sliding bodies. A smooth, steep slope which receives a heavy fall of snow will promptly

88

produce or throw off a sliding mass of snow. Raise, lower, or roughen this slope, increase or decrease the annual snow-fall, or change the direction of the wind, — and thus the position of snow-drifts, — and there will follow corresponding slide-action. Wind and calm, gravity, friction, adhesion, cohesion, geology, temperature and precipitation, all have a part and place in snow-piling and in slide-starting.

The Century slides are the damaging ones. These occur not only at unexpected times but in unexpected places. The Century slide is the deadly one. It usually comes down a course not before traversed by a slide, and sometimes crashes through a forest or a village. It may be produced by a record-breaking snow or by snow-drifts formed in new places by winds from an unusual quarter; but commonly the mass is of material slowly accumulated. This may contain the remnant snows and the wreckage spoils of a hundred years or more. Ten thousand snows have added to its slowly growing pile; tons of rock-dust have been swept into it by the winds; gravel has been deposited in it by water;

and gravity has conducted to it the crumbling rocks from above. At last — largely ice — it breaks away. In rushing down, it gathers material from its predestined way.

In the spring of 1901, one of these slides broke loose and came down the slope of Gray's Peak. For years the snow had accumulated on a ridge above timber-line. The mass shot down a steep slope, struck the woods, and swept to the bottom about four thousand feet below, mowing down every tree in a pathway about three hundred feet wide. About one hundred thousand trees were piled in wild, broken wreckage in the gorge below.

Although a snow-slide is almost irresistible, it is not difficult, in many localities, to prevent slides by anchoring the small snow-drift which would slip and start the slide. In the West, a number of slides have been suppressed by setting a few posts in the upper reaches of slopes and gulches. These posts pinned fast the snow that would slip. The remainder held its own. The Swiss, too, have eliminated many Alpine slides by planting hardy shrubbery in the slippery snowy areas. This anchorage gives the snow a hold until it can compact and freeze fast. Shrubbery thus is preventing the white avalanche!

A slide once took me with it. I was near the bottom of one snowy arm of a V gulch, waiting to watch Gravity, the world-leveler, take his next fragment of filling to the lowlands. Separating these arms was a low, tongue-like rock-ledge. A gigantic snow-cornice and a great snow-field filled, with full-heaped and rounded measure, the uppermost parts of the other arm.

Deep rumblings through the earth, echoings from crags and cañons through the communicative air, suddenly heralded the triumphant starting of an enormous slide. About three hundred feet up the heights, a broken end-on embankment of rocks and snow, it came coasting, dusting into view, plunging towards me. As a rock-ledge separated the two ravines above the junction, I felt secure, and I did not realize until too late that I was to coast down on the slide. Head-on, it rumbled heavily toward me with its mixed and crumbling front, making a most impressive riot of moving matter. Again and again the snowy monster smashed its shoulder into the impregnable farther wall. At last, one hundred feet high and twice as wide, came its impinging, crumbling front. At times the bottom caught and rolled under, leaving the overhanging front to cave and tumble forward with snowy splashes.

This crumbling front was not all snow; occasionally an iceberg or a cargo of stones fell forward. With snow flying from it as from a gale-swept, snow-piled summit, this monster of half a million tons roared and thundered by in a sound-burst and reverberation of incomparable depth and resonance, to plunge into a deeper, steeper rock-walled gorge. It probably was moving thirty-five or forty miles an hour and was gaining in velocity every second.

The noise of its passing suppressed the sounds of the slide that started in the gulch above me. Before I could realize it, this slide swept down, and the snow on which I was standing burst up with me into the air, struck and leaped the low ledge, rammed the rear end of the passing slide, and landed me, snowshoes down, on top of it.

The top was unstable and dangerous; it lurched, burst up, curled under, yawned, and gave off hissing jets of snow powder; these and the plunging movements kept me desperately active, even with my broad snowshoes, to avoid being swallowed up, or overturned and smothered, or crushed in the chaotic, fissuring mass.

As its speed increased, I now and then caught a glimpse, through flying, pelting snow-particles, of shooting rocks which burst explosively through the top. At timber-line the gorge walls abruptly ended and the channel curved swiftly to the left in a broad, shallow ravine. The momentum of this monster carried it out of the ravine and straight ahead over a rough, forested ridge.

Trees before it were crushed down, and those alongside were thrown into a wild state of excitement by the violence of swiftly created and entangling gale-currents. From the maelstrom on the top I looked down upon the panic through the snow-dust-filled air and saw trees flinging their arms wildly about, bowing and posturing to the snow. Occasionally a treetop was snapped off, and these broken tops swirled wildly about, hurried forward or backward, or were floated upward on rotating, slower currents. The sides of the slide crumbled and expanded; so it became lower, flatter, and wider, as it slid forward on a moderate up grade. A half-mile after leaving the gorge, the slide collided at right angles with a high moraine. The stop telescoped the slide, and the shock exploded the rear third and flung it far to right and left, scattering it over a wide area. Half a minute later I clawed out of the snow-pile, almost suffocated, but unhurt.

Toward the close of my last winter as government "Snow Observer" I made a snowshoe trip along the upper slopes of the Continental Divide and scaled a number of peaks in the Rocky Mountains of central Colorado. During this trip I saw a large and impressive snow-slide at a thrillingly close range. It broke loose and

"ran" — more correctly, plunged — by me
down a frightful slope. Everything before it
was overwhelmed and swept down. At the bottom of the slope it leaped in fierce confusion
from the top of a precipice down into a cañon.

For years this snowy mass had accumulated
upon the heights. It was one of the "eternal
snows" that showed in summer to people far
below and far away. A century of winters had
contributed snows to its pile. A white hill it was
in the upper slope of a gulch, where it clung,
pierced and anchored by granite pinnacles.
Its icy base, like poured molten lead, had covered and filled all the inequalities of the foundation upon which it rested. Time and its tools,
together with its own height and weight, at last
combined to release it to the clutch and eternal
pull of gravity. The expanding, shearing, breaking force of forming ice, the constant cutting of
emery-edged running water, and the under-
mining thaw of spring sent thundering downward with ten thousand varying echoes a half-
million tons of snow, ice, and stones.

Head-on the vast mass came exploding toward me. Wildly it threw off masses of snowy spray and agitated, confused whirlwinds of snow-dust. I was watching from the top of a precipice. Below, the wide, deep cañon was filled with fleecy clouds, — a bay from a sea of clouds beyond. The slide shot straight for the cloud-filled abyss and took with it several hundred broken trees from an alpine grove that it wrecked just above the precipice.

This swift-moving monster disturbed the air, and excited, stampeding, and cyclonic winds flung me headlong, as it tore by with rush and roar. I arose in time to see the entire wreckage deflected a few degrees upward as it shot far out over the cloud-made bay of the ocean. A rioting acre of rock-fragments, broken trees, shattered icebergs, and masses of dusting snow hesitated momentarily in the air, then, separating, they fell whirling, hurtling, and scattering, with varying velocities, — rocks, splintered trees, and snow, — in silent flight to plunge into the white bay beneath. No sound was given forth as they fell into, and disappeared beneath, the agitated sea of clouds. How strange this noiseless fall was! A few seconds later, as the wreckage reached the bottom, there came from beneath the silent surface the muffled sounds of crash and conflict.

# Wild Folk of the Mountain Summits

# Wild Folk of the Mountain-Summits

THE higher mountain-ranges rise far above the zone of life and have summits that are deeply overladen with ancient snow and ice, but the upper slopes and summits of the Rocky Mountains of Colorado and the Sierra of California are not barren and lifeless, even though they stand far above the timber-line. There is no other mountain-range on the earth that I know of that can show such a varied and vigorous array of life above the tree-line as do these ranges. In the Alps the upper slopes and summits stand in eternal desolation, without life even in summertime. The icy stratum that overlies the summit Alps is centuries old, and is perpetual down to nine thousand feet. Timber-line there is only sixty-four hundred feet above sea-level. How different the climatic conditions in the Rocky Mountains and in the Sierra, where timber-line is at approximately eleven thousand five hundred feet, or a vertical mile higher than it is in the Alps!

Even the high peaks of this region have touches of plant-life and are visited by birds and beasts. The list of living things which I have seen on the summit of Long's Peak (14,255 feet above sea-level) includes the inevitable and many-tinted lichens, spike-grass, dainty blue polemonium, and clumps of crimson purple primroses, all exquisitely beautiful. There are straggling bumblebees, grasshoppers, and at least two kinds of prettily robed butterflies. Among the mammals visiting the summit I have seen a mountain lion, a bob-cat, a rabbit, and a silver fox, though only one of each. The bird callers embrace flocks of rosy finches, ptarmigan, and American pipits, and numbers of white-crowned sparrows and juncos, together with a scattering of robins, bluebirds, golden eagles, red-tailed hawks, and hummingbirds!

The summit life zone in the Rocky Mountains not only sweeps up to exceptionally high altitudes, but it embraces vast territory. In Colorado alone the Arctic-Alpine territory above the tree-line probably extends over five million or more acres. Thrust high in this summit area are the tops of more than three hundred peaks. Many of these tower three thousand feet above the timber-line. Much of this region is made up of steep slopes, shattered summits, and precipitous walls, many of which bound cañons. There is a scattering of lakes, gentle slopes, stretches of rolling moorlands, and bits of wet meadow or arctic tundra. In this high and far-extending mountain land one may travel day after day always above the uppermost reaches of the forest. In this strange treeless realm there is a largeness of view. Up close to the clouds and the sky, the big world far below, the scene stretches away in boundless, magnificent distances.

The snow-fall of this region varies with locality, and ranges from a few feet up to fifty feet annually. In most localities this snow is rapidly evaporated by the exceedingly dry air of the heights. The remnants of each year's fall commonly rest upon the accumulations of preceding years, but during midsummer not one tenth of the heights is snow-covered. Vast areas are occupied by craggy peaks and barren rock-fields. The barrenness is due almost entirely to a lack of soil, not to altitude nor to the rigors of the climate. The climate is in many respects similar to that which wraps the Arctic Circle near sea-level, and it allows many forms of vigorous life.

Numerous moraines, terraces, steppes, and moorlands — the wide sky plains — have their soil, and this in the warmth of summer generously produces green grass and brilliant flowers. These, together with big game, birds, and circling butterflies, people this zone with life and turn the towering and terraced heights into the rarest of hanging wild gardens. In favored places for a mile or so above timber-line are scattered acres of heathy growths. Stunted by cold, clipped off by the wind, and heavily pressed by the snow, these growths are thickly tangled, bristly, and rarely more than a few inches in height. Among these are wintergreen, bunchberry, huckleberry, kalmia, currant, black birch, and arctic willow.

ALPINE PASTURES ABOVE TIMBER-LINE

Near Specimen Mountain in the Rocky Mountain National Park

# Wild Folk of Mountain-Summits

There are miles of moorlands covered with short, thin grasses, while deeply soil-covered terraces, cozy slopes, and wet meadows have plushy grass carpets several inches thick. These growths form the basic food-supply of both the insects and the warm-blooded life of the heights.

These alpine pastures are the home of many mountain sheep. Between Long's Peak and Mt. Meeker there is a shattered shoulder of granite that is fourteen thousand feet above sea-level and at all times partly covered with an ancient snow-field, the remains of a former glacier. During earlier years I occasionally used the sky-line by this snow-field for a view-point and a lingering-place. One day after a long outlook, I emerged from between two blocks of granite and surprised a flock of mountain sheep near by. A majority of them were lying comfortably among the stones. One was nosing about, another was scratching his side with his hind hoof, while the patriarchal ram was poised on a huge block of granite. He, too, was looking down upon the world, but he was also scouting for enemies. Upon my appearance, the flock broke away at good speed but in excellent order, the old ram leading the way. In scrambling up for a farewell view, I disturbed a mountain lion. He bounded among the scattered wreckage of granite and vanished. Here was big game and its well-fed pursuer, in the mountain heights, above the limits of tree growth and almost three miles above the surface of the sea. Many flocks live at an altitude of twelve thousand feet. Here the lambs are born, and from this place they all make spring foraging excursions far down the slopes into a warmer zone for green stuffs not yet in season on the heights. Their warm covering of soft hair protects them from the coldest blasts. Winter quarters appear to be chosen in localities from which winds regularly sweep the snow. This sweeping prevents the snow from burying food beyond reach, and lessens the danger of these short-legged mountaineers becoming snowbound. They commonly endure wind-storms by crowding closely against the lee side of a ledge. Now and then they are so deeply drifted over with snow that many of the weaker ones perish, unable to wallow out. The snow-slide, the white terror of the heights, occasionally carries off an entire flock of these bold, vigilant sheep.

The mountain lion is a prowler, a cowardly, rapacious slaughterer, and may visit the heights at any time. Though apparently irregular in his visits, he seems to keep track of the seasons and to know the date for spring lamb, and he is likely to appear while the sheep are weak or snowbound. He is a wanton killer and is ever vigilant to slay. He lurks and lies in wait and preys upon all the birds and beasts except the bear.

This treeless realm is roamed by both the grizzly and the black bear; both pay most visits during the autumn, and the grizzly occasionally hibernates in these uplands. In summer they range the forests far below, but with the coming of autumn they climb the slopes to dig out fat woodchucks and to get the last of the season's berries, with which to put on final fat for hibernating. They overturn stones for mice and lick up the accumulations of chilled insects which they find along the snow and ice fields. Myriads of flies, moths, grasshoppers, and other insects often accumulate along or on the edge of snow or ice fields in the heights, attracted, apparently, by the brilliant whiteness of the ice or the snow. The cold closely surrounding air zone appears to benumb or paralyze them, and they drop in great numbers near the margin. Occasionally swarms of insects are carried by storms up the heights and dropped upon the snow or ice fields which lie in the eddying-places of the wind.

One autumn I accompanied a gentleman to the Hallett Glacier. On arriving, we explored a crevasse and examined the bergschrund at the top. When we emerged from the bergschrund, the new snow on the glacier was so softened in the sunshine that we decided to have the fun of coasting down the steep face to the bottom of the slope. Just as we slid away, I espied a bear at the bottom, toward which we were speeding. He was so busily engaged in licking up insects that he had not noticed us. Naturally the gentleman with me was frightened, but it was impossible to stop on the steep, steel-like, and snow-lubricated slope. Knowing something of bear nature, the situation, though most interesting, did not appear serious to me. Meantime, the bear heard us and made lively and awkward efforts to be gone. He fled at a racing gallop, and gave us an excellent side view of his clumsy, far-outreaching lively hind legs going it flatfooted.

Deer are among the summer visitors in the cool uplands, climbing a thousand feet or more above the uppermost trees. With the first autumn snow they start to descend, and they commonly winter from three to six thousand feet below their summer range. There are a few woodchuck colonies as high as twelve thousand feet. The woodchuck, in the spring, despite short legs and heavy body, gives way to *wanderlust*, and as a change from hibernation wanders afar and occasionally climbs a mountain-peak. Sometimes, too, a mountain lion prevents his return. The silver fox is a permanent resident of these heights and ranges widely over them. He catches woodchucks and ptarmigan and feasts on big game that has met with accident or that has been left to waste by that wild game-hog, the mountain lion. In summer, and occasionally in winter, both the coyote and the wolf come into the fox's territory.

In slide rock and in bouldery moraines up as high as thirteen thousand feet, one finds the pika, or cony. Almost nothing is known of his domestic life. Apparently he does not hibernate, for on sunny days he may be seen the year round. Like the beaver he each autumn lays up supplies for winter. Hay is his harvest. This hay is frequently placed in conical piles in the shelter of shelving rocks. These piles are sometimes two feet in diameter. His haymaking is done with much hurry. After quickly biting off a number of plants or grasses, he commonly seizes these by their ends and simply scampers for the harvest pile. Quickly thrusting them in, he hurries away for more. His ways are decidedly in contrast to the beaver's deliberate movements. When he is sunning himself, one may, by moving slowly, approach within a few feet. He has a squeaky whistle and a birdlike call, each of which it is difficult to describe. He is a tailless little fellow, and has round ratlike ears; is dark gray above and whitish beneath. In appearance he reminds one of a small guinea-pig, or a young rabbit.

Up in this region, the most skyward of life zones, nature, as everywhere, is red in tooth and claw. There are strength and cunning, victor and vanquished, pursuit and death. One day, while watching a beetle, I saw a deadly attack. For more than an hour the beetle had been doing nothing except turn this way and then that without getting two inches from the grass-edge on the top of a stone. Suddenly a black bit darted past my face, struck the beetle, and knocked him over. It was a wasp, and for a few seconds these two warriors clinched, and fought with all their strength, cunning, and weapons. While locked in deadly struggle, they fell over a cliff that was twelve inches high; the fall broke their hold; this was instantly renewed, but presently they ceased to struggle, with the wasp victor.

The weasel is the white wolf among the small people of the heights. In winter his pure white fur allows him to slip almost unsuspected through the snow. He preys upon the cony and the birds of the alpine zone. Like the mountain lion and some human hunters, he does wanton killing just for amusement. He is bloodthirsty, cunning, and even bold. Many times, within a few feet, he has glared fiendishly at me, seeming almost determined to attack; his long, low-geared body and sinister and snaky eyes make him a mean object to look upon.

An experience with a number of rosy finches in the midst of a blizzard was one of the most cheerful ever given me by wild fellow creatures. While snowshoeing across one of the high passes, I was caught in a terrific gale, which dashed the powdered snow-dust so thickly and incessantly that breathing was difficult and at times almost strangling. Crawling beneath an enormous rock-slab to rest and breathe, I disturbed a dozen or so rosy finches already in possession and evidently there for the same purpose as myself. They moved to one side and made room for me, but did not go out. As I settled down, they looked at me frankly and without a fear. Such trust! After one calm look, they gave me no further attention. Although trustful and friendly, they were reserved and mannerly. From time to time there were comings and goings among them. Almost every snow-dashed incoming stranger gave me a look as he entered, and then without the least suspicion turned to his own feathers and affairs. With such honor, I forgot my frosted nose and the blizzard. Presently, however, I crawled forth and groped through the blinding hurricane and entered a friendly forest, where wind-shaped trees at timber-line barely peeped beneath the drifted snow.

The rosy finch, the brown-capped leucosticte of the Rockies (in the Sierra it is the gray-crowned), is a little larger than a junco and is one of the bravest and most trusting of the winged mountaineers. It is the most numerous of the resident bird-population. These cheery little bits live in the mountain snows, rarely descending below timber-line. Occasionally they nest as high as thirteen thousand five hundred feet.

The largest bird resident of the snowy heights is the ptarmigan. Rarely does this bird descend below the timber-line. But a late and prolonged winter storm may drive him and his neighbor the rosy finch a mile or so down the slopes. The first fine day he is back again to the happy heights. The ptarmigan lives in the heathery growths among huge rocky débris. Much of the winter-time he shelters himself in deeply penetrating holes or runs in the compacted snow. His food consists of the seeds and buds of alpine plants, grasses, and insects. His ways remind one of a grouse, though he is a smaller bird. During winter he appears in suit of white, stockings and all. In spring a few black and cinnamon-colored feathers are added, and by midsummer his dress is grayish-brown. During all seasons he is fairly well concealed from enemies by the protective coloration of his clothes, and he depends largely upon this for protection. He is preyed upon by the weasel, fox, bear, eagle, and lion.

Although the mountain-tops have only a few resident birds, they have numerous summer bird builders and sojourners. Many birds nest in these heights instead of going to similar conditions in the great Arctic Circle nursery. Thus most birds met with in the heights during the summer season are the migratory ones. Among the summer residents are the American pipit, the white-crowned sparrow, and the gray-headed junco, the latter occasionally raising two broods in a summer. Here, too, in autumn come flocks of robins and other birds for late berries before starting southward.

The golden eagle may soar above the peaks during all the seasons, but he can hardly be classed as a resident, for much of the winter he spends in the lower slopes of the mountains. Early in the spring he appears in the high places and nests among the crags, occasionally twelve thousand feet above sea-level. The young eaglets are fed in part upon spring lamb from the near-by wild flocks.

One day, while in a bleak upland above the timber-line, I paused by a berg-filled lake, a miniature Arctic Ocean, with barren rock-bound shores. A partly snow-piled, half-frozen moor stretched away into an arctic distance. Everything was silent. Near by a flock of ptarmigan fed upon the buds of a clump of arctic willow that was dwarfed almost out of existence. I felt as though in the polar world. "Here is the environment of the Eskimo," I discoursed to myself. "He ought to be found in this kind of place. Here are icebergs, frozen tundras, white ptarmigan, dwarf willows, treeless distances. If arctic plants were transported down here on the Big Ice Floe, surely some Eskimo must have been swept along. Why did n't he stay? The climate was better, but perhaps he missed his blubber and sea food, and there was no midnight sun and the nights were extremely short. The pale and infrequent aurora borealis must have reminded him of better nights, if not better days. Anyway, even for the Eskimo, there is no place like home, even though it be in a domed and dingy ice house amid the eternal snows and beneath the wonderful sky of northern lights."

There are fields of varied wild flowers. Brilliant in color, dainty, beautiful, and graceful, they appear at their best amid the wild magnificence of rocky peaks, alpine lakes, and aged snow-fields, and on the far-extending lonely

AT THE EDGE OF THE ARCTIC-ALPINE LIFE ZONE IN THE SAN JUAN MOUNTAINS

moorlands. Many of these flowers are your low-land friends, slightly dwarfed in some cases, but with charms even fresher, brighter, and more lovely than those of the blooms you know. Numerous upland stretches are crowded and colored in indescribable richness, — acres of purple, blue, and gold. The flowers, by crowd-ing the moist outskirts of snow-drifts, make striking encircling gardens of bloom. In con-tributed and unstable soil-beds, amid ice and boulders, they take romantic rides and bloom upon the cold backs of the crawling glaciers, and thus touch with color and beauty the most savage of wild scenes.

The distribution and arrangement of the flowers has all the charm of the irregular, and for the most part is strikingly effective and de-lightfully artistic. They grow in bunches and beds; the stalks are long and short; rock towers and barren débris frown on meadow gardens and add to the attractiveness of the millions of mixed blossoms that dance or smile. Ragged tongues of green and blossoms extend for miles. One of the peculiarities of a few of these plants

117

is that they have stems and axes horizontal rather than vertical. Others are masses of mossy, cushion-like bloom. In many cases there is a marked enlargement of the root-growth, but the flowers compare favorably in size, sweetness, and brilliancy of coloring with their lowland relatives.

Among the blossoms that shine in these polar gardens are the spring beauty, the daisy, the buttercup, and the forget-me-not. There are numbers of the pink and the saxifrage families, white and purple monkshood, purple asters, and goldenrod. Whole slopes are covered with paint-brushes, and among these commonly is a scattering of tall, white-tipped wild buckwheat. Some of these are scentless, while others diffuse a rich perfume.

There are numerous hanging gardens that are grander than all the kings of the earth could create! White cascades with the soft, fluttering veils of spray pour through the brilliant bloom and the bright green of the terraces. In these gardens may bloom the bluest of mertensia, gentians, and polemonium, the brightest of yellow avens, the ruddy stonecrop, and gaillardias as handsome as any black-eyed Susan; then there is a fine scattering of shooting-stars, starworts, pentstemons of prettiest shades, and the tall and stately columbine, a burst of silver and blue.

Many of the polar plants that bloom in this Arctic world were probably brought here from the Arctic Circle by the vast and prolonged flow of ice from the north during the last ice age. Stranded here by the receding, melting ice, they are growing up with the country under conditions similar to those in the Northland. They are quick to seize and beautify each new soil-bed that appears, — soil exposed by the shrinking of snow-fields, piled by landslides, washed down by water, or made by the dropped or deposited sweepings of the winds.

Bees and butterflies follow the flowers, and every wild garden has the buzz of busy wings and the painted sails of idle ones. Mountain sheep occasionally pose and group among the flowers and butterflies. Often sheep, crags, ptarmigan, and green spaces, flowers, and waterfalls are caught in one small space that sweeps up into the blue and cloud in one grand picture.

In many localities there are such numbers of dwarfed plants that one may blunder through a fairy flower-garden without seeing it. To see these tiny flowers at their best, one needs to lie down and use a reading-glass. There are diminutive bellflowers that rise only half an inch above the earth and masses of cushion pinks and tiny phlox still finer and shorter.

The Arctic-Alpine zone, with its cloud and bright sunshine, rests upon the elevated and broken world of the Rockies. This realm is full of interest through all the seasons, and with its magnificence are lovely places, brilliant flowers, and merry birds to cheer its solitudes. During winter these polar mountain-stretches have a strange charm, and many a time my snowshoe tracks have left dotted trails upon their snowy distances.

These cheerful wild gardens are threatened with ruin. Cattle and sheep are invading them farther and farther, and leaving ruin behind. With their steep slopes, coarse soil, and shallow root-growths these alpine growths cannot endure pasturage. The biting, the pulling, and the choppy hoof-action are ruinous. Destined to early ruin if pastured, and having but little value when so used, these sky gardens might rightly be kept unimpaired for ourselves. They would make delightful National Parks. They have a rapidly increasing value for parks. Used for recreation places, they would have a high commercial value; and thus used they would steadily pay dividends in humanity.

# Some Forest History

# Some Forest History

Two picturesque pine stumps stood for years in the edge of a grove near my cabin. They looked as old as the hills. Although they had wasted a little through weathering, they showed no sign of decay. Probably they were the ruins of yellow pine trees that before my day had perished in a forest fire. The heat of the fire that had caused their death had boiled the pores of these stumps full of pitch. They were thus preserved, and would endure a long, long time.

I often wondered how old they were. A chance to get this information came one morning when a number of old pines that grew around these stumps were blown over. Among those that went down were three large and ancient yellow pines and several smaller lodge-pole pines. These I dissected and studied, with the idea that their annual wood rings, together with the scars and embossments, might give information concerning the death of the old brown-gray stumps.

Two of the yellow pines showed two hundred and fifty-six annual rings; the other showed two hundred and fifty-five. All carried fire scars, received in the year 1781. Apparently, then, the stumps had been dead and weathering since 1781. The annual rings in the overthrown lodge-poles showed that they started to grow in 1782. Lodge-pole pines commonly spring up immediately after a fire; these had apparently taken possession of the ground as soon as it was laid bare by the fire that had killed and partly consumed the two yellow pines and injured the three scarred ones. Since the lodge-poles were free from fire scars, since the yellow pine showed no scar after 1781, and since all these trees had stood close about the stumps, it was plain that the stumps were the remnants of trees that perished in a forest fire in 1781.

Later, a number of trees elsewhere in the grove were called upon to testify, and these told a story that agreed with that of the trees that had stood close to the stumps. These

A WESTERN YELLOW PINE

stumps are now the newel-posts in a rustic stairway.

Near my home on the slope of Long's Peak are the records of an extraordinary succession of forest fires. During the last two hundred and fifty years eight large fires and numerous small ones have occurred. Each left a black, fire-engraved date-mark. The dates of some of these fires are 1675, 1707, 1753, 1781, 1842, 1864, 1878, 1885, and 1900. Each fire burned over from a few hundred to a few thousand acres. In part, nature promptly reforested after each fire; consequently some of the later fires swept over areas that had been burned over by the earlier ones. Here and there a fire-scarred tree, escaping with its life, lived on to preserve in its rings the date of the conflagration. In one old pine I found seven widely separated scars that told of seven different fires. In addition to the records in isolated trees, there were records also in many injured trees in groves that had survived and in ragged forest-edges where forest fires had stopped. An excellent check on the evidence given by the annual rings of fire-scarred trees was found in the age of the new tree-growth that came up in the fire-swept territory in which, or on the borders of which, were the telltale fire-injured trees.

Some fires swept so clean that they left behind no date of their ravages, but here and there the character of the forest and of the soil in which it stood made me feel certain that the growth had arisen from the ashes of a fire, and that I could tell the extent of the fire. In most localities the fire-killed forest is at once restored by nature. That ever enthusiastic sower, the wind, reseeds most burned areas within a year. Burns on the Western mountains commonly are covered with young lodge-pole or aspen within three years. There are a few dry wind-swept slopes or places left rocky for which years or even centuries may be required to re-earth and reforest.

Some members of the Pine Family endure fire much better than others. The "big tree," the redwood, and the yellow and sugar pines will survive far hotter fires than their relatives, for their vitals are protected by a thick sheath of slow-burning bark. The Western yellow pine is one of the best fire-fighters in the forest world. Its vitals appear able to endure unusual heat without death, and it will survive fires that kill neighboring trees of other kinds. In old trees the trunk and large limbs are thickly covered with heat-and-fire-resisting bark. In examining a number of these old fellows that were at last laid low by snow or landslide or the axe, I found that some had triumphantly survived a number of fiery ordeals and two or three lightning-strokes. One pine of eight centuries carried the scars of four thunderbolts and seven wounds that were received from fires decades apart.

The deciduous, or broad-leaf, trees resist fires better than the coniferous, or evergreen, trees. Pines and spruces take fire much more readily than oaks and maples, because of the resinous sap that circulates through them; moreover, the pines and spruces when heated give off an inflammable gas which, rising in front of a forest fire, adds to the heat and destructiveness, and the eagerness of the blaze. Considered in relation to a fire, the coniferous forest is a poor risk because it is more inflammable than a deciduous one.

Another advantage possessed by broad-leaf trees lies in the rapid growth of their seedlings. Surface fires annihilate most tiny trees. Two-year-old chestnuts, maples, and, in fact, many of the broad-leaf youngsters, are three or more feet high, and are able to survive a severe fire; but two-year-old white pine, Engelmann spruce, or long-leaf pine are barely two inches high, — just fuzzy-topped matches stuck in the earth that perish in a flash from a single breath of flame.

The ability to send up sprouts, which most deciduous trees possess, is also a very great advantage in the fight against fire. A fire may destroy a deciduous forest and all its seeds without injuring the potent roots beneath the surface. The year following the fire, most of these roots send up sprouts that swiftly grow to replace the fallen forest. Among the so-called Pine Family, the ability to send up sprouts or shoots is limited to a few kinds, most prominent of which is the redwood.

# Some Forest History

Repeated forest fires have injured enormously the Southern hardwood forests; they have damaged millions of trees so that they have become hollow or punky-hearted. These fires have burned off limbs or burned into the trunks or the roots and made openings through which many kinds of fungi have entered the hearts of the trees, to doom them to rot and decay.

Forest fires have been common through the ages. Charcoal has been found in fossil. This has a possible age of a million years. Charred logs have been found, in Dakota and elsewhere, several hundred feet beneath the surface. The big trees of California have fire scars that are two thousand years old.

The most remarkable forest fire records that I ever saw were found in a giant California redwood. This tree was felled a few years ago. Its trunk was cut to pieces and studied by scientific men, who from the number of its annual rings found the year of its birth, and also deciphered the dates of the various experiences the tree had had with fire.

This patriarch had stood three hundred feet

high, was sound to the core, and had lived through two thousand one hundred and seventy-one years. Its existence began in the year 271 B.C. After more than five centuries of life, in A.D. 245 it was in the pathway of a forest fire from which it received a bad burn on the lower trunk. It was one hundred and five years before this burn was fully covered with tissue and bark.

Following this fire came the peaceful procession of twelve centuries. Eleven hundred and ninety-six times the golden poppies came to glorify the green hills of spring, while the songs of mating birds filled woods and meadows. More than a thousand times the aspens ripened and scattered their golden leaves, while this serene evergreen grew and towered more and more noble through the centuries.

Elsewhere the forests were dim with smoke, and on the Sierra during these centuries the heroic "big trees" received many a scar from fire. But not until 1441 did fire again try this veteran. Soon after this burn was healed there came a third fire. This was less injurious than the preceding ones, for the wound that it inflicted healed in half a century.

Higher and more stately the tree grew, and in 1729 it attained the age of two thousand years. At the age of two thousand and eighty-eight years the fourth fire attacked it. This fire burned an eighteen-foot scar upon the trunk of the old tree. In 1900, after the lapse of almost a century, only a small part of this wound was overgrown. This year, 1900, came the reaper, the axeman, who laid low this aged and monumental tree!

What starts forest fires? Some are started by lightning; others are kindled by meteors that are flung from the sky, or by fire that is hurled or poured from a volcano; a few are caused by spontaneous combustion; and many are set by man. Down through the ages primitive and civilized men have frequently set fire to the forest. These fires are set sometimes accidentally, sometimes intentionally. The forest has been fired to drive out game, to improve pasturage, to bewilder the enemy during war, and to clear the land for the plow.

# Rocky Mountain Wonderland

During one of my Colorado camping-trips a high October wind brought me the information that spruce wood was burning near by. While I was searching for the fire in the thick needle carpet of the forest floor, a spark from above settled before me. A fire was sputtering and starting in a tree top about thirty feet above the earth. This fire was starting where a dead leaning tree-trunk was rasping and rubbing against an upright one. The bark of the standing tree was powdered and tufted with wood-dust which had been ground by friction from the trunks as they swayed and rotated in the wind. This inflammable wood-dust, together with accumulated bark-bits and needles, had been set on fire from the heat generated by these two big sticks rubbing together. Plainly this was a friction fire. The incessant swaying of treetops in the tireless wind occasionally causes a smoke from friction at points where overlapping limbs or entangled trees are rubbing. Within a few minutes after my discovery, this fire was roaring eagerly through the treetops.

Friction fires are rare, but my old notebooks

tell of numerous fires that were set by lightning. Before this fire, which was in the Sangre de Cristo Mountains, had died out, a lightning-set fire in the mountains of central Colorado had attracted my attention with massive, magnificent smoke-clouds, which were two or three thousand feet above the mountain-tops. Though thirty miles distant, these clouds occasionally took on the bossy white splendor of big cumuli assembling for summer rain. I resolved to see the fire at close range.

Until burned territory was reached, I followed along sky-line ridges through changing conditions of clear sky, smoke, and falling ashes, ready for swift retreat down a slope in case the fire advanced under smoke cover and surprised me. The burn was entered at the first edge I reached. Millions of seared and blackened trees were standing steadfastly where they had died at their post. All twigs and leafage were burned away, but the majority of the trees still carried their larger limbs and patches of bark. In places only the tree-trunk, a fire-carved totem pole, remained. Whirlwinds of flame had moved, and in places every burnable thing on the surface was consumed, and even tree-roots were burned out two and three feet beneath the surface.

Though weirdly interesting, these ashen fields of desolation were not wholly lifeless. Here, as elsewhere, feasters came to banquet, and good fortune brought favorites to the scene of panic and death. Flocks of gorged magpies were about, and unwontedly bold coyotes, both filled and foraging, were frequently met with. At one place a half-dozen beaver were portaging round a tumble of charred tree-trunks that obstructed the brook-channel. Fire had destroyed the food-supply, and the beaver were seeking home and harvest in other scenes. A grizzly bear was wading their pond and feasting on the dead trout that floated on the surface. Two black bears, despite terrible threats from the grizzly, claimed all the fish that came within reach of the shore. They discreetly kept out of the pond.

Two fawns and their mother lay dead at the foot of a cliff. Either blinded or terrorized by fire or smoke, they apparently had leaped or fallen to death. As I gained the top in climbing to investigate, an eagle swooped angrily at me from a topless trunk. Her mate with scorched feathers lay on the rocks near by. On returning a few days later I found her still watching the lifeless one from the same perch in the dead tree.

In the heart of the burned tract was a thirty-or-forty-acre tract of forest that had escaped the fire. It was surrounded with wide though broken barriers of rock ledges. In this green oasis were numerous wild-folk refugees. Chipmunks, rats, woodchucks, and birds were startlingly abundant, but no big game. Apparently the home people had welcomed the refugees, or had received them indifferently. The only fight noticed was between mountain rats. However, this crowding and overrunning of territory when the exciting fire was over, probably made many terrible pages of animal history, before exodus and death brought a normal readjustment of life to the territory.

Wandering on across the burn toward the

fire-line, I came to the place where a ragged-edged and beautiful glacier meadow had reposed, a poetic park among the spruces dark and tall. Commonly these meadows are sufficiently saturated to defy fire, but this one was burning, though slowly and with but little blaze or smoke. The fire was working toward the centre from the edges and eating downward from one to three feet. This kind of meadow usually carries a covering stratum of a kind of peat or turf which is composed almost entirely of matted grass or sedge roots that are almost free from earthy or mineral matter. These meadows lack warmth or soil sufficient to germinate tree seeds or to grow trees. Often they remain beautiful treeless gardens for generations, while wind and wash slowly bring sediment, or until a flood or landslip brings soil. The deep burning of the surface and the consequent deposit of ash on the new surface probably offered an abiding-place to the next adventurous tree seeds. Glacier meadows occasionally have this kind of ending.

Two prospectors were found at work in a

spruce forest near which the fire started but which it did not reach for a week. These men said that, an hour or so after a thunder-shower of a few days before, one of the brown beetle-killed pines had sent up a smoke-column. Apparently lightning had struck this tree. The following day a small fire was burning near it. This expanded into the forest fire. Commonly it is a standing dead tree that is set on fire by the lightning, but the bolt sometimes fires accumulated trash around the roots where it enters the earth.

Within this extensive burn the trees had stood from thirty to one hundred and forty feet high and from two hundred to three thousand to the acre, and they were from thirty to four hundred and fifty years old. A majority were about two centuries old. The predominating kinds were yellow pine, Douglas spruce, Engelmann spruce, and aspen. Different altitudes, forest fires, and a variety of slope-exposures, along with the peculiar characteristics of each species, had distributed these in almost pure stands, an area of each kind to itself. There was some overlapping and mixing, but lodge-pole pine noticeably stood by itself.

Where first encountered, this fire was roaring through a thick second growth of lodge-pole pine. Scattered through this young growth were hundreds of dead and limbless trees killed by a fire of thirty years before. The preservative effect of their fiery death had kept these great pillars sound, though they had become checked and weathered. They burned slowly, and that night while the fire-front was storming a ridge, these columns spread sparks and flames from split sides, or as gigantic candles blazed only at the top. Yellow pines and Douglas spruces killed in an intensely hot fire are so cooked and preserved that they will resist weathering or rot for decades. I have seen a few of these pitchy broken fellows standing erect in the depth of a century-old second generation of forest with the arms of the living trees about and above them.

Down a slope a fire moves more slowly and with lower temperature than upward on the same slope. A fire may rush in a minute up a slope which it would require a day to creep down. A fire is more all-consuming in going up, and even after years have passed, the remains left on a slope will often enable one to determine whether a fire swept up or crept down. One peculiarity of flames in young growths on steep slopes is that they sometimes dart up the heights in tongues, leaving narrow ragged stretches of unburned trees! Usually these fiery tongues sweep in a straight line up the slope.

The intense heat of a passing fire-front is withering at long distances. I have known a fire to blister aspen clumps that were seven or eight hundred feet from the nearest burned trees. The passing flames may have been pushed much closer than this by slow heavy air-swells or by the brief blasts of wild wind rushes.

The habits of forest fires are largely determined by slope-inclination, wind-speed, and the quantity and quality of the fuel. In places the fire slips quietly along with low whispering, then suddenly it goes leaping, whirling, and roaring. A fire may travel less than one mile or farther than one hundred miles in a day. The ever varying slope and forest conditions in the mountains are constantly changing the speed and the enthusiasm of a fire. Where all conditions are favorable, it sweeps level stretches at a mile-a-minute speed and rolls up slopes with the speed of sound!

One evening I climbed a high ridge that stood about half a mile in front of a heavily forested peninsula which the fire-front would reach in a few hours. The fire was advancing across the valley with a front of about two miles. On arriving at the top of the ridge, I came up behind a grizzly bear seated on his haunches like a dog, intently watching the fire below. On discovering me he took a second look before concentrating his mind on a speedy retreat. Along the ridge about a quarter of a mile distant, a number of mountain sheep could be seen through the falling ashes, with heads toward the fire, but whether they were excited or simply curious could not be determined.

The forested peninsula which extended from between two forested cañons had a number of meadow openings on the slopes closest to me.

# Some Forest History

Around these were many brilliant fiery displays. Overheated trees in or across these openings often became enveloped in robes of invisible gas far in advance of the flames. This gas flashed and flared up before the tree blazed, and occasionally it convoyed the flames across openings one hundred feet or so above the earth. Heated isolated trees usually went with a gushing flash. At other places this flaming sometimes lasted several seconds, and, when seen through steamy curtains or clouds of smoke, appeared like geysers of red fire.

At times there were vast scrolls and whirling spirals of sparks above and around the torrential, upstreaming flames of the fire-front. Millions of these sparks were sometimes formed by high outflowing air streams into splendid and far-reaching milky ways. In moments of general calm the sky was deeply filled with myriads of excited sparks, which gradually quieted, then floated beautifully, peacefully up to vanish in the night.

Meantime the fire-front was pushed by wind-currents and led by ridges. By the time the fire-line had advanced to the steeper slopes it was one vast U about three miles long. Its closed end was around the peninsula toward me. The fire-front rushed upward through the dense forest of the peninsula steeps more swiftly than the wildest avalanche could have plunged down. The flames swept across three-hundred-foot grassy openings as easily as breakers roll in across a beach. Up the final two thousand feet there were magnificent outbursts and sheets of flame with accompanying gale and stormy-ocean roars. Terrific were the rushes of whirled smoke-and-flame clouds of brown, ashen green, and sooty black. There were lurid and volcanic effects in molten red and black, while tattered yellow flames rushed, rolled, and tumbled everywhere.

An uprushing, explosive burst of flames from all sides wrapped and united on the summit. For a minute a storm of smoke and flame filled the heavens with riot. The wild, irresistible, cyclonic rush of fiery wind carried scores of tree-limbs and many blazing treetops hundreds of feet above the summit. Fire and sparks were

# Some Forest History

hurled explosively outward, and a number of blazing treetops rushed off in gale-currents. One of these blazing tops dropped, a destructive torch, in a forest more than a mile distant from the summit!

# Mountain Lakes

# Mountain Lakes

HIGH up in the Rocky Mountains are lakes which shine as brightly as dewdrops in a garden. These mountains are a vast hanging garden in which flowers and waterfalls, forests and lakes, slopes and terraces, group and mingle in lovely grandeur. Hundreds of these lakes and tarns rest in this broken topography. Though most of them are small, they vary in size from one acre to two thousand acres. Scores of these lakes have not been named. They form a harmonious part of the architecture of the mountains. Their basins were patiently fashioned by the Ice King. Of the thousand or more lakes in the Colorado mountains only a few are not glacial. The overwhelming majority rest in basins that were gouged and worn in solid rock by glaciers. John Muir says that Nature used the delicate snowflake for a tool with which to fashion lake-basins and to sculpture the mountains. He also says: "Every lake in the Sierra

149

is a glacier lake. Their basins were not merely remodeled and scoured out by this mighty agent, but in the first place were eroded from the solid." The Rocky Mountain lakes are set deep in cañons, mounted on terraces, and strung like uncut gems along alpine streams. The boulders in many of their basins are as clean and new as though just left by the constructive ice.

These lakes are scattered through the high mountains of Colorado, the greater number lying between the altitudes of ten thousand and twelve thousand feet. Few were formed above the altitude of twelve thousand, and most of those below ten thousand now are great flower-pots and hold a flower-illumined meadow or a grove. Timber-line divides this lake-belt into two nearly equal parts. Many are small tarns with rocky and utterly wild surroundings. Circular, elliptical, and long, narrow forms predominate. Some lie upon a narrow terrace along the base of a precipice. Many are great circular wells at the bottom of a fall; others are long and narrow, filling cañons from wall to wall.

Glaciers the world over have been the chief

CRYSTAL LAKE, A TYPICAL GLACIER LAKE

makers of lake-basins, large and small. These basins were formed in darkness, and hundreds and even thousands of years may have been required for the ice to carve and set the gems whose presence now adds so much to the light and beauty of the rugged mountain-ranges. The ponderous glaciers or ice rivers in descending from the mountain-summits came down steep slopes or precipitous walls and bore irresistibly against the bottom. The vast weight of these embankments of ice moving almost end-on, mixed with boulders, tore and wore excavations into the solid rock at the bottom of each high, steep descent.

Nature's ways are interestingly complicated. Both the number and the location of many of these glacier lakes are due in part to the prevailing direction of the wind during the last glacial epoch. This is especially true of those in the Snowy Range of the Rocky Mountains, which fronts the Great Plains. The majority of the lakes in this range are situated on its eastern slope. Westerly winds undoubtedly prevailed on these mountains during the depositing of the snows which formed and maintained the glaciers that excavated these lake-basins. As a result, much of the snow which fell on the summit and its westerly slope was swept across and deposited on the eastern slope, thus producing on the eastern side deeper ice, more glaciers, and more appreciable erosion from the glaciers. The eastern summit of this range is precipitous and is deeply cut by numerous ice-worn cirques which extend at right angles to the trend of this range. These cirques frequently lie close together, separated by a thin precipitous wall, or ridge. On the westerly side of the range the upper slopes descend into the lowlands through slopes and ridges rounded and but little broken. Over these it is possible to ride a horse to the summit, while foot travel and careful climbing over precipitous rocky walls is in most places required to gain the summit from the east.

Westerly winds still blow strongly, sometimes for weeks, and the present scanty snowfall is largely swept from the western slopes and deposited on the eastern side. So far as I know, all the remaining glaciers in the front ranges are on the eastern slope. The Arapahoe, Sprague, Hallett, and Andrews Glaciers and the one on Long's Peak are on the eastern slope. They are but the stubs or remnants of large glaciers, and their presence is due in part to the deep, cool cirques cut out by the former ice-flows, and in part to the snows swept to them by prevailing westerly winds.

Though these lakes vary in shape and size, and though each is set in a different topography, many have a number of like features and are surrounded with somewhat similar verdure. A typical lake is elliptical and about one fifth of a mile long; its altitude about ten thousand feet; its waters clear and cold. A few huge rock-points or boulders thrust through its surface near the outlet. A part of its circling shore is of clean granite whose lines proclaim the former presence of the Ice King. Extending from one shore is a dense, dark forest. One stretch of low-lying shore is parklike and grassy, flower-crowded, and dotted here and there with a plume of spruce or fir. By the outlet is a filled-in portion of the lake covered with sedge and willow.

In summer, magpies, woodpeckers, nuthatches, and chickadees live in the bordering woods. In the willows the white-crowned sparrow builds. By the outlet or in the cascades above or below is the ever-cheerful water-ouzel. The solitaire nesting near often flies across the lake, filling the air with eager and melodious song. Along the shore, gentians, columbines, paintbrushes, larkspur, and blue mertensia often lean over the edge and give the water-margin the beauty of their reflected colors.

These lakes above the limits of tree-growth do not appear desolate, even though stern peaks rise far above. The bits of flowery meadow or moorland lying close or stretching away, the songful streams arriving or departing, soften their coldness and give a welcome to their rockbound, crag-piled shores. Mountain sheep are often visitors. They come to drink, or to feed and play in the sedgy meadow near by. Ptarmigan have their homes here, and all around them nest many birds from the southland.

# Mountain Lakes

Into these lakes swift waters run, and here the snowy cataract leaps in glory. From the overshadowing cliffs, flattened and lacy streams flutter down. During the summer there is the ever-flowing harmony, the endless animation, of falling water; and in winter there is the silent and architectural symphony of the frozen waterfall. Many lakes during summer are partly edged with inthrusting snow and ice piles; from time to time fragments of these piles break away and become miniature icebergs in these small arctic seas.

Although filled with the purest and clearest water, from a distant height they often appear to contain a brilliant heavy liquid. Under different lights and from different points of view they are emerald, opal, inky black, violet, indigo-blue, and sea-green. I have approached one from a high distant point, and as I descended and waveringly advanced, the lake took on a number of deep colors, each melting like a passing shadow from one into the other. Occasionally, too, it almost vanished in dull gray or flashed up in molten silver. The colors shown

155

were as vivid as if made of the brilliant fire of the northern lights. All these changing colors played on the lake, while the surrounding peaks towered in cold and silent desolation, changeless except when occasionally swept with the filmy bluish shadows of the clouds.

Below the timber-line these lakes are more appealing, and many in the midst of groves and meadows help to form delightful wild parks. Others are hidden away in black forests; tall, crowding firs and spruces rise from their edges and hide them completely, even when one is only a yard or two from their shores. I camped for a week within a stone's throw of one of these forest-embowered gems without suspecting its presence. Returning to camp one evening from an encircling ramble, I was startled by stepping into a lake-edge. For a moment I was puzzled. Instinctively I felt that my camp was about the width of the lake ahead of me. Although I felt certain of my bearings, my mental processes were such that I was unwilling to trust this strange lake. Instead of walking around its poetic shore, I lashed two water-soaked logs

156

together with willows and on this rude raft made my way directly across. My camp was within fifty feet of the place where I landed.

Elements of peculiar attractiveness are combined in the lakes that are situated along the timber-line. Some have a treeless mountain or a rugged snow-piled peak rising boldly behind, and an acre or so of meadow between one shore and the forest. A segment of wind-distorted trees, a few enormous rock domes, a fine pile of boulders, and a strip of willow with clumps of spruces and firs combine to give a charming border.

Among the best known of these Colorado lakes are Grand, Trapper's, Bierstadt, Trout, San Cristoval, Chicago, Thunder, Silver, Moraine, and Twin Lakes. Grand Lake, probably the largest, is about three miles long by one mile wide. Its basin appears to be largely due to a morainal dam. The San Cristoval basin appears to have been formed by a mud stream which blockaded a mountain valley. The lakes of the Long's Peak region are my favorites. These are numerous and show a variety of forms.

Grand Lake and a few others lie to the west; Thunder Lake, Ouzel Lake, and a dozen others are in Wild Basin to the south; Odessa, Bierstadt, and the score of lakes in Loch Vale and Glacier Gorge are to the north. All are within ten miles of the summit of this peak. These lakes and their splendid mountain setting will in time give scenic fame to the region.

The alpine lakes in the mountains of the West are but little known to travelers. Many Western people appreciate the beauty of the Swiss and Italian lakes but do not even know of the existence of the shining lakes in their own mountains. But the unexcelled beauty and grandeur of these lakes, their scenic surroundings, and the happy climate in which they repose will in due time give them fame and bring countless travelers to their shores.

In exploring the mountains I have often camped on a lake-shore. These camps were conveniently situated for the exploration of neighboring slopes and the valley below; or for making excursions to the more rugged scenes, — the moraines, snow-fields, cirques, and peaks

TRAPPER'S LAKE

above. Many an evening after a day with the moraines and the forests, or with the eagles and the crags, I have gone down to one of these ideal camping-places. Here through the night my fire blazed and faded in the edge of a meadow before a templed cluster of spruces on a rocky rim above the lake.

Many times camp was so situated that splendid sunsets or the lingering pink and silver afterglow were at their best behind a broken sky-line ridge. My camp-fire was reflected in the lake, which often sparkled as if enamel-filled with stars. Across one corner lay softly the inverted Milky Way. Shooting stars passed like white rockets through the silent waters. The moon came up big and yellow from behind a crag and in the lake became a disc of gold. Many a night the cliffs repeated the restlessness of the wind-shaken water until the sun quieted all with light. During the calm nights there were hours of almost unbroken silence, though at times and faintly a far-off waterfall could be heard, the bark of a fox sounded across the lake, or the weird and merry cries of the coyote were echoed and reëchoed around the shore. More often the white-crowned sparrow sang hopefully in the night. Morning usually was preceded by a horizon of red and rose and gold. Often, too, vague sheep and deer along the farther shore were slowly developed into reality by the morning light. From all around birds came to bathe and drink, and meet in morning song service.

Occasionally I remained in camp almost motionless from early morning until the stars of evening filled the lake, enjoying the comings and goings and social gatherings of the wilderness folk.

These lakes, if frozen during calm times, have ice of exceeding clearness and smoothness. In early winter this reflects peak, cloud, and sky with astonishing faithfulness. In walking across on this ice when the reflective condition was at its best, I have marveled at my reflection, or that of Scotch, my dog, walking on what appeared to be the surface of the water. The lakes above timber-line are frozen over about nine months of the year, some of them even longer.

Avalanches of snow often pile upon them, burying them deeply.

Gravity and water are filling with débris and sediment these basins which the glaciers dug. Many lakes have long since faded from the landscape. The earthy surface as it emerges above the water is in time overspread with a carpet of plushy sedge or grass, a tangle of willow, a grove of aspen, or a forest of pine or spruce. The rapidity of this filling is dependent on a number of things, — the situation of the lake, the stability of the watershed, its relation to forests, slopes, meadows, and other lakes, which may intercept a part of the down-coming sediment or wreckage. This filling material may be deposited evenly over the bottom, the lake steadily becoming shallower, though maintaining its original size, with its edge clean until the last; or it may be heaped at one end or piled along one side. In some lakes the entering stream builds a slowly extending delta, which in time gains the surface and extends over the entire basin. In other lakes a side stream may form an expanding dry delta which the grass, willows or aspens eagerly follow outward and cover long before water is displaced from the remainder of the lake's rock-bound shores. With many, the lower end of the basin, shallow from the first, is filled with sediment and changed to meadow, while the deep upper end lies almost unchanged in its rock basin. Now and then a plunging landslide forms an island, on which the spruces and firs make haste to wave triumphant plumes. Lake Agnes on the northern slope of Mt. Richthofen was formed with a ,rounded dome of glaciated rock remaining near the centre. This lake is being filled by the slow inflow of a "rock stream."

Landslides, large and small, often plunge into these lakes. One of the largest rock avalanches that I ever saw made one wild leap into Chasm Lake and buried itself. This was about the middle of June. This glacier lake is on the eastern side of Long's Peak and is in a most utterly wild place. The lake was still covered with thick ice, and on the ice the snow lay deep. But spring was melting and loosening things in the alpine heights. As I stood on a talus slope above the outlet of the lake, an echoing on the opposite cliffs told me that a rock-slide was coming down. Almost instantly there was the ripping whizz of falling stone. A huge stone struck and pierced twenty feet of snow and more than four feet of ice, which covered the lake. At the same instant there came sounds of riot from above. More stones were coming down. The crash of their striking, repeated and reëchoed by surrounding cliffs and steeps, made an uproarious crashing as though the top of Long's Peak had collapsed. It was an avalanche of several thousand tons off the slope of Mt. Washington.

This avalanche was formed of a quantity of broken granite sufficient to load a number of freight-trains. It smashed through the icy cover of the lake. The effect was like a terrific explosion. Enormous fragments of ice were thrown into the air and hurled afar. Great masses of water burst explosively upward, as if the entire filling of water had been blown out or had leaped out of its basin. The cliffs opposite were deluged. The confused wind-current which this created shredded and separated much of the water into spray, dashing and blowing it about. I was thoroughly drenched. For half a minute this spray whirled so thickly that it was almost smothering.

Water and ice are incessantly at work tearing down the heights. Water undermines by washing away the softer parts and by leaching. Every winter ice thrusts its expansive wedge into each opening. Places are so shattered by this explosive action that thousands of gallons of water are admitted. This collects in openings, and the following winter the freezing and forcing continues. During the winter the irresistible expansion of freezing water thus pushes the rocks and widens the openings with a force that is slow but powerful. Winter by winter rocks are moved; summer by summer the water helps enlarge the opening. Years or centuries go by, and at last during a rainy time or in the spring thaw a mass slips away or falls over. This may amount to only a few pounds, or it may be a cliff or even a mountain-side.

The long ice-ages of the earth appear to have their sway, go, and return. These alternate with

# Mountain Lakes

long climatic periods made up of the short winters and the other changing seasons such as we know. The glacier lake is slowly created, but an avalanche may blot it out the day after it is completed. Other lakes more favorably situated may live on for thousands of years. But every one must eventually pass away. These lakes come into existence, have a period of youth, maturity, and declining years; then they are gone forever. They are covered over with verdure— covered with beauty — and forgotten.

# A Mountain Pony

# A Mountain Pony

OUR stage in the San Juan Mountains had just gained the top of the grade when an alert, riderless pony trotted into view on a near-by ridge. Saddled and bridled, she was returning home down a zigzag trail after carrying a rider to a mine up the mountain-side. One look at this trim, spirited "return horse" from across a narrow gorge, and she disappeared behind a cliff.

A moment later she rounded a point of rocks and came down into the road on a gallop. The stage met her in a narrow place. Indifferent to the wild gorge below, she paused unflinchingly on the rim as the brushing stage dashed by. She was a beautiful bay pony.

"That is Cricket, the wisest return horse in these hills," declared the stage-driver, who proceeded to tell of her triumphant adventures as he drove on into Silverton. When I went to hire Cricket, her owner said that I might use her as long as I desired, and proudly declared that if she was turned loose anywhere within thirty miles she would promptly come home or die. A trip into the mountains beyond Telluride was my plan.

A "return horse" is one that will go home at once when set free by the rider, even though the way be through miles of trailless mountains. He is a natural result of the topography of the San Juan Mountains and the geographic conditions therein. Many of the mines in this region are situated a thousand feet or so up the precipitous slopes above the valleys. The railroads, the towns, society, are down in the cañons, — so near and yet so far, — and the only outlet to the big world is through the cañon. Miners are willing to walk down from the boarding-house at the mine; but not many will make the vigorous effort, nor give the three to four hours required, to climb back up the mountain. Perhaps some one wants to go to a camp on the opposite side of the mountain. As there is no tunnel through, he rides a return horse to the summit, turns the horse loose, then walks down the opposite side. The return horse, by coming back undirected, meets a peculiar transportation condition in a satisfactory manner.

The liverymen of Silverton, Ouray, and Telluride keep the San Juan section supplied with these trained ponies. With kind treatment and experience the horses learn to meet emergencies without hesitation. Storm, fallen trees, a landslide, or drifted snow may block the way — they will find a new one and come home.

The local unwritten law is that these horses are let out at the owner's risk. If killed or stolen, as sometimes happens, the owner is the loser. However, there is another unwritten law which places the catching or riding of these horses in the category of horse-stealing, — a serious matter in the West.

I rode Cricket from Silverton to Ouray, and on the way we became intimately acquainted. I talked to her, asked questions, scratched the back of her head, examined her feet, and occasionally found something for her to eat. I walked up the steeper stretches, and before evening she followed me like a dog, even when I traveled out of the trail.

For the night she was placed in a livery-barn in Ouray. Before going to bed I went out and patted and talked to her for several minutes. She turned to watch me go, and gave a pleasant little whinny as the barn-door closed.

Telluride and Ouray are separated by a mountain that rises four thousand feet above their altitude. By trail they are twelve miles apart; by railroad, forty miles. Many people go by trail from one to the other, usually riding to the summit, one half the distance, where the horse is set free, and walking the rest of the way.

When Cricket and I set out from Ouray, we followed the road to the Camp Bird Mine. We met horses returning with empty saddles, each having that morning carried a rider from Ouray to the mine. Three of these horses were abreast, trotting merrily, sociably along, now and then giving a pleasant nip at one another.

We stopped at the Camp Bird Mine, and while in the office I overheard a telephone inquiry concerning a return horse, Hesperus,

CRICKET AT THE SUMMIT OF THE PASS

who had been sent with a rider to the summit and was more than an hour overdue. Half a mile above the mine we met Hesperus coming deliberately down. He was not loafing, but was hampered by a loose shoe. When he reached the Camp Bird barn he stopped, evidently to have the shoe removed. As soon as this was done, he set off on a swinging trot down the trail.

As Cricket and I went forward, I occasionally gave her attention, such as taking off her saddle and rubbing her back. These attentions she enjoyed. I walked up the steep places, an act that was plainly to her satisfaction. Sometimes I talked to her as if she were a child, always speaking in a quiet, conversational manner, and in a merry make-believe way, pretending that she understood me. And doubtless she did, for tone is a universal language.

At the summit Cricket met some old friends. One pony had been ridden by a careless man who had neglected to fasten the bridle-reins around the saddle-horn, — as every rider is expected to do when he starts the pony homeward. This failure resulted in the pony's entangling a foot in the bridle-rein. When I tried to relieve him there was some lively dodging before he would stand still enough for me to right matters. Another pony was eating grass by walking in the bottom of a narrow gully and feeding off the banks. Commonly these horses are back on time. If they fail to return, or are late, there is usually a good reason for it.

The trail crossed the pass at an altitude of thirteen thousand feet. From this point magnificent scenes spread away on every hand. Here we lingered to enjoy the view and to watch the antics of the return ponies. Two of them, just released, were rolling vigorously, despite their saddles. This rolling enabled me to understand the importance of every liveryman's caution to strangers, "Be sure to tighten the saddle-cinches before you let the pony go." A loose cinch has more than once caught the shoe of a rolling horse and resulted in the death of the animal. A number of riderless ponies who were returning to Telluride accompanied Cricket and me down the winding, scene-commanding road into this picturesque mining town.

# A Mountain Pony

I spent a few days about Telluride riding Cricket up to a number of mines, taking photographs on the way. Whenever we arrived at an exceptionally steep pitch, either in ascending or in descending, Cricket invited me to get off and walk. Unbidden she would stop. After standing for a few seconds, if I made no move to get off, she turned for a look at me; then if I failed to understand, she laid back her ears and pretended to bite at my feet.

One day we paused on a point to look down at a steep trail far below. A man was climbing up. A riderless pony was trotting down. Just as they met, the man made a dash to catch the pony. It swerved and struck with both fore feet. He dodged and made another bold, swift grab for the bridle-rein, but narrowly missed. He staggered, and, before he could recover, the pony wheeled and kicked him headlong. Without looking back, the pony trotted on down the trail as though nothing had happened. For a moment the man lay stunned, then, slowly rising, he went limping up the slope.

A well-meaning tenderfoot, that afternoon in

Telluride, saw a riderless pony and concluded that he had broken loose. After lively work he cornered the pony in an alley and caught it. The owner appeared just as the stranger was tying the pony to a hitching-post. A crowd gathered as the owner, laughing heartily, dragged the stranger into a saloon. I leaped off Cricket and went into the saloon after them. To the astonishment of every one Cricket also walked in.

We left Telluride one sunny October morning with a sleeping-bag and a few supplies. I had made plans to have a few days for the study of forest conditions around Lizard Head and Mt. Wilson. In the neighborhood of Ophir Loop, the first night out, the moonlight on the mountains was so enchanting that I rode on until nearly morning.

Cricket and I were chummy. The following afternoon, while waiting for sunset over Trout Lake, I lay down for a sleep on the grass in a sun-filled opening surrounded by clumps of tall spruces. Trusting Cricket to stay near, I threw her bridle-rein over her head to the ground and thus set her free. In the sunny, dry air I quickly fell asleep. An hour later, a snorting explosion on the top of my head awakened me. Though I was somewhat startled, the situation was anything but alarming. Cricket was lying beside me. Apparently, while dozing, she had dropped her head against mine, and had snorted while her nostrils were against my ear.

We wandered far from the trail, and, after a few perfect days in the mountain heights, big clouds came in and snow fell thickly all night long. By morning it was nearly two feet deep, and before noon several snow-slides were heard. Being a good rustler, Cricket had all the morning been pawing into the snow, where she obtained a few mouthfuls of snowy grass. But she must be taken where she could get enough to eat.

After thirty-six hours of storm we started down a cañon out of the snowy wilderness under a blue sky. No air stirred. The bright sun cast purple shadows of the pines and spruces upon the clean white snow. After a few hours we came to a blockade. The cañon was filled with an enormous mass of snow. A snow-slide had run in from a side gulch. We managed to get into the upper edge of this snow, where it was thin and not compressed.

Cricket fought her way through in the most matter-of-fact manner, notwithstanding her head and neck were all that showed above the snow. As these return horses are often caught out in deep drifts, it is important that they be good "snow horses." She slowly forced her way forward, sometimes pawing to make an opening and again rearing and striking forward with both fore feet. From time to time she paused to breathe, occasionally eating a mouthful of snow while she rested. All the time I talked encouragingly to her, saying, "Of course you can make it!" "Once more!"

When more than halfway through the snow-slide mass, one of the saddle-cinches caught on the snag of a fallen log and held her fast. Her violent efforts were in vain. Wallowing my way along the rocks several yards above, I descended to her side, cut both saddle-cinches, threw the saddle and the sleeping-bag off her

178

back, and removed the bridle. Cricket was thus left a naked horse in the snow.

When after two hours she had made her way out, I went for the saddle and sleeping-bag. As it was impossible to carry them, I attached the bridle to them and wallowed my way forward, dragging them after me. Meantime Cricket was impatiently waiting for me and occasionally gave an encouraging hurry-up neigh.

When I had almost reached her, a mass of snow, a tiny slide from a shelving rock, plunged down, sweeping the saddle and the bag down into the cañon and nearly smothering me. As it was almost night, I made no attempt to recover them. Without saddle or bridle, I mounted Cricket and went on until dark. We spent the night at the foot of an overhanging cliff, where we were safe from slides. Here we managed to keep warm by a camp-fire. Cricket browsed aspen twigs for supper. I had nothing. A number of slides were heard during the night, but none were near us.

At daylight we again pushed forward. The

snow became thinner as we advanced. Near Ophir Loop, we passed over the pathway of a slide where the ground had been swept bare. Having long been vigilant with eyes and ears for slides, while on this slide-swept stretch, I ceased to be alert. Fortunately Cricket's vigilance did not cease. Suddenly she wheeled, and, with a quickness that almost took her from beneath me, she made a frantic retreat, as a slide with thunderous roar shot down into the cañon. So narrowly did it miss us that we were heavily splashed with snow-fragments and almost smothered by the thick, prolonged whirl of snow-dust. Cricket's vigilance had saved my life.

The masses of snow, stones, and broken timber brought down by this slide blockaded the cañon from wall to wall. These walls were too steep to be climbed, and, after trying until dark to make a way through the wreckage, we had to give it up.

We spent a cold night alongside a cliff. Cricket and I each ate a few willow twigs. The night was of refined clearness, and from time to time I moved away from the pungent camp-

LOOKING EASTWARD FROM LIZARD HEAD

fire smoke to look at the myriads of stars that pierced with icy points the purple sky.

The clear morning brought no solution of my problem of getting Cricket through. I could not abandon her. While she was trying to find something to eat, I made my way up a side gulch, endeavoring to find a way for her to the summit. From the top we could get down beyond the slide blockade. After a time a way was found that was impossible for her at only one point. This point was a narrow gulch in the summit. I climbed along a narrow ledge, swept bare by the slide, then turned into a rocky gulch which came in from the side. I was within fifteen feet of success. But this was the width of a rocky gulch. Beyond this it would be comparatively easy to descend on the other side of the slide wreckage and land in the road to Telluride.

But how was Cricket to get to the other side of this gorge? Along the right I made my way through great piles of fallen fire-killed timber. In places this wreckage lay several logs deep. I thought to find a way through the four or five hundred feet of timber-wreckage. Careful examination showed that with much lifting and numerous detours there was a way through this except at four places, at which the logs that blocked the way were so heavy that they could not be moved. Without tools the only way to attack this confusion of log-masses was with fire. In a short time the first of these piles was ablaze. As I stepped back to rub my smoke-filled eyes, a neigh came echoing to me from the side cañon below.

Cricket had become lonesome and was trying to follow me. Reared in the mountains, she was accustomed to making her way through extremely rugged places, over rocks and fallen trees. Going to the rim of the cañon, I looked down upon her. There she stood on a smoothly glaciated point, a splendid statue of alertness. When I called to her she responded with a whinny and at once started to climb up toward me. Coaching her up the steep places and along narrow ledges, I got her at last to the burning log obstruction. Here several minutes of wrestling with burning log-ends opened a way for her.

182

# A Mountain Pony

The two or three other masses were more formidable than the first one. The logs were so large that a day or more of burning and heavy lifting would be required to break through them. More than two days and nights of hard work had been passed without food, and I must hold out until a way could be fought through these other heavy timber-heaps. Cricket, apparently not caring to be left behind again, came close to me and eagerly watched my every move. To hasten the fire, armfuls of small limbs were gathered for it. As limbs were plentiful on the other side of the gorge, I went across on a large fallen log for a supply, shuffling the snow off with my feet as I crossed. To my astonishment Cricket came trotting across the slippery log after me! She had been raised with fallen timber and had walked logs before. As she cleared the edge, I threw my arms around her neck and leaped upon her back. Without saddle, bridle, or guiding, she took me merrily down the mountainside into the wagon-road beyond the snow-slide blockade. At midnight we were in Telluride.

# The Grizzly Bear

# The Grizzly Bear

ONE day in North Park, Colorado, I came on the carcass of a cow that wolves had recently killed. Knowing that bears were about, I climbed into the substantial top of a stocky pine near by, hoping that one would come to feast. A grizzly came at sundown.

The carcass lay in a grassy opening surrounded by willow-clumps, grassy spaces, and a sprinkling of low-growing, round-topped pines. When about one hundred feet from the carcass, the bear stopped. Standing erect, with his fore paws hanging loosely, he looked, listened, and carefully examined the air with his nose. As the air was not stirring, I felt that he had not, and probably would not, scent me in the treetop perch.

After scouting for a minute or two with all his keen senses, he dropped on all fours and slowly, without a sound, advanced toward the carcass. He circled as he advanced; and, when

187

within thirty feet of the waiting feast, he redoubled his precautions against surprise and ambush. My scent by the carcass probably had nothing to do with these precautions. A grizzly is ever on guard and in places of possible ambush is extremely cautious. He is not a coward; but he does not propose to blunder into trouble.

Slipping cautiously to the edge of a thick willow-clump, he suddenly flung himself into it with a fearful roar, then instantly leaped out on the other side. Evidently he planned to start something if there was anything to start.

Standing fully erect, tense at every point, he waited a moment in ferocious attitude, ready to charge anything that might plunge from the willows; but nothing started. After a brief pause he charged, roaring, through another willow-clump. It was a satisfaction to know that the tree-limb on which I sat was substantial. That a grizzly bear cannot climb a tree is a fact in natural history which gave me immense satisfaction. Every willow-clump near the carcass was charged, with a roar.

Not finding an enemy, he at last went to the

carcass. After feasting for a few minutes he rose and snarled. Then, sniffing along my trail a few yards, he stopped to mutter a few growling threats and returned to the feast.

After eating contentedly and to his satisfaction, he moved round the carcass, raking and scraping grass and trash on it. Then, pausing for a minute or two in apparently peaceful contemplation, he doubled back on the trail over which he had come and faded into the twilight.

Alertness and brain-power are characteristics of the grizzly bear. He is eternally vigilant. He has the genius for taking pains. He is watchful even in seclusion; and when he is traveling his amazingly developed senses appear never to rest, but are constantly on scout and sentinel duty, — except on rare occasions when he is temporarily hypnotized by curiosity. I believe his intelligence to be greater than that of the dog, the horse, or the elephant. Apparently he assumes that some one is ever stealthily in pursuit.

In repeatedly following the grizzly with photographic intentions I was almost invariably outwitted. On one occasion I followed one almost constantly for eight days and nights; and though many times I almost had him, yet I never succeeded. Now and then he climbed a rocky crag to look about; or he doubled back a short distance on his trail to some point of vantage, where he rose on his hind legs, sniffed the air, looked and listened. At other times he turned at right angles to his general course, went a short distance to a point favorable for seeing, hearing, or smelling his possible pursuer, and there remained for a few minutes. If all seemed well, he commonly returned to his trail and again went forward.

Usually he traveled in the face of the wind; commonly he promptly changed his course if the wind changed. In crossing a grassy opening in the woods he sometimes went boldly across; but on the farther side, concealed by the trees, he waited to see whether a pursuer appeared across the opening. Sometimes he went round an opening to the right or to the left. Apparently there lay a plan behind his every move.

# The Grizzly Bear

The third day he was well started diagonally down the wall of a cañon. I naturally concluded that he would on this course descend to the bottom and there continue down-stream. Instead of doing this, he stopped at a point about midway down for a long stay. Then from this place he pointed his nose up-stream and descended diagonally to the bottom of the cañon. At the bottom he again made an acute angle to ascend to the top of the opposite wall.

The last three days of this pursuit he knew that I was following him, but there seemed to be no change in his tactics. He simply moved a little more rapidly. Though well acquainted with grizzly habits, I was unable to anticipate his next important move, and he defeated every plan I put into operation.

For several years an outlaw or cattle-killing grizzly terrorized an extensive cattle-grazing section in the mountains of Utah. For months at a stretch he killed a cow or steer at least every other day. He would make a kill one day and on the next would appear across the mountains, forty or more miles away.

Organized expeditions, made up of from thirty to fifty men, with packs of dogs, pursued him day and night for a week or longer; but each time he escaped. Large rewards were offered for his capture. Old trappers and hunters came from afar, but after weeks of trial gave up the pursuit.

The grizzly has a well-developed bump of curiosity. This sometimes betrays him into forgetfulness. On a few occasions I have come on one — and twice one unwittingly came close to me — while he was intent on solving something that had awakened that curiosity.

Once, while watching a forest fire, I climbed a mountain to a point above the tree-line in order to reach a safe and commanding spot from which to view the flames on a near-by slope. At the summit I came upon a grizzly within a few yards of me. He was squatting on his haunches like a dog, and was intently watching the fire-fount below. A deep roar at one place, high-leaping flames at another, a vast smoke-cloud at another, — each in turn caught his attention. None of his keen senses warned him of my presence, though I stood near him for two or three minutes. When I yelled at him he slowly turned his head and stared at me in a half-dazed manner. Then he angrily showed his teeth for a second or two, and finally — much to my relief — fled like a frightened rabbit.

On another occasion I saw a grizzly on the opposite side of a narrow cañon, with his fore paws on a boulder, watching with the greatest interest the actions of a fisherman on the bank of the stream below. Every cast of the fly was followed by the head of the bear. The pulling-up of a trout caused him almost excited interest. For some minutes he concentrated all his faculties on the fisherman; but suddenly, with no apparent reason that I could discern, he came to his senses and broke away in a most frightened manner, apparently condemning himself for briefly relapsing into dullness.

Two pet grizzlies that I raised always showed marked curiosity. An unusual sound near by or a glimpse of some distant object brought them to tiptoe height, roused their complete attention, and held it until the mystery was solved.

# Rocky Mountain Wonderland

The grizzly is not ferocious. On the contrary, he uses his wits to keep far away from man. He will not make a wanton attack. He will fight in self-defense; or if surprised, and thinking himself cornered, he at once becomes the aggressor. If a mother grizzly feels that her cubs are in danger, she will face any danger for their defense; but the grizzly does not fight unless he thinks a fight cannot be avoided.

He is a masterful fighter. He has strength, endurance, powerful jaws, deadly claws, courage, and brains. Before the white man and the repeating rifle came, he boldly wandered over his domain as absolute master; there was nothing to fear, — not a single aggressive foe existed. I doubt whether toward man the grizzly was ever ferociously aggressive.

That he has changed on account of contact with the white man and the repeating rifle there can be no doubt. Formerly the rightful monarch of the wilds through capability, he roamed freely about, indifferent as to where he went or whether he was seen. He feared no foe and knew no master. The bow and arrow, and the spear, he held in contempt; for the powerful re-peating rifle he has a profound respect. He has been wise to adjust himself to this influential factor of environment or evolutionary force. He has thus become less inquisitive and aggressive, and more retiring and wary. He has learned to keep out of sight and out of man's way.

A grizzly acts so promptly in emergencies that he has often been misunderstood. He fights because he thinks he has to, not because he wants to.

On one occasion in Wyoming I was running down a mountain-side, leaping fallen fire-killed timber. In the midst of this I surprised a grizzly by landing within a few feet of him. He leaped to his feet and struck at me with sufficient force to have almost cut me in two had the blow landed. Then he instantly fled.

On other occasions I have seen grizzlies sur-prised, when, though not cornered, they thought they were and instantly commenced a fierce and effective fight. Dogs, horses, and men were charged in rapid succession and either knocked down or put to flight; yet in these fights he was not the aggressor. He does not belong to the criminal class.

Almost every one is interested in bears; children, the tenderfeet, and Westerners are always glad to have a good bear story. Countless thousands of bear stories have been written, — and generally written by people unacquainted with the character of grizzly bears. Most of these stories are founded on one or another of three fundamental errors. One of these is that the grizzly has a bad temper, — "as cross as a bear" is an exceedingly common expression; another is that bears are ferocious, watchful, and aggressive, always ready to make an attack or to do wanton killing; and the third is that it is almost impossible to kill him. After a desperate fight — in the story — the grizzly at last succumbs, but not, as a rule, until his body is numerously perforated or changed into a lead mine. As a matter of fact, a shot in the brain, in the upper part of the heart, or properly placed in the spine instantly ends the life of a grizzly. Most hunters when facing a grizzly do not shoot accurately.

# The Grizzly Bear

One day I saw three men fire from twelve to sixteen shots at a small grizzly bear on a mountain-side only a short distance away. That evening these men sincerely asserted that he must have weighed at least a ton — when he probably did not weigh more than five hundred pounds — and that though they shot him full of lead, he refused to die. I doubt whether a single one of their shots hit the grizzly. Most of the shots went wild, and some of them hit a rocky cliff about two hundred yards distant and fifty or sixty feet higher than the bear. At another time I saw a hunter kill four huge grizzly bears with just four successive shots. Of course he knew the vital point at which to aim, was a good shot, and had perfect self-control during the few seconds of shooting.

As a rule, the grizzly does not kill cattle or big game. There were buffalo-killing grizzlies, and an occasional one now kills cattle. These killers commonly slay right and left, often killing a dozen head in a short time, but they do not often kill big game. I have a number of times seen elk, deer, and mountain sheep feeding near a grizzly without showing the slightest concern.

The grizzly is an omnivorous feeder. He will eat anything that is edible, — fresh meat or carrion, bark, grass, grasshoppers, ants, fruit, grubs, and leaves. He is fond of honey and with it will consume rotten wood, trash, and bees, — stings and all. He is a destroyer of many pests that afflict man, and in the realm of economic biology should be rated high for work in this connection. I doubt whether any dozen cats, hawks, or owls annually catch as many mice as he. But in some localities the grizzly is almost a vegetarian. In western Montana and in the southern Selkirks of Canada he lives almost exclusively on plants and plant-roots, together with berries and bark.

All grizzlies are fond of fish and in some sections they become successful fishermen. Sometimes they capture fish by wading along a brook, and catching, with claws or teeth, the fish that conceal themselves beneath banks or roots. Commonly the bear makes a stand in driftwood on a bank, or on a log that has fallen into or across a stream. From this stand he knocks fish entirely out of the water with a lightning-like stroke of his paw. The bears that range along the water-sheds of the Columbia and its tributaries feed largely on fish, mostly salmon.

I saw a grizzly make a stand in the ripple of an Idaho stream, where he was partly concealed by a willow-clump. In about half an hour he knocked five large salmon out of the water. With a single stroke of his fore paw each fish was flung on the shore, fifteen or twenty feet away. He made only one miss. These salmon weighed between five and twenty pounds each.

One autumn day, along the timber-line in the Rocky Mountains, wild folk were feeding on the last of the season's berries. Birds were present in such numbers that it appeared like a cosmopolitan bird picnic. There were flocks of grouse and robins, numerous jays and camp-birds; and noisiest and liveliest of all were the Clarke crows. I watched the scene from the top of a tall spruce. This annual autumn feast is common to both bears and birds. In this region, and in the heights above, the bears sometimes fatten themselves before retiring for their long winter's sleep.

While I was up in the tree, out of the woods below a mother grizzly and her two cubs ambled into an opening and made their way slowly up the slope toward me. Mother Grizzly stopped near my tree to dig out some mice. Just after this operation she evidently caught a faint scent of me and instantly stood on tiptoe, all concentration. Motionless as a statue, she looked, listened, and gathered information with her nostrils; but just one whiff of danger was all that came to her through the calm air.

Presently she relaxed and stood for a moment on all fours before moving on. One of the cubs concluded to suckle. Either this violated an ancient grizzly custom or else it was something that in the face of danger was too thoughtless to be excused; at all events the mother knocked the cub headlong with a side swing of her left fore paw. He landed heavily some yards away and tumbled heels over head. The instant he rolled on his feet he sniffed the earth eagerly, as though a remarkable discovery had been made; and immediately he started to dig rapidly with his fore paws, as if some good thing were buried just beneath. He may have been only pretending, however. Without uncovering a thing, he presently raced forward to overtake Mother Grizzly.

The hibernating habits of the grizzly are not completely understood. The custom probably originated, as did the hibernation of other animals, from the scarcity of food. In a long acquaintance with the grizzly my study of his hibernation has brought scanty returns, though all that I have actually seen has been of the greatest interest.

The grizzly hibernates each winter, — "dens up" from three to four months. The length of time is determined apparently by latitude and altitude, by the snow-fall, weather conditions, — whether severe or mild, — and the length of the winter; and perhaps, also, by the peculiarities or the condition of the individual animal. Commonly he hibernates in high altitudes, many going to sleep near or above the timber-line.

# Rocky Mountain Wonderland

The place where he hibernates preferably is a natural cave or a large opening beneath rocks. If completely sheltered in a cave, he is commonly satisfied to lie on bare rocks, with nothing over him. In other places, where the snow might come in contact with him, he commonly crawls beneath a huge pile of trash, leaves, sticks, and roots. Snow had drifted deeply over each hibernating-place I have found.

That his winter-sleep is more or less restless is shown in the spring by his hairless hips and sides, the hair having been worn off during the winter. This probably is due to frequent turnings from side to side.

He is generally fat when he turns in for his winter's sleep; but usually he does not eat anything for a few days before going in. On the few occasions on which I was able to keep track of a bear for several days before he went to sleep he did not eat a single thing during the four or five days that immediately preceded retiring. I have examined a number of grizzlies that were killed while hibernating, and in every instance the stomach and intestines were entirely empty and clean. These facts lead me to think that bears do not eat just before hibernating.

Nor do they at once eat heartily on emerging. The instances in which I was able to watch them for the first few days after they emerged from winter quarters showed each time almost a fast. Those observed ate only a few ounces of food during the four or five days immediately after emerging. Each drank a little water. The first thing each ate was a few willow-twigs. Apparently they do not eat heartily until a number of days elapse.

On one occasion I carefully watched a grizzly for six days after he emerged from his hibernating-cave. His winter quarters were at timberline on Battle Mountain, at an altitude of nearly twelve thousand feet. The winter had been of average temperature but scanty snow-fall. I saw him, by chance, just as he was emerging. It was the first day of March. I watched him with a field-glass. He walked about aimlessly for an hour or more, then returned to his sleeping-place without eating or drinking anything.

The following morning he came forth and

wandered about until afternoon; then he broke his fast with a mouthful of willow-twigs. Soon after eating these he took a drink of water. After this he walked leisurely about until nearly sundown, then made himself a nest at the foot of a cliff in the woods. Here he remained until late the following afternoon, apparently sleeping. Just before sundown he walked out a short distance, smelled of a number of things, licked the snow a few times, and then returned to his nest.

The next morning he went early for a drink of water and ate more willow-twigs. In the afternoon of this day he came on a dead bird, — apparently a junco, — which he ate. Another drink, and he lay down at the foot of a tree for the night. The next morning he drank freely of water, surprised a rabbit, which he entirely devoured, and then lay down and probably slept until noon the following day. On this day he found a dead grouse, and toward evening he caught another rabbit.

The following day he started off with more spirit than on any of the preceding ones. Evidently he was hungry, and he covered more distance that day than in all those preceding. He caught another rabbit, apparently picked up three or four dead birds, and captured a mouse or two.

Grizzlies are born about midwinter, while the mother is in the hibernating-cave. The number at birth is commonly two, though sometimes there is only one, and occasionally there are as many as four. The period between births is usually two years. Generally the young bears run with their mother a year and sleep in the cave with her the winter after their birth.

At the time of birth the grizzly is a small, blind, almost hairless, ugly little fellow, about the size of a chipmunk. Rarely does he weigh more than one pound! During the first two months he grows but little. When the mother emerges from the cave the cubs are often no larger than cottontail rabbits; but from the time of emergence their appetites increase and their development is very rapid.

They are exceedingly bright and playful youngsters. I have never seen a collie that learned so easily or took training so readily as grizzly bear cubs. My experience, however, is confined to five cubs. The loyalty of a dog to his master is in every respect equaled by the loyalty of a grizzly cub to his master. A grizzly, young or old, is an exceedingly sensitive animal. He is what may be called high-strung. He does unto you as you do unto him. If you are invariably kind, gentle, and playful, he always responds in the same manner; but tease him, and he resents it. Punish him or treat him unfairly, and he will become permanently cross and even cruel.

Grizzly bears show great variations in color. Two grizzlies of a like shade are not common, unless they are aged ones that have become grizzled and whitish. Among their colors are almost jet black, dark brown, buff, cinnamon, gray, whitish, cream, and golden yellow. I have no way of accounting for the irregularity of color. This variation commonly shows in the same litter of cubs; in fact it is the exception and not the rule for cubs of the same litter to be of one color. In the Bitter Root Mountains,

# The Grizzly Bear

Montana, I saw four cubs and their mother all five of which were of different colors.

The color of the grizzly has been and still is the source of much confusion among hunters and others who think all grizzlies are grayish. Other names besides grizzly are frequently used in descriptions of this animal. Such names as silver-tip, baldface, cinnamon, and range bear are quite common. Within the bounds of the United States there are just two kinds of bears, — the grizzly and the black; these, of course, show a number of local variations, and five subspecies, or races, of the grizzly are recognized. Formerly he ranged over all the western part of North America.

The great Alaskan bears are closely allied to the grizzly, but the grizzly that is found in the United States is smaller than most people imagine. Though a few have been killed that weighed a thousand pounds or a trifle more, the majority of grizzlies weigh less than seven hundred pounds. Most of the grizzly's movements appear lumbering and awkward; but, despite appearances, the grizzly is a swift runner. He is agile, strikes like lightning with his fore paws, and, when fighting in close quarters, is anything but slow. The life of a grizzly appears to be from fifteen to forty years.

In only a few localities is there any close season to protect him. Outside the National Parks and a few game preserves he is without refuge from the hunter throughout the year. It is not surprising that over the greater portion of his old territory he rarely is seen. He is, indeed, rapidly verging on extermination. The lion and the tiger are often rapacious, cruel, sneaking, bloodthirsty, and cowardly, and it may be better for other wild folk if they are exterminated; but the grizzly deserves a better fate. He is an animal of high type; and for strength, mentality, alertness, prowess, superiority, and sheer force of character he is the king of the wilderness. It is unfortunate that the Fates have conspired to end the reign of this royal monarch. How dull will be the forest primeval without the grizzly bear! Much of the spell of the wilderness will be gone.

# Bringing back the Forest

# Bringing back the Forest

DURING the last fifty years repeated fires have swept through Western forests and destroyed vast quantities of timber. As a result of these fires, most species of trees in the West have lost large areas of their territory. There is one species of tree, however, that has, by the very means of these fires, enormously extended its holdings and gained much of the area lost by the others. This species is the lodge-pole pine.

My introduction to this intrepid tree took place in the mountains of Colorado. One day, while watching a forest fire, I paused in the midst of the new desolation to watch the behavior of the flames. Only a few hours before, the fire had stripped and killed the half-blackened trees around me. All the twigs were burned off the tree beneath which I stood, but the larger limbs remained; and to each of these a score or more of blackened cones stuck closely. Know-

211

ing but little of trees and being interested in the fire, I paid no attention to these cones until a number of thin, brownish bits, like insects' wings, came fluttering and eddying easily down from the treetop.

The ashes and the earth around me were still warm, and the air was misty with smoke. Near by, a tall snag and some fallen logs smoked and blazed by turns. Again, a number of these tissue bits came fluttering and whirling lightly down out of the fire-killed treetop. Watching carefully, I saw brown tissue bits, one after another, silently climb out of a blackened cone and make a merry one-winged flight for the earth. An examination of these brown bits showed that they were the fertile seeds of the lodge-pole pine. With heroic and inspiring pioneer spirit, this indomitable tree was sowing seeds, beginning the work of reconstruction while its fire-ruined empire still smoked.

It is the first tree to be up and doing after destructive flames sweep by. Hoarded seeds by the million are often set free by fire, and most of these reach the earth within a few hours or a few days after the fiery whirlwind has passed by. Being winged and exceedingly light, thousands are sometimes blown for miles. It would thus appear that the millions of lodge-pole seeds released by fire begin under most favorable conditions. Falling as they do, upon earth cleaned for their reception, there is little or no competition and but few enemies. The fire has banished most of the injurious animals, consumed competitors and their seeds, and prepared an ashen, mineralized seed-bed; not a leaf shades it, and altogether it is an ideal place for the lodge-pole seed and seedlings.

It seems extraordinary that fire, the arch-enemy of the lodge-pole pine, should so largely contribute to the forest extension of this tree. It is not only one of the most inflammable of trees but it is easily killed by fire. Despite these weaknesses, such are the remarkable characteristics of this species that an increase in the number of forest fires in the West will enable this tree to extend its holdings; on the other hand, a complete cessation of fires would, in time, almost eliminate it from the forest!

The lodge-pole pine (*Pinus contorta*, var. *Murrayana*) lives an adventurous frontier life, and of the six hundred kinds of North American trees no other has so many pioneer characteristics. This species strikingly exhibits some of the necessary requisites in trees that extend or maintain the forest-frontier. The characteristics which so largely contribute to its success and enable it to succeed through the agency of fire are its seed-hoarding habit and the ability of its seedling to thrive best in recently fire-cleaned earth, in the full glare of the sun. Most coniferous seedlings cannot stand full sunlight, but must have either completely or partly shaded places for the first few years of their lives.

Trees grow from seed, sprouts, or cuttings. Hence, in order to grow or to bring back a forest, it is necessary to get seeds, sprouts, or cuttings upon the ground. The pitch pine of New Jersey and the redwood of California, whether felled by fire or by axe, will sprout from root or stump. So, too, will the aspen, chestnut, cherry, cottonwood, elm, most of the oaks, and many other kinds of trees. The extensive areas in New Brunswick and Maine that were cleared by the fires of 1825 were in large part at once regrown with aspen, most of which sprouted from the roots of burned aspens. Willow is easily propagated from a short section of the root, trunk, or limb. These sections may be broken from the tree by accident, be carried miles downstream, lodge on shore or shoal, and there take root and grow. Beaver dams made of willow poles are commonly overgrown in a short time with willow. Several years ago a tornado wrecked hundreds of willows along a Kansas stream. Each willow was broken into scores of pieces, which were carried and dropped along the track of the tornado. Countless numbers of them were stuck into the earth. Several thousand willow trees were thus successfully planted by this violent wind.

Seeds are the chief means by which the forest is extended or produced. They are sown by wind and gravity, by water, by birds and beasts. I have dwelt at length upon the romance of seed-scattering in "The Spell of the Rockies," in the chapter concerning "The Fate of a Tree Seed." Each species of tree has its own way of scattering its seeds. Once upon the earth, they and the seedlings that may spring from them have peculiar limitations and special advantages. In some cases — as, for instance, with most willows and poplars — these seeds must in an extremely short time find a place and germinate or they perish; the seeds of few trees will stand exposure for two years and still be fertile.

It is only a question of a few years until seeds are carried to every treeless locality. They may journey down-stream or across lakes on a log, fly with birds across mountain-ranges, ride by easy stages clinging to the fur of animals, or be blown in storms across deserts; but these adventurous seeds may find grass in possession of the locality and so thickly sodded that for a century or longer they may try in vain to establish a forest.

Commonly wind-blown seeds are first upon the ground and the most numerous. Though it is of advantage to be the first upon the ground, it is of immense importance that the seed which falls in an opening produce a seedling which thrives in the sun-glare, — which grows without shade. The seedlings of our great oaks and most strong and long-lived trees cannot thrive unless shielded from the sun, sheltered from the wind, and protected from the sudden temperature-changes which so often afflict openings. While these maintain the forest areas, they extend it but little. Only a small number of trees have the peculiar frontier characteristics. Young trees which cannot live in the sun are called tolerant, — they tolerate shade and need it. Species which conquer sunny territory are called intolerant, — they cannot stand shade and need sunlight. It will thus be seen that the acquirement of treeless territory by any species of tree demands not only that the tree get its seeds upon the earth in that territory, but also that the seeds, once there, have the ability to survive in the sunlight and endure the sudden changes of the shelterless opening. Most species of oaks, elms, firs, and spruces require shade during their first few years, and though they steadfastly defend possessions, they can do but little toward winning new territory. On the other hand, aspens, willows, gray birch, cottonwood, old-field pine, and lodge-pole pine produce seedlings that glory in the sunlight and seek to gain more territory, — to push forward the forest-frontier.

Again and again the forest has been swept away by fire; but again and again a few aggressive species have retaken speedily the lost territory. In this pioneer reclamation the aspen and the lodge-pole are leaders. The aspen follows the water-courses, running along the muddy places, while the lodge-pole occupies the dry and rocky slope of the burned area. Seen from a distance the aspen groves suggest bright ribbons and pockets on the sombre cloak with which lodge-pole drapes the mountain. And even beneath the trees the contrast between the methods of these two agents of reforestation is marked. The lodge-pole pine is all for business. Its forest floor is swept clean and remains uncarpeted. The aspen groves, on the other hand, seem like the haunts of little women. Here the floor has a carpet of grass gay with columbines, sweet peas, and wild roses. While the aspens and the lodge-poles are still young they begin to shelter the less hardy coniferous seedlings. But sooner or later both the aspens and the lodge-poles themselves are smothered by their nurslings. They then surrender their areas to forest trees that will live to be many times their age.

But that species which is preëminently successful in bringing back the forest to a burned-over area is the lodge-pole pine. It produces seeds each year and commonly hoards them for many years. Its seeds are light, winged, and easily carried by the wind. As they are frequently released by fire, they are sown at the most opportune time, scattered in profusion, and, in windy weather, transported long distances.

Commonly lodge-pole pine holds on to, or hoards, a percentage of the seeds it bears; that is to say, these seeds remain in the cone, and the cone remains on the tree. In some situations it begins to bear at eight years of age, and in most localities by the time it is twelve.

Year after year the cones, with their fertile seeds safely enclosed, are borne and cling to the tree. Some of these cones remain unopened from three to nine years. A small percentage of them do not open and distribute their seeds until they have been on the tree from twelve to twenty years, and many of the cones cling to the tree through life.

Under favorable conditions the lodge-pole is a rapidly growing conifer. In a forty-five-year growth near my home, the varied light and soil conditions were so spotted that in a small area marked differences in growth were shown. A few clusters were vigorous, and the trees showed an average diameter of six inches and a height of thirty-four feet. From this the size dropped, and in one group the individuals were less than one inch in diameter and scarcely tall enough to be used as a cane; yet all were forty-five years old.

The lodge-pole is not long-lived. The oldest one I ever measured grew upon the slope of Long's Peak. It was three hundred and forty-six years of age, measured twenty-nine inches in diameter, and stood eighty-four feet high. A study of its annual rings showed that at the age of two hundred it was only eleven inches in diameter, with a height of sixty-nine feet. Evidently it had lived two centuries in an overcrowded district. The soil and moisture conditions were good, and apparently in its two hundred and second year a forest fire brought it advantages by sweeping away its crowding, retarding competitors. Its annual ring two hundred and two bore a big fire-scar, and after this age it grew with a marked increase of rapidity over the rate of previous years. A mature lodge-pole of average size and age measures about eighteen inches in diameter and stands sixty feet high, with an age of between one hundred and twenty-five and one hundred and seventy-five years.

The clinging habit of the cones of the lodge-pole pine in rare cases causes numbers of them to be caught by the expanding tissues, held, and finally overgrown and completely buried up in the tree like a knot. Commonly the first crop of cones is the one caught. These are usually stuck a few inches apart in two vertical opposite rows along the slender trunk. Each knob-like cone is held closely against the trunk by a short, strong stem.

I have a ten-foot plank from the heart of a large tree which shows twenty-eight imbedded cones. The biography of this tree, which its scroll of annual rings pictured in the abstract, is of interest. The imbedded cones grew upon the sapling before it was thirty years old and when it was less than twenty-five feet high. They appeared upon the slender trunk before it was an inch in diameter. Twenty-six annual wood-rings formed around them and covered them from sight as completely as the seeds the cone-scales clasped and concealed. The year of this completed covering, as the annual rings showed, was 1790. Then the tree was sixty-six years of age; it came into existence in 1724, and apparently, from the forest-history of the place, in the pathway of a fire. This lodge-pole lived on through one hundred and eighty-two years. In the spring of 1906 a woodsman cut it down. A few weeks later two-inch planks

OVERGROWN CONES IN THE HEART OF A LODGE-POLE PINE
(Showing also the cones as borne on the twigs and an early stage of the
overgrowing process)

were sliced from the log of this tree in a sawmill. The fourth cut split the pith of the tree, and the startled sawyer beheld a number of imbedded cones stuck along and around the pith, the heart of this aged pine. These cones and the numerous seeds which they contained were approximately one hundred and fifty years old. I planted two dozen of the seeds, and three of these were fertile and sprouted.

Old trees may carry hundreds or even thousands of seed-filled cones. Once I counted 14,137 of these on the arms of one veteran lodge-pole. If we allow but twenty seeds to the cone, this tree alone held a good seed-reserve. Commonly a forest fire does not consume the tree it kills. With a lodge-pole it usually burns off the twigs and the foliage, leaving many of the cones unconsumed. The cones are excellent fire-resisters, and their seeds usually escape injury, even though the cones be charred. The heat, however, melts the resinous sealing-wax that holds the cone-scales closed. I have known the heat of a forest fire to be so intense as to break the seals on cones that were more than one hundred feet beyond the side line of the fire.

In most cases the seedlings spring up on a burned-over area the year following the fire. Often they stand as thickly as grain in the field. Under favorable conditions as many as one hundred and fifty thousand will appear upon an acre, and a stand of fifty thousand to the acre is not uncommon. Starting in a close, even growth, they usually suppress for years all other species of trees and most other plants. Their growth is mostly upward — about the only direction possible for expansion — with moderate rapidity. In a few years they are tall but exceedingly slender, and they become poles in from twenty-five to fifty years. The trappers named this tree lodge-pole because of its common use by the Indians for lodge, or tepee, poles.

In overcrowded stands, especially those in which groups or individual trees have slight advantages over their neighbors, a heavy percentage of the growth may die annually for the want of nutrition. If equal opportunities prevail in a crowded tract, all will grow slowly until some have an advantage; these will then grow more rapidly, and shade and suppress neighboring competitors.

The lodge-pole does good work in developing places that are inhospitable to other and longer-lived trees, but it gives way after preparing for the coming and the triumph of other species. By the time lodge-poles are sixty years of age their self-thinning has made openings in their crowded ranks. In these openings the shade-enduring seedlings of other species make a start. Years go by, and these seedlings become great trees that overtop the circle of lodge-poles around them. From this time forward the lodge-pole is suppressed, and ultimately its fire-acquired territory is completely surrendered to other species. It holds fire-gained areas from seventy-five to one hundred and fifty years. It is often supplanted by Douglas or Engelmann spruce. Let fire sweep these, and back comes the lodge-pole pine.

Though it distances all competitors in taking possession of fire-cleared territory, it is less successful than its fellows in entering a territory already occupied by other trees or by grass, because its seedlings cannot endure shade, and its seeds will not germinate or take root except they be brought directly into contact with clean mineral soil. The lodge-pole, therefore, needs the assistance of fire both to acquire and to hold territory. Increase the number of forest fires, and the lodge-pole extends its holdings; if we could stop fires altogether, the lodge-pole would become almost extinct.

The lodge-pole has an astonishing altitudinal as well as latitudinal range. Scattered pretty well over the mountain region of the western United States, thence northward along the coast over much of the head-waters of the Yukon in Alaska, it occupies an enormous area. Over this it adapts itself with marked success to a variety of soil, moisture, and climatic conditions, and covers ragged tracts from warm sea-beaches to dry, cold mountain slopes eleven thousand feet above the sea. In many places it surrenders the traditional pole form of its race and wins success by becoming thick-barked, stocky, and limb-covered from top to bottom.

# Mountain Parks

# Mountain Parks

THE grassy park openings within the mountain forests are among the great charms of the outdoor world. These are as varied in their forms as clouds, delightfully irregular of outline. Their ragged-edged border of forest, with its grassy bays and peninsulas of trees, is a delight. Numbers are bordered by a lake or a crag, and many are crossed by brooks and decorated with scattered trees and tree-clumps. Others extend across swelling moraines. All are formed on Nature's free and flowing lines, have the charms of the irregular, and are model parks which many landscape gardeners have tried in vain to imitate. They vary in size from a mere grass-plot to a wide prairie within the forest.

"Park" is the name given to most of these openings, be they large or small. There are many of these scattered through the Rocky Mountains. North, South, and Middle Parks of Colorado are among the largest. These larger ones are simply meadows on a magnificent scale. Each is an extensive prairie of irregular outline surrounded by high forest-draped mountains with snowy peaks, — an inter-mountain plain broken by grassy hills and forested ridges. Here a mountain peninsula thrusts out into the lowland, and there a grassy bay extends a few miles back into the forested mountains. Samuel Bowles, in the "Springfield Republican," gave the following description of Middle Park while it was still primeval: "Above us the mountain peaks go up sharp with snow and rock, and shut in our view; but below and beyond through wide and thick forests lies Middle Park, a varied picture of plain and hill, with snowy peaks beyond and around. . . . It offers as much of varied and sublime beauty in mountain scenery as any so comparatively easy a trip within our experience possibly can. . . . A short ride brought us into miles of clear prairie, with grass one to two feet high, and hearty streams struggling to be first into the Pacific Ocean. This was the Middle Park, and we had a long twenty-five miles ride northerly through

A MOUNTAIN PARK IN THE SAN JUAN MOUNTAINS

it that day. It was not monotonous by any means. Frequent ranges of hills break the prairie; the latter changes from rich bottom lands with heavy grass, to light, cold gravelly uplands, thin with bunch grass and sage brush; sluggish streams and quick streams alternate; belts of hardy pines and tender-looking aspens (cottonwood) lie along the crests or sides of the hills; farther away are higher hills fully wooded, and still beyond the range that bounds the Park and circles it with eternal snows."

During one of his early exploring expeditions, John C. Frémont visited North Park and wrote of it as follows: "The valley narrowed as we ascended and presently degenerated into a gorge, through which the river passed as through a gate — a beautiful circular valley of thirty miles in diameter, walled in all around with snowy mountains, rich with water and with grass, fringed with pine on the mountain sides below the snow line and a paradise to all grazing animals. We continued our way among the waters of the park over the foothills of the bordering mountains."

# Rocky Mountain Wonderland

Hayden Valley in the Yellowstone National Park is another large grassy opening in a mountain forest. This valley apparently was once a vast arm of Yellowstone Lake.

Estes Park, in Colorado, is one of the most attractive as well as the best known of the mountain parks. Although much smaller than Middle or South Park, it is much larger than hundreds of the other beautiful mountain parks. The Estes Park region embraces about one hundred square miles, though only one third of this is open. The approximate altitude of the ragged lowland park is a trifle less than eight thousand feet. This is entirely surrounded by high mountains which uphold a number of rocky, snowy peaks. In 1875 Dr. F. V. Hayden, father of the Yellowstone Park, wrote of this region: "Within the district treated we will scarcely be able to find a region so favorably distinguished as that presented by Estes Park. Not only has nature amply supplied this valley with features of rare beauty and surroundings of admirable grandeur, but it has thus distributed them that the eye of an artist may rest with perfect satisfaction on the complete picture presented." Erosion and glacial action have given this region its form, while fire made the beautiful opening or park within a forest.

The majority of parks or meadow gardens which decorate the forests of the Rocky Mountains probably owe their existence to fire. Trees and grass are endlessly contending for the possession of the earth. In this incessant silent struggle a sweeping fire is generally of advantage to the grass. Trees suffer more from fire than does grass. It is probable that repeated fires enable the grass to hold the plains and prairies against the encroachments of the trees. Each forest fire commonly gives the grass possession of a part of the area formerly dominated by the forest. Usually both grass and trees are prompt to seize any fire-cleared area. The grass may be first to come, or some space may be wet or in some other way unfavorable to tree seed but encouraging to grass seed.

While forest fires bring many of these parks, others are glacier meadows, lake-basins which time has filled with sediment and sodded with grass. Many are due to the presence of water, either outspreading surface water or an excess of underground water just beneath the surface, — to streams visible or invisible. A few result from boggy places which result from impaired drainage caused by landslips or fallen trees. Thousands were made by beaver dams, — are old beaver ponds that filled with sediment and then grassed over.

Most parks that owe their origin to forest fires have charcoal beneath the surface. A little digging commonly reveals charred logs or roots. Occasionally, too, a blackened tree-snag stands suggestively in these treeless gardens. In the competition for this territory, in which grass, spruces, aspens, and kinnikinick compete, grass was successful. Just what conditions may have been favorable to grass cannot be told, though probably one point was the abundance of moisture. Possibly the fire destroyed all near-by seed trees, or trees not destroyed may not have borne seed until the year following the fire. Anyway, grass often seizes and covers fire-cleared areas so thickly and so continuously with sod that tree seeds find no opening, and grass thus holds possession for decades, and, in favorable places, possibly for a century.

Trees grow up around these areas and in due time the grassy park is surrounded by a forest. The trees along the edge of this park extend long limbs out into it. These limbs shade and kill the grass beneath. Tree seeds sprout where the grass is killed, and these seedlings in turn produce trees with long limbs reaching into the park. These shade and smother more grass and thus advance the forest another limb's length. Slowly but surely the park is diminished.

Struggling trees may sometimes obtain a place in advance of the others or a start in the centre of the park, and thus hasten the death of the park and speed the triumph of the trees. A mere incident may shorten the life of a park. A grizzly bear that I followed one day, paused on a dry point in a park to dig out some mice. In reaching these he discovered a chipmunk burrow. By the time he had secured all these he had torn up several square yards of sod. In this fresh earth the surrounding trees sowed triumphant seeds, from which a cluster of spruces expanded and went out to meet the surrounding advancing forest. Fighting deer sometimes cut the sod and thus allow a few tree seeds to assert themselves. Wind may blow down a tall tree which lands in the edge of the park. Along its full length grows a line of invading forest. Occasionally the earth piled out by a gopher, or by a coyote in digging out a gopher, offers an opportunity that is seized by a tree seed. An ant-hill in a meadow may afford a footing for invading tree seeds. On one occasion a cliff tumbled and a huge rock-fragment bounded far into the sloping meadow. Trees sprang up in each place where the rock tore the sod and also around where it came to rest in the grass.

These breaks in the sod made by animals or other agencies do not always give triumph to the trees. Seedlings may eagerly start in these openings, but, being isolated, they are in greater danger, perhaps, than seedlings in the forest. Rabbits may nibble them, woodchucks devour, or insects overrun them. The surrounding grass may smother them and reclaim the temporarily lost opening.

But, though only one tree may grow, this in due time shades the grass, a circle of young trees rise around it, and these in turn carry forward the work of winning territory. At last the park is overgrown with trees!

Glacier meadows may be seen in all stages of evolution. The lake-basin gouged by a glacier goes through many changes before it is covered by a forest and forgotten. No sooner does ice vanish and a glacier lake appear than its filling-in is commenced. Landslips and snow-slides thrust boulders and cliff-fragments into it; running water is constantly depositing sand and sediment upon its bottom. Sedge and moss commence covering its surface as soon as its water becomes shallow. In due time it becomes a bog with a thick covering like a wet mattress, composed of the matted roots of sedge and grass. Over this, wind and water deposit earthy matter, but centuries may pass before the bog is filled in sufficiently to have a dry surface and produce grass and flowers and finally trees.

Once while strolling through a forested flat in central Colorado, I concluded from the topography of the country that it must formerly have been a glacier lake. I procured tools and sank a shaft into the earth between the spruces. At a depth of two feet was a gravelly soil-deposit, and beneath this a matting of willow roots and sedge roots and stalks. These rested in a kind of turf at water-level, beneath which were boulders, while under these was bed-rock. Numerous romantic changes time had made here.

Many of these meadows are as level as the surface of a lake. Commonly the surface is comparatively smooth, even though one edge may be higher than the other. I measured one meadow that was three thousand feet long by two hundred and fifty feet wide. Tree-ranks of the surrounding forest crowded to its very edge. On the north the country extended away only a foot or two higher than meadow-level. On the south a mountain rose steeply, and this surface of the meadow was four feet higher than the one opposite. The up-the-mountain end was about three feet higher than the end which had been the old outlet of the lake. The steep south shore had sent down more material than the level one on the north. In fact, water-level on the north shore, though concealed by grass, was almost precisely the same as when the waters of the lake shone from shore to shore. In one corner of the meadow was an aspen grove. From the mountain-side above, a landslide had come down. Rains had eroded this area to bed-rock and had torn out a gully that was several feet wide on the slope below. This washed material was spread out in a delta-like deposit on the surface of the meadow. Aspens took possession of this delta.

Glacier meadows are usually longer-lived than other mountain parks. In favorable places they sometimes endure for centuries. Commonly they are slowly replaced by the extending forest. The peaty, turfy growth which covers them is of fine matted roots, almost free of earthy or mineral matter, and often is a saturated mattress several feet in thickness. The water-level is usually at the surface, but during an extremely dry time it may sink several inches or even a few feet. If fires run during a dry period of this kind, the fire will burn to water-level. The ashes of this fire, together with the mineral matter which it concentrates, commonly form a soil-bed which promptly produces trees. Sometimes, however, grass returns. Thus, while fire brings forth many meadows in the forest, it sometimes is the end of one evolved from glacial action. A landslip often plunges a peninsula of soil out upon a glacial meadow. This is usually captured by trees in a year or two.

These parks make ideal camping-places, — wild, beautiful, and alluring in every season. I have enjoyed them when they were white with snow, mysterious with cloud and mist, romantic with moonlight, and knee-deep in the floral wealth of June. Often I have burst out upon a sunny meadow hidden away in the solitude of the forest. As it lies silent in the sunshine, butterflies with beautifully colored wings circle lightly above its brilliant masses of flowers. Here bears prowl, deer feed, and birds assemble in such numbers that the park appears to be their social centre. In these wild gardens the matchless solitaire is found. Often he sings from the top of a spruce and accompanies his song by darting off or upward on happy wings, returning and darting again, singing all the time as if enchanted.

Among the hundreds of these happy resting-grounds in which I have camped, one in the San Juan Mountains has left me the most memories. I came there one evening during a severe gale. The wind roared and thundered as impressively as breakers on a rock-bound shore. By midnight the storm ceased, and the tall trees stood as quietly as if content to rest after their vigorous exercise in the friendly wrestling-match with the wind. The spruces had become towering folded flags of fluffy black. After the gale the sky was luminous with crowding stars. I lingered in the centre of the opening to watch them. The heavens appeared to be made of many star-filled skies, one behind the other. The farthest one was very remote, while the closest seemed strangely near me, just above the tops of the trees.

# Rocky Mountain Wonderland

Many times I have come out of the subdued light of the pathless forest to enjoy these sunny openings. Often I have stood within them watching the butterflies circling in the sun or a deer and her fawns feeding quietly across, and, as I looked, I have listened to the scolding of the squirrel and the mellow ringing of the woodpecker far away in the forest. Here I have watched the coming storm, have enjoyed its presence, and in its breaking have seen the brilliant bow rest its foundations in front of the trees just across the meadow. Sometimes the moon showed its soft bow in the edge of the advancing or the breaking storm.

One evening, before the moon looked into this fairy garden, I watched a dance of crowding fireflies. They were as thick as snowflakes, but all vanished when the moonlight turned the park into fairyland. Rare shadow etchings the tall, short-armed spruces made, as they lay in light along the eastern border of this moon-filled park. A blue tower of shadow stretched from a lone spruce in the open to the forest wall beyond. As the moon rose higher, one of the

CAPITOL PEAK AND SNOW MASS MOUNTAIN FROM GALENA PARK

dead trees in the edge of the forest appeared to rise out of the darkness and stand to watch or to serve. Then another rose, and presently two appeared side by side and edged into the light. They might have been conversing. As the night advanced, the shadow of the spruces shortened as their shadow points moved round to the north. As the moon sank behind a mountain, the dead trees settled back into the darkness, and, just before light left the park, the two broken trees moved behind a shadow and vanished. They were scarcely out of sight when the weird cries of a fox sounded from the farther edge of the woods.

Those who believe in fairies will receive the most from Nature. The unfenced wilderness is full of wild folk, full of fairy gardens and homes. With these a careless prowler is rarely welcome. Wasps and bees early gave me sharp hints on blundering, hurried intrusion, and a mother grizzly with two cubs by her side also impressed me concerning this matter. Birds sometimes made me ashamed for breaking in upon them. I did no shooting, carried only a kodak, and was careful to avoid rushing from one place to another; but refined wilderness etiquette was yet to be learned. Usually I felt welcome in the most secluded place, but one day, having wandered out into the corner of the meadow, I felt that I was not only an uninvited guest, but a most unwelcome intruder.

The meadow was a deeply secluded one, such as the fairies would naturally reserve for themselves. Towering spruces shut it out from the world. A summer play was surely in progress when I blundered upon the scene. With my intrusion everything stopped abruptly. Each flower paused in the midst of its part, the music of the thrush broke off, the tall spruces scowled stiffly, and the slender, observant young trees stood unwillingly still. Plainly all were annoyed at my presence, and all were waiting impatiently for me to be gone. As I retreated into the woods, a breeze whispered and the spruces made stately movements. The flowers in the meadow resumed their dance, the aspen leaves their merry accompaniment, the young trees their graceful swaying and bowing, and the fairies and bees became as happy as before.

# Mountain Parks

A camp-fire anywhere in the wilderness appeals strongly to the imagination. To me it was most captivating in a little mountain meadow. Even in a circle of friends it may shut out all else, and with it one may return through "yesterday's seven thousand years." But to be completely under its spell one must be alone with its changing flame. Although I have watched the camp-fire all alone in many scenes, — in the wilderness, at the shore of the sea, at timber-line, and on the desert in the shadow of the prehistoric cactus, — nowhere has my imagination been more deeply stirred than it was one night by my camp-fire in a little mountain meadow. Around were the silent ranks of trees. Here the world was new and the fire blazed in primeval scenes. Its strange dance of lights and shadows against the trees rebuilt for me the past. Once more I felt the hopes and dreads of savage life. Once more I knew the legends that were told when the first camp-fire burned.

# Drought in Beaver World

# Drought in Beaver World

NOT until one year of drought did I realize how dependent the beaver is upon a constant water-supply that is both fresh and ample. A number of beaver colonies close to my cabin were badly afflicted by this dry period. I was already making special studies of beaver ways among the forty-odd beaver colonies that were within a few miles of my mountain home, and toward the close of this droughty summer I made frequent rounds among the beaver. By the middle of September I confined these attentions to five of the colonies that were most affected by low water. Two were close to each other, but upon separate brooks. The other three were upon one tumbling streamlet.

Autumn is the busiest time of the year in beaver world. Harvest is then gathered, the dam is repaired, sometimes the pond is partly dredged, and the house is made ready for winter, — all before the pond freezes over. But drought had so afflicted these colonies that in only one had any of the harvest been gathered. This one I called the Cascade Colony. It was the uppermost of the three that were dependent upon this one stream. Among the five colonies that I observed that autumn, this one had the most desperate and tragic experience.

Toward the close of September the colonists in each of the five colonies gave most of their attention to the condition of their dam. Every leak was stopped, and its water face was given a thick covering of mud, most of which was dredged from the bottom of the pond.

The beaver is intimately associated with water. He is not a landsman, and only necessity will cause him to go far from the water. The water in a main beaver pond is usually three or more feet deep, a depth needed all the year around. Where nature has provided a place of this kind that is close to his food-supply, the beaver uses it; he will not trouble to build a dam and form a pond of deep water unless this is necessary. But deep water he must have; to him it is a daily necessity in getting a living, moving about the easiest way, and protecting his life.

Early in October the first colony below the Cascade had to leave the old home because of the scarcity of water. There were seven or eight of them, and all went down-stream and joined another colony. From what I know of the two colonies I judge that this was probably a case of the old folks being forced to take refuge with their fortunate children. Apparently they were welcome.

A few days later the lowest of the three colonies on the Cascade streamlet was also abandoned. Two days before leaving home the beaver had commenced to harvest aspen for winter food. A few aspens were standing partly cut; a number untrimmed were lying where they fell; several had been dragged into the pond. But suddenly the beaver deserted the place.

The fifteen or sixteen in this colony went down-stream and took possession of an old and abandoned house and pond. They hastily repaired the dam and the house, and they had only just begun to gather supplies for the winter when the pond froze over. In the bottom of the pond, below the ice, there may have been an abundance of the tuberous growths of the pond-lily or a supply of intruding willow roots; both of these the beaver often dig out even while the pond is frozen over. These beaver in this old pond may have pieced out their scanty food-supply with these roots and endured until springtime; but I fear that at best they had a close squeak.

One brook went dry and the beaver folk on it moved up-stream. They left the dam well repaired, a new house, and a pile of green aspen cuttings in the pond. They were ready for winter when the water-failure forced them to find a new home. They scooped out a small basin by a spring in the top of a moraine, used the material for a dam, and into the pond thus formed dragged a few aspens and willows. A winter den was dug in the bank.

The colonists at the other low-water place abandoned their home and moved three miles down-stream. The tracks in the mud, a few bits of fur, told too well a story of a tragedy during

this enforced journey. While traveling along
the almost dry bed of the stream and at a point
where the water was too shallow to allow them
to dive and escape, two, and probably three, of
their number were captured by coyotes. The
survivors found a deep hole in a large channel,
and here they hurriedly accumulated a scanty
supply of green aspen. As winter came on, they
dug a burrow in the bank. This had a passage-
way which opened into the water about two
feet below the surface and close to their food-
supply.

The Cascade colonists held on for the winter.
Their pond was deep, and their careful repair
of the dam had enabled them to retain water
to the very top of it. However, beaver cannot
long endure water that is stagnant. This is
especially true in winter-time. A beaver house
is almost without ventilation, but its entrance
ways are full of water; the fresh water of the
pond appears to absorb impurities from the air
of the house. Apparently stagnant water will
not do this. Then, too, a stagnant pond freezes
much more rapidly than the waters of a pond

that are constantly stirred and aerated by the inflow of fresh water. The Cascade colonists entered the winter with an abundant food-supply that was stored close to the house. The pond was full of water, but it was becoming stagnant. The drought continued and no snow fell. This was another disadvantage to the colony. If a pond is thickly blanketed with snow, it does not freeze so deeply nor so rapidly as when its surface is bare. By the middle of October the pond was solidly frozen. Drought and continued cold weather came and stayed. Christmas week not a drop of water was flowing from the pond and apparently none was flowing into it. The ice was clear, and, the day I called, there appeared to be digging going on in the pond beneath the ice; close to the dam the water was so roily that I could not see into it.

On the first of February I sounded the ice in a number of places. It seemed to be frozen solidly to the bottom. This pond was circular in outline, and the house stood near the centre in about three feet of water. I climbed up on the house and stood there for some time. Commonly in the winter an inhabited beaver house gives a scent to the small amount of air that escapes from the top, and this tells of the presence of the living beaver inside. But I was unable to detect the slightest beaver scent in the air. Apparently the water in the pond was frozen from top to bottom; probably all the beaver had perished, unless they had managed to dig out, as they sometimes do, by tunneling beneath the dam into the brook-channel below. Many old beaver ponds have a subway in the mud of the bottom. One opening is close to the entrance of the house; the other at a point on shore a few feet or several yards beyond the edge of the pond. This offers a means of escape from the pond in case it is frozen to the bottom or if it be drained. A careful search failed to reveal any tunnel, new or old, through which these beaver might have escaped.

I determined to know their fate and went to my cabin for an axe and a shovel. A hole was cut in the ice midway between the beaver house and the food-pile, — a pile of green aspen cuttings about twelve feet away from the house. The pond was solidly frozen to the bottom, and the beaver had all been caught. The entrances to their house were full of ice. One beaver was found at the food-pile, where he apparently had been gnawing off a bark-covered stick. One was dead between the food-pile and the house. The others were dead by the entrance of an incomplete tunnel beneath the dam, which they apparently had been digging as a means of escape when death overtook them. One had died while gnawing at the ice-filled entrance of the house. Inside of the house were the bodies of two very old beaver and four young ones, frozen solid.

The death of these little people, one and all, in their home under the ice, may have come from suffocation, from cold, from starvation, or from a combination of all these; I do not know. But my observations made it clear that the drought was at the bottom of it all.

# In the Winter Snows

# In the Winter Snows

FOR years I wondered how big game managed to live through the hard winters. How did they obtain food while the snows lay deep? Two winters of snowshoeing through the Rocky Mountains as Snow Observer often brought me in contact with wild game. These wanderings, together with numerous winter camping-excursions through the woods in other scenes, gave me many a glimpse of the winter manners and customs of big wild folk.

One autumn a heavy snow-storm caught me in the mountains of Colorado without snowshoes. In getting out of this I found it easier to wade down a shallow unfrozen stream than to wallow through deep snow. Presently I came upon a herd of deer who were also avoiding the deep snow by using a water-way. They were traveling along in the river and occasionally paused to feed off the banks. Out all floundered into the snow to let me pass. They reëntered the water before I was out of sight.

A few days later I returned on snowshoes to see how they were faring. Deep snow had not seriously concerned them. They were in a snowless place near the river. During the storm an accumulation of sludgy, floating snow had formed a temporary dam in the stream, which raised the water and flooded a near-by flat. Presently the dam went out, and the water ran off; but the water carried with it some of the snow, and it had dissolved much of the remainder. In this cleared place the deer were feeding and loitering.

Wild life easily stands an ordinary storm and usually manages to survive even a deep, long-lying snow. The ability of big game to endure storms must in part be due to their acquaintance with every opportunity afforded by the restricted district in which they live. Big wild folk do not range afar nor at random, nor do they drift about like gypsies. Most animals range in a small locality, — spend their lives in a comparatively small territory. They are

A DEER IN DEEP SNOW, ROCKY MOUNTAIN NATIONAL PARK

familiar with a small district and thus are able to use it at all times to the best advantage. They know where to find the earliest grass; where flies are least troublesome; the route over which to retreat in case of attack; and where is the best shelter from the storm.

With the coming of a snow-storm big game commonly move to the most sheltered spot in their district. This may or may not be close to a food-supply. A usual place of refuge is in a cover or sheltered spot on a sunny southern slope, — a place, too, in which the snow will first melt. Immediately after a storm there may often be found a motley collection of local wild folk in a place of this kind. Bunched, the big game hope and wait. Unless the snow is extremely deep they become restless and begin to scatter after two or three days.

There are a number of places in each locality which may offer temporary, or even permanent, relief to snow-hampered game. These are open streams, flood-cleared flats, open spots around springs, wind-cleared places, and openings, large and small, made by snow-slides.

# Rocky Mountain Wonderland

During long-lying deep snows the big game generally use every local spot or opening of vantage.

In many regions a fall of snow is followed by days of fair weather. During these days most of the snow melts; often the earth is almost free of one snow before another fall comes. In places of this kind the game have periods of ease. But in vast territories the snow comes, deepens, and lies deep over the earth for weeks. To endure long-lying deep snows requires special habits or methods. The yarding habit, more or less intensely developed, is common with sheep, elk, deer, and moose of all snowy lands.

The careful yarding habit of the moose is an excellent method of triumphing over deep snow. In early winter, or with the deepening snow, a moose family proceed to a locality where food is abundant; here they restrict themselves to a small stamping-ground, — one of a stone's throw or a few hundred feet radius. Constant tramping and feeding in this limited area compacts the snow in spaces and in all the trails so that the animals walk on top of it. Each additional snow is in turn trampled to sustaining compactness.

At first the low-growing herbage is eaten; but when this is buried, and the animals are raised up by added snow, they feed upon shrubs; then on the willow or the birch tops, and sometimes on limbs well up in the trees, which the platform of deeply accumulated snow enables them to reach. Commonly moose stay all winter in one yard. Sometimes the giving-out of the food-supply may drive them forth. Then they try to reach another yard. But deep snow or wolves may overcome one or all on the way.

During one snowshoe trip through western Colorado I visited seven deer-yards. One of these had been attacked by wolves but probably without result. Apparently five of the others had not as yet been visited by deadly enemies. The seventh and most interesting yard was situated in a deep gorge amid rugged mountains. It was long and narrow, and in it the deer had fed upon withered grass, plant stalks, and willow twigs. All around the undrifted snow lay deep. The limbless bases of the spruces were set deep in snow, and their lower limbs were pulled down and tangled in it. These trees had the appearance of having been pushed part way up through the snow. In places the cliffs showed their bare brown sides. Entire spruce groves had been tilted to sharp angles by the slipping and dragging snow weight on steep places; among them were tall spruces that appeared like great feathered arrows that had been shot into snowy steeps. The leafless aspens attractively displayed their white and greenish-white skin on limbs that were held just above the snow.

With a curve, the yard shaped itself to the buried stream. It lay between forested and moderately steep mountains that rose high. In this primeval winter scene the deer had faced the slow-going snow in the primitive way. At the upper end of the yard all the snow was trampled to compactness, and over this animals could walk without sinking in. Firm, too, were the surfaces of the much looped and oft trodden trails. The trail nearest to the stream passed beneath a number of beautiful snow-piled arches. These arches were formed of outreaching and interlacing arms of parallel growths of willow and birch clusters. The stream gurgled beneath its storm window of rough ice.

I rounded the yard and at the lower end I found the carcasses of the entire herd of deer, — nine in all, — evidently recently killed by a mountain lion. He had eaten but little of their flesh. Wolves had not yet discovered this feast, but a number of Rocky Mountain jays were there. The dark spruces stood waiting! No air stirred. Bright sunlight and bluish pine shadows rested upon the glazed whiteness of the snow. The flock of cheerful chickadees feeding through the trees knew no tragedy.

The winter food of big game consists of dead grass, shrubs, twigs, buds and bark of trees, moss, and dry plants. At times grass dries or cures before the frost comes. When thus cured it retains much nutrition, — is, in fact, unraked hay. If blighted by frost it loses its flavor and most of its food value.

During summer both elk and deer range high on the mountains. With the coming of winter they descend to the foothill region, where the elk collect in large herds, living in yards in case of prolonged deep snow. Deer roam in small herds. Occasionally a herd of the older elk will for weeks live in the comparatively deep snow on northern slopes, — slopes where the snow crusts least. Here they browse off alder and even aspen bark.

The present congestion of elk in Jackson Hole represents an abnormal condition brought about by man. The winter feed on which they formerly lived is devoured by sheep or cattle during the summer; a part of their former winter range is mowed for hay; they are hampered by fences. As a result of these conditions many suffer and not a few starve.

Wolves are now afflicting both wild and tame herds in Jackson Hole. Apparently the wolves, which formerly were unknown here in winter, have been drawn thither by the food-supply which weak or dead elk afford.

The regular winter home of wild sheep is among the peaks above the limits of tree growth. Unlike elk and deer, the mountain sheep is found in the heights the year round. He may, both in winter and summer, make excursions into the lowlands, but during snowy times he clings to the heights. Here he usually finds a tableland or a ridge that has been freed of snow by the winds. In these snow-free places he can feed and loiter and sometimes look down on unfortunate snow-bound deer and elk.

The bunching habit of big game during periods of extreme cold or deep snow probably confers many benefits. It discourages the attacks of carnivorous enemies, and usually renders such attacks ineffective. Crowding also gives the greatest warmth with the least burning of fat fuel. The conservation of energy by storm-bound animals is of the utmost importance. Cold and snow make complicated endurance tests; the animals must with such handicaps withstand enemies and sometimes live for days with but little or nothing to eat.

Big game, on occasions, suffer bitterly through a combination of misfortunes. Something may prevent a herd reaching its best shelter, and it must then endure the storm in poor quarters;

pursuit may scatter and leave each one stranded alone in a bad place; in such case each will suffer from lonesomeness, even though it endure the cold and defy enemies. Most animals, even those that are normally solitary, appear to want society during emergencies.

A deep snow is sometimes followed by a brief thaw, then by days of extreme cold. The snow crusts, making it almost impossible for big game to move, but encouragingly easy for wolves to travel and to attack. Of course, long periods separate these extremely deadly combinations. Probably the ordinary loss of big game from wolves and mountain lions is less than is imagined.

Some years ago an old Ute Indian told me that during a winter of his boyhood the snow for weeks lay "four ponies deep" over the Rocky Mountains, and that "most elk die, many ponies die, wolves die, and Indian nearly die too." A "Great Snow" of this kind is terrible for wild folk.

Snow and cold sometimes combine to do their worst. The snow covers everything deeply;

then follows an unbroken period of extreme cold; the Ice King is again enthroned; the snow fiendishly refuses to melt, and lies for weeks; the endurance of most wild folk becomes exhausted, and birds, herds, and wolves perish. Similar calamities used occasionally to afflict our primitive ancestors.

Over the vast Northwest a feature of the climate is the winter-annihilating Chinook wind. This occasionally saves the people of the wilds when other relief is impossible. The snowy earth is quickly transformed by this warm, dry wind. In a few hours conditions become summer-like. Fortunately, the Chinook often follows a blizzard. Many a time at the eleventh hour it has dramatically saved the waiting, suffering birds and rescued the snow-buried and starving folk of the wilds.

The beaver and the bear are often benefited by the deep snows which afflict their wild neighbors. During the prolonged hibernating sleep, the bear does not eat, but he commonly needs a thick snowy blanket to keep him comfortable. The beaver has his winter stores on the bottom of the pond beneath the ice. These he reaches from his house by swimming beneath the ice from the house to the food-pile. If the ice is not covered by snow, it may, during a cold winter, freeze thickly, even to the bottom, and thus cause a starving time in the beaver colony.

Deep snow appears not to trouble the "stupidest animal in the woods," the porcupine. A deeper snow is for him a higher platform from which the bark on the tree may be devoured. Rabbits, too, appear to fare well during deep snow. This uplift allows them a long feast among the crowded, bud-fruited bush-tops at which they have so often looked in vain.

The chipmunk is not concerned with ground-hog day. Last summer he filled his underground granaries with nuts and seeds, and subways connect his underground winter quarters with these stores. But heavy snows, with their excess of water, flood him out of winter quarters in spring earlier than he planned.

One March at the close of a wet snow-fall I went out into a near-by pine grove to see the squirrels. One descended from a high hole to the snow and without trouble located and bored down through the snow to his cone-deposit. With difficulty he climbed up through the heavy snow with a cone. He did not enjoy floundering through the clinging snow to the tree-trunk. But at last up he started with a snow-laden cone, in search of a dry seat on which to eat. After climbing a few feet he tumbled back into the unpleasant snow. In some manner the wet snow on the tree-trunk had caused his downfall. With temper peppery he gathered himself up, and for a moment glared at me as though about to blame me for his troubles. Then, muttering, he climbed up the tree. Sometimes the chipmunk, and the squirrel also, indulge in hibernating periods of sleep despite their ample stores of convenient food.

The ptarmigan is preëminently the bird of the snows; it is the Eskimo of the bird world. It resides in the land realm of the Farthest North and also throughout the West upon high mountain-tops. In the heights it lives above the limits of tree growth, close to snow-drifts that never melt, and in places above the altitude of twelve thousand feet. It is a permanent resident of the heights, and apparently only starvation will drive it to the lowlands. Its winter food consists of seeds of alpine plants and the buds of dwarf arctic willow. This willow is matted, dwarfed, and low-growing. When drifted over, the ptarmigan burrow into the snow and find shelter beneath its flattened growth. Here they are in reach of willow buds.

Buds are freely eaten by many kinds of birds; they are the staff of life of the ptarmigan and often of the grouse. They are sought by rabbits and go in with the browse eaten by big game. Buds of trees and shrubs are a kind of fruit, a concentrated food, much of the nature of nuts or tubers.

The cheerful water-ouzel, even during the winter, obtains much of its food from the bottom of brooks and lakes. The ouzel spends many winter nights in nooks and niches in the bank between the ice and the water. This is a strange place, though one comparatively safe and sheltered. In getting into the water beneath the ice, the ouzel commonly finds opportunity at the outlet or the inlet of the lake; sometimes through an opening maintained by spring water. There are usually many entrances into the waters of a frozen brook, — openings by cascades and the holes that commonly remain in the ice over swift waters. Excessive snow or extreme cold may close all entrances and thus exclude the ouzel from both food and water. Down the mountain or southward the ouzel then goes.

Woodpeckers and chickadees fare well despite any combination of extreme cold or deep snow. For the most part their food is the larvæ or the eggs that are deposited here and there in the tree by hundreds of kinds of insects and parasites which afflict trees. Nothing except a heavy sleet appears to make these food-deposits inaccessible.

Most birds spend the winter months in the South. But bad conditions may cause resident birds and animals to migrate, even in midwinter. Extremely unfavorable winters in British Columbia will cause many birds that regularly winter in that country to travel one or two thousand miles southward into the mountains of Colorado. Among the species which thus modify their habits are the red crossbill, the redpoll, the Lapland longspur, and the snowy owl.

After all, there are points in common between the animal life of the wild and the human life of civilization. Man and the wild animals alike find their chief occupation in getting food or in keeping out of danger. Change plays a large part in the life of each, and abnormal conditions affect them both. Let a great snow come in early winter, and both will have trouble, and both for a time may find the struggle for existence severe.

The primitive man slaughtered storm-bound animals, but civilized man rescues them. A deep snow offers a good opportunity for more intimate acquaintance with our wild neighbors. And snowy times, too, are good picture-taking periods. In snowy times, if our wild neighbors already respect us, tempting food and encouraging hunger will place big, shy, and awkward country fellows and nervous birds close to the camera and close to our hearts.

# My Chipmunk Callers

# My Chipmunk Callers

ABOUT a score of chipmunks have their homes in my yard. They are delightfully tame and will climb upon my head or shoulder, eat nuts from my hand, or go into my pockets after them. At times three or four make it lively for me. One day I stooped to give one some peanuts. While he was standing erect and taking them from my fingers, a strange dog appeared. At once all the chipmunks in the yard gave a chattering, scolding alarm-cry and retreated to their holes. The one I was feeding dashed up into my coat pocket. Standing up with fore paws on the edge of the pocket, and with head thrust out, he gave the dog a tempestuous scolding. This same chipmunk often played upon the back of Scotch, my collie. Occasionally he stood erect on Scotch to sputter out an alarm-cry and to look around when something aroused his suspicions.

Chipmunks are easily tamed and on short

acquaintance will come to eat from one's hand. Often they come into my cabin for food or for paper to use for bedding. Occasionally one will sit erect upon my knee or shoulder, sometimes looking off intently into the yard; at other times apparently seeing nothing, but wrapped in meditation. More often, however, they are storing peanuts in their pouches or deliberately eating a kernel. Rarely is the presence of one agreeable to another, and when four or five happen to call at the same time, they sometimes forget their etiquette and I am the centre of a chipmunk scrimmage.

Once five callers came, each stringing in behind another. Just as the fifth came in the door, there was a dispute among the others and one started to retreat. Evidently he did not want to go, for he retreated away from the open door. As number two started in pursuit of him, number three gave chase to number two. After them started number four, and the fifth one after all the others. The first one, being closely pressed and not wanting to leave the room, ran round the centre table, and in an instant all

ENTERTAINING A CHIPMUNK CALLER

five were racing single file round the table. After the first round they became excited and each one went his best. The circle they were following was not large, and the floor was smooth. Presently the rear legs of one skidded comically, then the fore feet of another; and now and then one lost his footing and rolled entirely over, then arose, looking surprised and foolish, but with a leap entered the circle and was again at full speed.

I enjoy having them about, and spend many a happy hour watching them or playing with them. They often make a picnic-ground of my porch, and now and then one lies down to rest upon one of the log seats, where, outstretched, with head up and one fore paw extended leisurely upon the log, he looks like a young lion.

Often they climb up and scamper over the roof of my cabin; but most of their time on the roof is spent in dressing their fur or enjoying long, warm sun baths. Frequently they mount the roof early in the morning, even before sunrise. I am sometimes awakened at early dawn by a chipmunk mob that is having a lively time upon the roof.

In many things they are persistent. Once I closed the hole that one had made in a place where I did not want it. I filled the hole full of earth. Inside of two hours it was reopened. Then I pounded it full of gravel, but this was dug out. I drove a stake into the hole. A new hole was promptly made alongside the stake. I poured this full of water. Presently out came a wet and angry chipmunk. This daily drowning out by water was continued for more than a week before the chipmunk gave it up and opened a hole about thirty feet distant.

For eight years I kept track of a chipmunk by my cabin. She lived in a long, crooked underground hole, or tunnel, which must have had a total length of nearly one hundred feet. It extended in a semicircle and could be entered at three or four places through holes that opened upon the surface. Each of these entrance holes was partly concealed in a clump of grass by a cluster of plants or a shrub.

I have many times examined the underground works of the chipmunk. Some of these examinations were made by digging, and others

# My Chipmunk Callers

I traced as they were exposed in the making of large irrigation ditches. The earth which is dug from these tunnels is ejected from one or more holes, which are closed when the tunnel is completed. Around the entrance holes there is nothing to indicate or to publish their presence; and often they are well concealed.

These tunnels are from forty to one hundred feet long, run from two to four feet beneath the surface, and have two or more entrances. Here and there is a niche or pocket in the side of the tunnel. These niches are from a few inches to a foot in diameter and in height. In one or more of these the chipmunk sleeps, and in others is stored his winter food-supply. He uses one of these pockets for a time as a sleeping-place, then changes to another. This change may enable the chipmunk to hold parasites in check. The fact that he has a number of sleeping-places and also that in summer he frequently changes his bedding, indicates that these efforts in sanitation are essential for avoiding parasites and disease.

Commonly the bedding is grass, straw, and

leaves; but in my yard the chipmunks eagerly seize upon a piece of paper or a handkerchief. I am compelled to keep my eyes open whenever they come into the cabin, for they do not hesitate to seize upon unanswered letters or incomplete manuscripts. In carrying off paper the chipmunk commonly tears off a huge piece, crumples it into a wad, and, with this sticking from his mouth, hurries away to his bedchamber. It is not uncommon to see half a dozen at once in the yard, each going his own way with his clean bed-linen.

Chipmunks take frequent dust and sun baths, but I have never seen one bathe in water. They appear, however, to drink water freely. One will sip water several times daily.

In the mountains near me the chipmunks spend from four to seven months of each year underground. I am at an altitude of nine thousand feet. Although during the winter they indulge in long periods of what may be called hibernating sleep, they are awake a part of the time and commonly lay in abundant stores for winter. In the underground granaries of one

# My Chipmunk Callers

I once found about a peck and a half of weed seeds. Even during the summer the chipmunk occasionally does not come forth for a day or two. On some of these occasions I have found that they were in a heavy sleep in their beds.

These in my yard are fed so freely upon peanuts that they have come to depend upon them for winter supplies. They prefer raw to roasted peanuts. The chipmunk near my cabin sometimes becomes a little particular and will occasionally reject peanuts that are handed to her with the shell on. Commonly, however, she grabs the nut with both fore paws, then, standing erect, rapidly bites away the shell until the nut is reached. This she usually forces into her cheek pocket with both hands. Her cheek pouches hold from twelve to twenty of these. As soon as these are filled she hurries away to deposit her stores in her underground granary. One day she managed to store twenty-two, and her cheek pouches stood out abnormally! With this "swelled" and uncouth head she hurried away to deposit the nuts in her storehouse, but when she reached the hole her cheeks were so distended that she was unable to enter. After trying again and again she began to enlarge the hole. This she presently gave up. Then she rejected about one third of the nuts, entered, and stored the remainder. In a few minutes she was back for more. One day she made eleven round trips in fifty-seven minutes. Early one autumn morning a coyote, in attempting to reach her, dug into her granary and scattered the nuts about. After sending him off I gathered up three quarts of shelled nuts and left about as many more scattered through the earth! Over these the jays and magpies squabbled all day.

One day a lady who was unsympathetic with chipmunks was startled by one of the youngsters, who scrambled up her clothes and perched upon her head. Greatly excited, she gave wild screams. The young chipmunk was in turn frightened, and fled in haste. He took consolation with his mother several yards away. She, standing erect, received him literally with open arms. He stood erect with one arm upon her shoulder, while she held one arm around him. They thus stood for some seconds, he screeching a frightened cry, while she, with a subdued muttering, endeavored to quiet him.

Once, my old chipmunk, seeing me across the yard, came bounding to me. Forgetting, in her haste, to be vigilant, she ran into a family of weasels, two old and five young ones, who were crossing the yard. Instantly, and with lion-like ferocity, the largest weasel leaped and seized the chipmunk by the throat. With a fiendish jerk of his head the weasel landed the chipmunk across his shoulders and, still holding it by the throat, he forced his way, half swimming, half floundering, through a swift brook which crossed the yard. His entire family followed him. Most savagely did he resent my interference when I compelled him to drop the dead chipmunk.

The wise coyote has a peculiar habit each autumn of feasting upon chipmunks. Commonly the chipmunks retire for the winter before the earth is frozen, or before it is frozen deeply. Apparently they at once sink into a hibernating sleep. Each autumn, shortly after the chipmunks retire, the coyotes raid all localities in my neighborhood in which digging is good. Scores of chipmunks are dug out and devoured. Within a quarter of a mile of my cabin one October night forty-two holes were dug. Another night fifty-four holes were dug near by. In a number of these a few scattered drops of blood showed that the coyote had made a capture. In one week within a few miles of my cabin I found several hundred freshly dug holes. Many holes were dug directly down to the granary where the stores were scattered about; and others descended upon the pocket in which the chipmunk was asleep. In a few places the digging followed along the tunnel for several yards, and in others the coyote dug down into the earth and then tunneled along the chipmunk's tunnel for several feet before reaching the little sleeper.

So far as I know, each old chipmunk lives by itself. It is, I think, rare for one to enter the underground works of another. Each appears to have a small local range upon the surface, but this range is occasionally invaded by a neighboring chipmunk. This invasion is always resented, and often the invader is angrily ejected by the local claimant of the territory.

In my locality the young are born during the first week in June. The five years that I kept track of the mother chipmunk near my cabin, she usually brought the youngsters out into the sunlight about the middle of June. Three of these years there were five youngsters. One year the number was four, and another year it was six. About the middle of July the young were left to fight the battle of life alone. They were left in possession of the underground house in which they were born, and the mother went to another part of the yard, renovated another underground home, and here laid up supplies for the winter.

A few days before the mother leaves the youngsters, they run about and find most of their food. One year, a day or two before the one by my cabin bade her children good-bye, she brought them — or, at any rate, the children came with her — to the place where we often distributed peanuts. The youngsters, much lighter in color, and less distinctly marked than

287

the mother, as well as much smaller, were amusingly shy, and they made comic shows in trying to eat peanuts. They could not break through the shell. If offered a shelled nut, they were as likely to bite the end of your finger as the nut. They had not learned which was which. With their baby teeth they could eat but little of the nut, but they had the storing instinct and after a struggle managed to thrust one or two of the nuts into their cheek pockets.

The youngsters, on being left to shift for themselves, linger about their old home for a week or longer, then scatter, each apparently going off to make an underground home for himself. The house may be entirely new or it may be an old one renovated.

I do not know just when the mother returns to her old home. Possibly the new home is closely connected with the one she has temporarily left, and it may be that during the autumn or the early spring she digs a short tunnel which unites them. The manner of this aside, I can say that each summer the mother that I watched, on retiring from the youngsters, carried supplies into a hole which she had not used before, and the following spring the youngsters came forth from the same hole, and presumably from the same quarters, that the children of preceding years had used.

Chipmunks feed upon a variety of plants. The leaves, seeds, and roots are eaten. During bloom time they feast upon wild flowers. Often they make a dainty meal off the blossoms of the fringed blue gentian, the mariposa lily, and the harebell. Commonly, in gathering flowers, the chipmunk stands erect on hind feet, reaches up with one or both hands, bends down the stalk, leisurely eats the blossoms, and then pulls down another. The big chipmunk, however, has some gross food habits. I have seen him eating mice, and he often catches grasshoppers and flies. It is possible that he may rob birds' nests, but this is not common and I have never seen him do so. However, the bluebirds, robins, and red-winged blackbirds near me resent his close approach. A chipmunk which has unwittingly climbed into a tree or traveled into a territory close to the nest of one of these birds receives a beating from the wings of the birds and many stabs from their bills before he can retreat to a peaceful zone. Many times I have seen birds battering him, sometimes repeatedly knocking him heels over head, while he, frightened and chattering, was doing his best to escape.

There are five species of chipmunks in Colorado. Two of these are near me, — the big chipmunk and the busy chipmunk. The latter is much smaller, shyer, and more lively than the former and spends a part of its time in the tree-tops; while the big, although it sometimes climbs, commonly keeps close to the earth.

Among their numerous enemies are coyotes, wild-cats, mountain lions, bears, hawks, and owls. They appear to live from six to twelve years. The one near my place I watched for eight years. She probably was one or more years of age when I first saw her.

Almost every day in summer a number of children come, some of them for miles, to watch and to feed my chipmunks. The children enjoy this as keenly as I have ever seen them enjoy anything. Surely the kindly sympathies which

# My Chipmunk Callers

are thus aroused in the children, and the delightful lesson in natural history which they get, will give a helpful educational stimulus, and may be the beginning of a sympathetic interest in every living thing.

# A Peak by the Plains

# A Peak by the Plains

**P**IKE'S PEAK rises boldly from the plains, going steeply up into the sky a vertical mile and a half. There is no middle distance or foreground; no terraced or inclined' approach. A spectator may thus stand close to its foot, at an altitude of six thousand feet, and have a commanding view of the eight thousand feet of slopes and terraces which culminate in the summit, 14,110 feet above the sea. Its steep, abrupt ascent makes it imposing and impressive. It fronts the wide plains a vast broken tower. The typical high peak stands with other high peaks in the summit of a mountain-range. Miles of lesser mountains lie between its summit and the lowlands. Foothills rise from the edge of the lowland; above these, broken benches, terrace beyond terrace, each rising higher until the summit rises supreme. With Pike's Peak this typical arrangement is reversed.

Pike's Peak probably is the most intimately

known high mountain. It has given mountain-top pleasure to more people than any other fourteen thousand foot summit of the earth. One million persons have walked upon its summit, and probably two million others have climbed well up its slopes. Only a few thousand climbers have reached the top of Mont Blanc. Pike's is a peak for the multitude.

Climbing it is comparatively easy. It stands in a mild, arid climate, and has scanty snowfall; there are but few precipitous walls, no dangerous ice-fields; and up most of its slopes any one may ramble. One may go up on foot, on horseback, in a carriage, or by railroad, or even by automobile. It is not only easy of ascent, but also easy of access. It is on the edge of the plains, and a number of railroads cross its very foot.

This peak affords a unique view, — wide plains to the east, high peaks to the west. Sixty thousand or more square miles are visible from the summit. It towers far above the plains, whose streams, hills, and level spaces stretch away a vast flat picture. To the west it commands a wondrous array of mountain topog-

PIKE'S PEAK FROM THE TOP OF CASCADE CAÑON

raphy, — a two-hundred-mile front of shattered, snow-drifted peaks.

The peak is an enormous broken pyramid, dotted with high-perched lakes, cut with plunging streams, broken by cañons, skirted with torn forests, old and young, and in addition is beautiful with bushes, meadows, and wild flowers. The major part of the peak's primeval forest robe was destroyed by fire a half-century ago. Many ragged, crag-torn areas of the old forest, of a square mile or less, are connected with young growths from thirty to sixty years old. Much of this new growth is aspen. From the tree-studies which I have made, I learn that two forest fires caused most of the destruction. The annual rings in the young growth, together with the rings in the fire-scarred trees which did not perish, indicate that the older and more extensive of these fires wrapped most of the peak in flames and all of it in smoke during the autumn of 1850. The other fire was in 1880.

Pike's Peak exhibits a number of scenic attractions and is bordered by other excellent ones.

Near are the Royal Gorge, Cripple Creek, and the fossil-beds at Florissant. The Garden of the Gods, Manitou Mineral Springs, Glen Eyrie, Crystal Park, the Cave of the Winds, and Williams, Ruxton, and South Cheyenne Cañons are some of its attractions.

The fossil-beds at Florissant are one of the most famous of fossil-deposits. Here was an old Tertiary lake-basin. In the deposit which filled it—a deposit of fine volcanic sand or ash, sediment, and other débris—is a wonderful array of fossilized plants and insects of a past age. All are strangely preserved for us in stone. A part of the lake appears to have been filled by a volcanic catastrophe which overwhelmed animals, plants, and insects. Whole and in fragments, they are lying where they fell. Here have been found upwards of one hundred recognizable plants, eleven vertebrate animals, and a few hundred insects. Among the fossil trees are the narrow-leaf cottonwood, the ginkgo, the magnolia, the incense cedar, and the giant redwood. Water erosion through the ages has cut deeply into these fossil-beds and worn and washed away their treasures. This deposit has been but little studied. But what it has yielded, together with the magnitude of the unexamined remainder, makes one eager concerning the extent and the nature of the treasures which still lie buried in it.

Helen Hunt, whose books helped awaken the American people to the injustice done the Indian and to an appreciation of the scenic grandeur of the West, lived for many years at the foot of this peak. Much of her writing was done from commanding points on the peak. She was temporarily buried on Cheyenne Mountain, and on her former grave has accumulated a large cairn of stones, contributed singly by appreciative pilgrims.

South Cheyenne Cañon, like Yosemite, gives a large, clear, and pleasing picture to the mind. This is due to the individuality and the artistic grouping of the beauty and grandeur of the cañon. The cañon is so narrow, and its high walls so precipitous, that it could justly be called an enormous cleft. At one point the walls are only forty feet apart; between these a road and

a swift, clear stream are crowded. Inside the
entrance stand the two "Pillars of Hercules."
These magnificent rock domes rise nearly one
thousand feet, and their steep, tree-dotted walls
are peculiarly pleasing and impressive. Prospect Dome is another striking rock point in
this cañon. The cañon ends in a colossal cirque,
or amphitheatre, about two hundred and fifty
feet deep. Down one side of this a stream makes
its seven white zigzag jumps.

Pike's Peak wins impressiveness by standing
by itself. Cheyenne Cañon is more imposing by
being alone, — away from other cañons. This
cañon opens upon the plains. It is a cañon that
would win attention anywhere, but its situation
is a most favorable one. Low altitude and a
warm climate welcome trees, grass, bushes, and
many kinds of plants and flowers. These cling
to every break, spot, ledge, terrace, and niche,
and thereby touch and decorate the cañon's
grim and towering walls with lovely beauty.
Walls, water, and verdure — water in pools and
falls, rocks in cliffs, terraces, and domes, grass
and flowers on slopes and terraces, trees and

groves, — a magnificence of rocks, a richness of verdure, and the charm of running water — all unite in a picturesque association which makes a glorious and pleasing sunken garden.

It is probable that Pike's Peak was discovered by Spanish explorers either in 1598 or in 1601. These are the dates of separate exploring expeditions which entered Colorado from the south and marched up the plains in near view of this peak. The discovery is usually accredited, however, to Captain Pike, who caught sight of it on the 15th day of November, 1806. Pike's journal of this date says: "At two o'clock in the afternoon I thought I could distinguish a mountain to our right which appeared like a small blue cloud; viewed it with a spyglass and was still more confirmed in my conjecture. . . . In half an hour it appeared in full view before us. When our small party arrived on a hill, they with one accord gave three cheers to the Mexican Mountains." It appears not to have been called Pike's Peak until about twenty-five years after Pike first saw it. He spoke of it as the Mexican Mountains and as Great Peak. The first ascent by white men was made July 14, 1819, by members of Major Long's exploring expedition. For a number of years this peak was called James Peak, in honor of the naturalist in the Long exploring party.

Pike's Peak has what Montesquieu calls the "most powerful of all empires, the empire of climate." It stands most of the time in the sun. All over it the miner and the prospector have searched for gold, mutilating it here and there with holes. Fires have scarred the sides, and pasturing has robbed it of flowers and verdure. The reputed discovery of gold at its base started a flood of gold-seekers west with "Pike's Peak or bust" enthusiasm. But the climate and scenery of this peak attract people who come for pleasure and to seek for health. It has thus brought millions of dollars into Colorado, and it will probably continue to attract people who seek pleasure and refreshment and who receive in exchange higher values than they spend. Pike's Peak is a rich asset.

The summit of Pike's Peak is an excellent place to study the effect of altitude upon lowland visitors. Individual observations and the special investigations of scientific men show that altitude has been a large, unconscious source of nature-faking. During the summer of 1911 a number of English and American scientists, the "Anglo-American Expedition," spent five weeks on Pike's Peak, making special studies of the effects of altitude. Their investigations explode the theory that altitude is a strain upon the heart, or injurious to the system. These men concluded that the heart is subjected to no greater strain in high altitudes than at sea-level, except under the strain of physical exertion. The blood is richer in high altitudes. For every hundred red corpuscles found at sea-level there are in Colorado Springs, at six thousand feet, one hundred and ten; and on the summit of Pike's Peak, from one hundred and forty to one hundred and fifty-four.

"The danger to people suffering from heart trouble coming into high altitudes is grossly exaggerated," says Dr. Edward C. Schneider, one of the Anglo-American expedition. "The rate of circulation is not materially increased. The blood-pressure on the Peak is not increased; it is even lowered. The heart — if a person exercises — may beat a little faster but it does not pump any more blood. The pulse is a little more rapid. If a man suffering from heart trouble rode up the peak on a train, remained in his seat, and did not exert himself physically, his heart would not beat a bit faster at the summit than when he left Manitou. But if he walked about on the summit there would be a change, for the exercise would make the heart work harder." But exercise is not injurious; it is beneficial.

As I found in guiding on Long's Peak, the rarefied air of the heights was often stimulating, especially to the tongue. Rarefied air is likened by the scientists to "laughing-gas" and furnishes a plausible explanation of the queerness which characterizes the action of many people on mountain-summits. "We saw many visitors at the summit," said Dr. Schneider in explaining this phase, "who appeared to be intoxicated. But there was no smell of liquor on their breath. They were intoxicated with rarefied atmosphere, not with alcohol. The peculiar effects of laughing-gas and carbon-monoxide gas on people are due to the lack of oxygen in the gas; and the same applies to the air at high altitudes."

The summit of Pike's Peak is roomy and comparatively level, and is composed of broken granite, many of the pieces being of large size. A stone house stands upon the top. In this for many years was a government weather-observer. A weather station has just been re-established on its summit. This will be one of a line of high weather stations extending across the continent. This unique station should contribute continuously to the weather news and steadily add to the sum of climatic knowledge.

This one peak has on its high and broken slopes a majority of the earth's climatic zones, and a numerous array of the earth's countless kinds of plant and animal life. One may in two hours go from base to summit and pass through as many life zones as though he had traveled northward into the Arctic Circle. Going from base to summit, one would start in the Upper Sonoran Zone, pass through the Transition,

Canadian, and Hudsonian Zones, and enter the Arctic-Alpine Zone. The peak has a number of places which exhibit the complexity of climatic zones. In a deep cañon near Minnehaha Falls, two zones may be seen side by side on opposite sides of a deep, narrow cañon. The north side of the cañon, exposed to the sun, has such plants as are found in the Transition Zone, while the cool south side has an Hudsonian flora. Here is almost an actual contact of two zones that outside the mountains are separated by approximately two thousand miles.

The varied climate of this peak makes a large appeal to bird-life. Upward of one hundred species are found here. People from every part of the Union are here often startled by the presence of birds which they thought were far away at home. At the base the melodious meadowlark sings; along the streams on the middle slopes lives the contented water-ouzel. Upon the heights are the ptarmigan and the rosy finch. Often the golden eagle casts his shadow upon all these scenes. The robin is here, and also the bluebird, bluer, too, than you have ever seen him. The Western evening grosbeak, a bird with attractive plumage and pleasing manners, often winters here. The brilliant lazuli bunting, the Bullock oriole, the red-shafted flicker, and the dear and dainty goldfinch are present in summer, along with mockingbirds, wrens, tanagers, thrushes, and scores of other visitants.

A few migratory species winter about the foot of the peak. In summer they fly to the upper slopes and nest and raise their young in the miniature arctic prairies of the heights. With the coming of autumn all descend by easy stages to the foot. The full distance of this vertical migration could be covered in an hour's flight. Many of the north-and-south-migrating birds travel a thousand times as far as these birds of vertical migration.

The big game which formerly ranged this peak included buffalo, deer, elk, mountain sheep, the grizzly, the black bear, the mountain lion, the fox, the coyote, and the wolf. Along the descending streams, through one vertical mile of altitude, were beaver colonies, terrace upon terrace. No one knows how many varieties of wild flowers each year bloom in all the Peak's various ragged zones, but there are probably no fewer than two thousand. Along with these are a number of species of trees. Covering the lower part of the mountain are growths of cottonwood, Douglas spruce, yellow pine, white fir, silver spruce, and the Rocky Mountain birch. Among the flowering plants are the columbine, shooting-star, monkshood, yucca or Spanish bayonet, and iris. Ascending, one finds the wintergreen, a number of varieties of polemonium, the paintbrush, the Northern gentian, the Western yarrow, and the mertensia. At timber-line, at the altitude of about eleven thousand five hundred feet, are Engelmann spruce, arctic willow, mountain birch, foxtail pine, and aspen. At timber-line, too, are the columbine, the paintbrush, and a number of species of phlox. There are no trees in the zone which drapes the uppermost two thousand feet of the summit, but in this are bright flowers, — cushion pinks, the spring beauty, the alpine gentian, the mountain buckwheat, the white and yellow mountain avens, the arctic harebell, the marsh-marigold, the stonecrop, and the forget-me-not. One summer I found a few flowers on the summit.

Isolation probably rendered the summit of this peak less favorable for snow-accumulation during the Ice Age than the summits of un-isolated peaks of equal altitude. During the last ice epoch, however, it carried glaciers, and some of these extended down the slopes three miles or farther. These degraded the upper slopes, moved this excavated material toward the bottom, and spread it in a number of places. There are five distinct cuplike hollows or depressions in this peak that were gouged by glaciers. The one lying between Cameron's Cone and the summit is known as the "Crater." A part of this is readily seen from Colorado Springs. Far up the slopes are Lake Moraine and Seven Lakes, all of glacial origin.

The mountain mass which culminates in Pike's Peak probably originated as a vast uplift. Internal forces appear to have severed this mass from its surroundings and slowly upraised it seven thousand or more feet. The slow uprising probably ended thousands of years ago. Since that time, disintegration, frost, air, and stream erosion have combined to sculpture this great peak. Pike's Peak might well be made a National Park.

# The Conservation of Scenery

# The Conservation of Scenery

THE comparative merits of the Alps and the Rocky Mountains for recreation purposes are frequently discussed. Roosevelt and others have spoken of the Colorado Rockies as "The Nation's Playground." This Colorado region really is one vast natural park. The area of it is three times that of the Alps. The scenery of these Colorado Rocky Mountains, though unlike that of the Alps, is equally attractive and more varied. Being almost free from snow, the entire region is easily enjoyed; a novice may scale the peaks without the ice and snow that hamper and endanger even the expert climbers in the icy Alps. The Alps wear a perpetual ice-cap down to nine thousand feet. The inhabited zone in Colorado is seven thousand feet higher than that zone in Switzerland. At ten thousand feet and even higher, in Colorado, one finds railroads, wagon-roads, and hotels. In Switzerland there are but few hotels above five thousand feet, and most people live below the three-thousand-foot mark. Timber-line in Colorado is five thousand feet farther up the heights than in Switzerland. The Centennial State offers a more numerous and attractive array of wild flowers, birds, animals, and mineral springs than the land of William Tell. The Rocky Mountain sheep is as interesting and audacious as the chamois; the fair phlox dares greater heights than the famed edelweiss. The climate of the Rocky Mountains is more cheerful than that of the Alps; there are more sunny days, and while the skies are as blue as in Switzerland, the air is drier and more energizing.

But the attractions in the Alps are being preserved, while the Rocky Mountains are being stripped of their scenery. Yet in the Rocky Mountains there are many areas rich in perishable attractions which might well be reserved as parks so that their natural beauties could be kept unmarred. It is to be hoped that the growing interest in American scenery will bring this

THE CONTINENTAL DIVIDE NEAR ESTES PARK

about before these wild mountain gardens are shorn of their loveliness.[1]

The United States is behind most nations in making profitable use of scenery. Alpine scenery annually produces upward of ten thousand dollars to the square mile, while the Rocky Mountains are being despoiled by cattle and sawmills for a few dollars a square mile. Though Switzerland has already accomplished much along scenic conservation lines, it is working for still better results. It is constructing modern hotels throughout the Alps and is exploiting the winter as well as the summer use of these. The Canadian Government has done and is doing extensive development work in its national parks. It is preparing a welcome for multitudes of travelers; travelers are responding in numbers.

The unfortunate fact is that our scenery has

---

[1] Since this was put into type, the Rocky Mountain National Park, after a campaign of six years, has been established, and campaigns have started to make National Parks of Mount Evans and Pike's Peak. And the Secretary of the Interior has appointed a Superintendent of National Parks and called attention to the great need of legislation for these Parks.

never had a standing. To date, it has been an outcast. Often lauded as akin to the fine arts, or something sacred, commonly it is destroyed or put to base uses. Parks should no longer be used as pigpens and pastures. These base uses prevent the parks from paying dividends in humanity.

There is in this country a splendid array of Nature's masterpieces to lure and reward the traveler. In mountain-peaks there are Grand Teton, Long's Peak, Mt. Whitney, and Mt. Rainier; in cañons, the vast Grand Cañon and the brilliantly colored Yellowstone; in trees, the unrivaled sequoias and many matchless primeval forests; in rivers, few on earth are enriched with scenes equal to those between which rolls the Columbia; in petrified forests, those in Arizona and the Yellowstone are unsurpassed; in natural bridges, those in Utah easily arch above the other great ones of the earth; in desert attractions, Death Valley offers a rare display of colors, strangeness, silences, and mirages; in waterfalls, we have Niagara, Yellowstone, and Yosemite; in glaciers, there are those of the

# The Conservation of Scenery

Glacier and Mount Rainier National Parks and of Alaska; in medicinal springs, there is an array of flowing, life-extending fountains; in wild flowers, the mountain wild flowers in the West are lovely with the loveliest anywhere; in wild animals of interest and influence, we have the grizzly bear, the beaver, and the mountain sheep; in bird music, that which is sung by the thrushes, the cañon wren, and the solitaire silences with melodious sweetness the other best bird-songs of the earth. In these varied attractions of our many natural parks we have ample playgrounds for all the world and the opportunity for a travel industry many times as productive as our gold and silver mines — and more lasting, too, than they. When these scenes are ready for the traveler we shall not need to nag Americans to see America first; and Europeans, too, might start a continuous procession to these wonderlands.

In the nature of things, the United States should have a travel industry of vast economic importance. The people of the United States are great travelers, and we have numerous and

317

extensive scenic areas of unexcelled attractiveness, together with many of the world's greatest natural wonders and wonderlands which every one wants to see. All these scenes, too, repose in a climate that is hospitable and refreshing. They should attract travelers from abroad as well as our own people. The traveler brings ideas as well as gold. He comes with the ideals of other lands and helps promote international friendship. Then, too, he is an excellent counter-irritant to prevent that self-satisfied attitude, that deadening provincialism, which always seems to afflict successful people. Develop our parks by making them ready for the traveler, and they will become continuously productive, both commercially and spiritually.

Our established scenic reservations, or those which may be hereafter set aside, are destined to become the basis of our large scenic industry. The present reservations embrace fourteen National Parks and twenty-eight National Monuments. Each Park and Monument was reserved because of its scenic wonders, to be a recreation place for the people. The name

# The Conservation of Scenery

Monument might well be changed to Park. The Monuments were set aside by executive orders of the President; the Parks were created by acts of Congress. Each Park or Monument is a wonderland in itself. All these together contain some of the strangest, sublimest scenes on the globe. Each reservation is different from every other, and in all of them a traveler could spend a lifetime without exhausting their wonders.

I suppose that in order to lead Americans to see America first, or to see it at all, and also to win travel from Europe, it is absolutely necessary to get America ready for the traveler. Only a small part of American scenery is ready for the traveler. The traveler's ultimatum contains four main propositions. These are grand scenery, excellent climate, good entertainment, and swift, comfortable transportation. When all of these demands are supplied with a generous horn of plenty, then, but not until then, will multitudes travel in America.

Parks now have a large and important place in the general welfare, and the nation that neglects its parks will suffer a general decline. The people of the United States greatly need more parks, and these are needed at once. I do not know of any city that has park room extensive enough to refresh its own inhabitants. Is there a State in the Union that has developed park areas that are large enough for the people of the State? With present development, our National Parks cannot entertain one fifth of the number of Americans who annually go abroad. As a matter of fact, the entertainment facilities in our National Parks are already doing a capacity business. How, then, can our Parks be seen by additional travelers?

For a travel industry, the present needs in America are for cities at once to acquire and develop into parks all near-by scenery; for each State to develop its best scenic places as State Parks; and for the nation to make a number of new National Parks and at once make these scenic reservations ready for the traveler. Systems of good roads and trails are necessary. In addition to these, the Parks, Monuments, and Reservations need the whole and special attention of a department of their own.

# The Conservation of Scenery

A park requires eternal vigilance. The better half of our scenic attractions are the perishable ones. The forests and the flowers, the birds and the animals, the luxuriant growths in the primeval wild gardens, are the poetry, the inspiration, of outdoors. Without these, how dead and desolate the mountain, the meadow, and the lake! If a park is to be kept permanently productive, its alluring features must be maintained. If the beaver ceases to build his picturesque home, if the deer vanishes, if the mountain sheep no longer poses on the crags, if the columbine no longer opens its "bannered" bosom to the sun, if the solitaire no longer sings, — without these poetic and primeval charms, marred nature will not attract nor refresh. People often feel the call of the wild, and they want the wild world beautiful. They need the temples of the gods, the forest primeval, and the pure and flower-fringed brooks.

It would be well to save at once in parks and reservations the better of all remaining unspoiled scenic sections of the country, — the lake-shores and the seashore, the stream-side,

321

the forests primeval, and the Rocky Mountains. There is a great and ragged scenic border of varying width that extends entirely around the United States. This includes the Great Lake region and the splendid Olympic Mountains at the northwest corner of the country. Inside of this border are other localities richly dowered with natural beauty and dowered, too, with hospitable climate. The Rocky Mountain region is one splendid recreation-ground. There are many beauty-spots in the Ozark Mountains of Missouri and Arkansas, and there are scenic regions in New York, Pennsylvania, and western North Carolina, and the State of Idaho embraces many scenic empires. These contain scores of park areas that will early be needed.

Every park is a place of refuge, a place wherein wild life thrives and multiplies. As hunters are perpetually excluded from all parks, these places will thus become sanctuaries for our vanishing wild life. All wild life quickly loses its fear and allows itself to be readily seen in protected localities. Wild life in parks thus affords enjoy-

LONG'S PEAK FROM LOCH VALE

ment by being readily seen, and from now on this life will become a factor in education. Children who go into parks will be pleasantly compelled to observe, delightfully incited to think, and will thus become alert and interested, — will have the very foundation of education. Perhaps it is safe to predict that from now on the tendency will be to multiply the number of parks and decrease the number of zoölogical gardens.

Scenic places, if used for parks, will pay larger returns than by any other use that can be made of their territory. Parks, then, are not a luxury but a profitable investment. Switzerland is supporting about half of her population through the use of her mountain scenery for recreation purposes. Although parks pay large dividends, they also have a higher, nobler use. They help make better men and women. Outdoor life is educational. It develops the seeing eye, supplies information, gives material for reflection, and compels thinking, which is one of the greatest of accomplishments. Exercise in the pure air of parks means health, which is the greatest of personal resources, and this in turn makes for efficiency, kindness, hopefulness, and high ideals. Recreation in parks tends to prevent wasted life by preventing disease and wrong-doing. The conservation of scenery, the use of scenic places for public recreation parks, is conservation in the highest sense, for parks make the best economic use of the territory and they also pay large dividends in humanity.

The travel industry is a large and direct contributor to many industries and their laborers. It helps the railroads, automobile-makers, hotels, guides, and the manufacturers of the clothing, books, souvenirs, and other articles purchased by travelers. Perhaps the farmer is the one most benefited; he furnishes the beef, fruit, butter, chickens, and in fact all the food consumed by the traveling multitude. A large travel industry means enlarging the home market to gigantic proportions.

The courts have recently expressed definite and advanced views concerning scenic beauty. In Colorado, where water has a high economic value, a United States Circuit Court recently decided that the beneficial use of a stream was not necessarily an agricultural, industrial, or commercial use, and that, as a part of the scenery, it was being beneficially used for the general welfare. The question was whether the waters of a stream, which in the way of a lakelet and a waterfall were among the attractions of a summer resort, could be diverted to the detriment of the falls and used for power. The judge said "No," because the waters as used, were contributing toward the promotion of the public health, rest, and recreation; and that as an object of beauty — "just to be looked at" — they were not running to waste but were in beneficial use. He held that objects of beauty have an important place in our lives and that these objects should not be destroyed because they are without assessable value. The judge, Robert E. Lewis, said in part: —

"It is a beneficial use to the weary that they, ailing and feeble, can have the wild beauties of Nature placed at their convenient disposal. Is a piece of canvas valuable only for a tentfly, but worthless as a painting? Is a block of stone beneficially used when put into the walls of a dam, and not beneficially used when carved into a piece of statuary? Is the test dollars, or has beauty of scenery, rest, recreation, health and enjoyment something to do with it? Is there no beneficial use except that which is purely commercial?" This decision is epoch-marking.

Taken as a whole, our National Parks and Monuments and our unreserved scenic places may be described as an undeveloped scenic resource of enormous potential value. These places should be developed as parks and their resources used exclusively for recreation pur-poses. Thus used, they would help all interests and reach all people. South America, Switzer-land, Canada, and other countries are making intensified and splendid use of their parks by reserving that wild scenic beauty which appeals to all the world.

Parks are dedicated to the highest uses. They are worthy of our greatest attentions. It is of utmost importance that the management of Forest Reserves and the National Parks be sep-arate. In 1897 the National Academy of Sciences in submitting a plan for the management of the Forest Reserves recommended that places specially scenic be separated from the Forest Reserves and set aside as Parks and given the separate and special administration which parks need. If scenery is to be saved, it must be saved for its own sake, on its own merits; it cannot be saved as something incidental.

Multitudes will annually visit these places, provided they be developed as parks and used for people and for nothing else. Grazing, lumbering, shooting, and other commercial, conflicting, and disfiguring uses should be rigidly prohibited. Scenery, like beauty, has superior merit, and its supreme use is by people for rest and recreation purposes.

Switzerland after long experience is establishing National Parks and giving these a separate and distinct management from her forest reserves. For a time Canadian National Parks were managed by the Forest Service. Recently, however, the parks were withdrawn from the Forest Service and placed in a Park Department. This was a most beneficial change. Forestry is commercial, radically utilitarian. The forester is a man with an axe. Trees to the forester mean what cattle do to the butcher. Lumber is his product and to recite "Woodman, Spare that Tree!" to a forester would be like asking the butcher to spare the ox. The forester is a scientific slaughterer of the forest; he must keep trees falling in order to supply lumber. A forester is not concerned with the conservation of scenery. Then, too, a forester builds his roads to facilitate logging and lumbering. The Park man builds roads that are scenic highways, places for people.

We need the forest reserve, and we need the National Park. Each of these serves in a distinct way, and it is of utmost importance that each be in charge of its specialist. The forester is always the lumberman, the park man is a practical poet; the forester thinks ever of lumber, the park man always of landscapes. The forester must cut trees before they are over-ripe or his crop will waste, while the park man wants the groves to become aged and picturesque. The forester pastures cattle in his meadows, while the park man has only people and romping children among his wild flowers. The park needs the charm of primeval nature, and should be free from ugliness, artificiality, and commercialism. For the perpetuation of scenery, a landscape artist is absolutely necessary. It would be folly to put a park man in charge of a forest reserve, a lumbering proposition. On the other hand, what a blunder to put a tree-cutting forester in charge of a park! We need both these men; each is important in his place; but it would be a double misfortune to put one in charge of the work of the other. A National Park service is greatly needed.

Apparently William Penn was the first to honor our scenery, and Bryant, with poetry, won a literary standing for it. Official recognition came later, but the establishment of the Yellowstone National Park was a great incident in the scenic history of America — and in that of the world. For the first time, a scenic wonderland was dedicated as "a public park or pleasure ground for the benefit and enjoyment of all the people." The Yellowstone stands a high tribute

to the statesmanship, the public spirit, and the
energy of F. V. Hayden and the few men who
won it for us.

During the last few years the nation, as well
as the courts, has put itself on record concerning the higher worth of scenery. The White
House conference of governors recommended
that "the beauty . . . of our country should be
preserved and increased"; and the first National Conservation Commission thought that
"public lands more valuable for conserving
. . . natural beauties and wonders than for
agriculture should be held for the use of the
people."

The travel industry benefits both parties, —
the entertained as well as the entertainer. In-
vestments in outdoor vacations give large returns; from an outing one returns with life
lengthened, in livelier spirits, more efficient,
with new ideas and a broader outlook, and more
hopeful and kind. Hence parks and outdoor
recreation places are mighty factors for the general welfare; they assist in making better men
and women. A park offers the first aid and often

# The Conservation of Scenery

the only cure for the sick and the overworked.
Looking upon our sublime scenes arouses a love
for our native land and promotes a fellow feeling. Nature is more democratic even than
death; and when people mingle amid primeval
scenes they become fraternal. Saving our best
scenes is the saving of manhood. These places
encourage every one to do his best and help all
to live comfortably in a beautiful world. Scenery is our noblest resource. No nation has ever
fallen from having too much scenery.

# The Rocky Mountain National Park

# The Rocky Mountain National Park

**E**XTEND a straight line fifty-five miles northwest from Denver and another line sixty miles southwest from Cheyenne and these lines meet in approximately the centre of the Rocky Mountain National Park. This centre is in the mountain-heights a few miles northwest of Long's Peak, in what Dr. F. V. Hayden, the famous geologist, calls the most rugged section of the Continental Divide of the Rocky Mountains.

This Park is a mountain realm lying almost entirely above the altitude of nine thousand feet. Through it from north to south extends the Snowy Range, — the Continental Divide, — and in it this and the Mummy Range form a vast mountain Y. Specimen Mountain is the north end of the west arm of this Y, while Mummy Mountain is at the tip of the east arm. Mt.

Clarence King on the south forms the base of the stem, while Long's Peak is against the eastern side of the stem, about midway.

Long's Peak, "King of the Rockies," is the dominating peak and rises to the altitude of 14,255 feet. There are ten or more peaks in the Park that tower above thirteen thousand, and upwards of forty others with a greater altitude than twelve thousand feet. Between these peaks and their out-jutting spurs are numerous cañons. The Park is from ten to eighteen miles wide, its greatest length is twenty-five miles, and its total area is about three hundred and sixty square miles.

A line drawn around the Park on the boundary line would only in two or three places drop below the altitude of nine thousand feet. The area thus is high-lying and for the most part on edge. About one fifth of the entire area is above the limits of tree-growth. The peaks are rocky, rounded, and sharp. Here and there they are whitened by comparatively small snow and ice fields. From the summits the mountains descend through steeps, walls, slopes, ter-

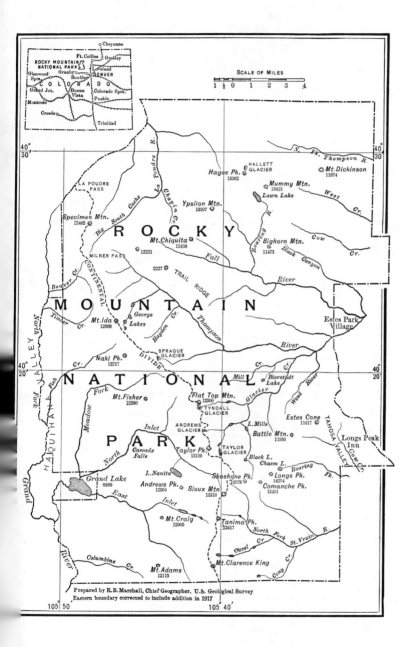

Prepared by R.B. Marshall, Chief Geographer. U.S. Geological Survey
Eastern boundary corrected to include addition in 1917

races, tablelands, spurs, gorges, and mountain valleys.

This Park is a wilderness. Though entirely surrounded by settlers and villages, it is an almost unbroken wild. Many of its peaks are as yet unclimbed. There are pathless forests, unvisited gorges, unnamed lakes, and unknown localities.

Gray and red granite form the larger portion of its surface. Here and there are mixtures of schist, gneiss, and porphyry. The northwest corner is volcanic and is made up of rhyolite, obsidian, and lava. The Indians have a tradition concerning the volcanic activity of Specimen Mountain, though I doubt if this mountain has been active within a century. It is a dead or sleeping volcano. A part of its old crater-rim has fallen away, and brilliant flowers cover the cold ashes in the crater.

Most of the territory was glaciated during the last ice age, and there still remain five small glaciers and a number of ice-fields. The Hallett Glacier is on the north shoulder of Hague's Peak, the Sprague Glacier on the south side of

Stone's Peak, Tyndall Glacier between Flat-Top and Mt. Hallett, and Andrews Glacier in a cirque of Loch Vale, while an unnamed small one is at the bottom of the east precipice of Long's Peak.

There can hardly be found a greater and more closely gathered area of imposing, easily read glacial records than those which centre about Long's Peak. These works of the Ice King, both intact and partly ruined, have attracted the attention and study of a number of prominent geologists and glaciologists. Among these ice works Dr. Hayden and Dr. David Starr Jordan have climbed and wandered. Vernon L. Kellogg has here gathered material for a book, and Dr. Edward L. Orton, former State Geologist of Ohio, has spent many weeks here in study. Within a six-mile radius of the top of Long's Peak are more than thirty glacier lakes and perhaps twice as many lakelets or mountain tarns. Immediately south of the Peak, Wild Basin is literally filled with glacier-records. To the north is Moraine Park; to the northwest, Glacier Gorge and Loch Vale; to the west, lying between the Peak and Grand Lake, there is a wondrous area of the Ice King's topography.

Bierstadt, St. Vrain, and Mills Moraines are imposing deposits of glacial débris. Of these Mills Moraine has been the most studied. It apparently holds the story of two widely separated ice ages. This moraine evidently was formed by the glacier which made the basin of Chasm Lake. It extends eastward from Long's Peak, its uppermost end being at twelve thousand five hundred feet. At timber-line its trend is toward the southeast. It is about one mile wide, five miles long, and in places apparently more than one thousand feet deep.

The ice-stream which piled the enormous Bierstadt Moraine took its rise on the west summit slope of Long's Peak. It flowed first toward the west, and in the upper amphitheatre of Glacier Gorge it united with the ice-stream from the north slope of Shoshone Peak and the stream off the eastern slope of Mt. McHenry. Although a part of this enlarged flow appears to have been thrust across the Continental Divide, the larger portion of it was deflected to the north through Glacier Gorge. Emerging from this gorge and enlarged by the ice-streams from Mt. Otis, Mt. Hallett, and other peaks in the Continental Divide, it flowed on to thrust against the eastern base of Flat-Top Mountain. This bent it to the east, and from this turning-point it began to unload its débris on Bierstadt Moraine. A part of its débris was dropped in a smaller parallel moraine on the opposite side of Glacier Creek, and finally a terminal moraine was piled against the western front of Green Mountain, where it almost united with the terminal part of the Moraine on the south side of Moraine Park.

The glaciers have formed and distributed much of the soil of this region. Above timberline there are wide, sedgy meadows and tundras and dry, grassy moorlands. Everywhere on the heights where there is soil there is a growth of Arctic-Alpine vegetation. Above the limits of tree-growth are enormous ragged areas and tiny ledge gardens that are crowded with a variety of brilliantly colored wild blossoms.

ESTES PARK ENTRANCE TO THE ROCKY MOUNTAIN NATIONAL PARK

# Rocky Mountain National Park

The average altitude of the timber-line is about eleven thousand three hundred feet, nearly a vertical mile higher than the timber-line in the Alps. Timber-line the world over is a place of striking interest, but nowhere have I found or heard of a timber-line which exhibits so many telling features as does the forest-frontier on the eastern side of the Continental Divide. The prevailing tree on the drier slopes at timber-line is *Pinus flexilis*, the limber pine. In the moist places Engelmann spruce predominates, and in many of the moister places there are dwarfed and tangled growths of arctic willow, black birch, and aspen.

Among the least broken and most enchanting of the primeval forests of the Park are a few that are grand. One of these is between the head of Fall River and the Poudre; another is in Forest Cañon; one is in the southern part of Wild Basin; still another is on the western slope of Stone's Peak and Flat-Top Mountain. These forests are mostly Engelmann spruce, with a scattering of sub-alpine fir. Around the lower, warmer slopes grows the Western yellow pine,

341

and on the cold lower slopes the Douglas spruce. There are a number of extensive lodge-pole pine forests. These are from thirty to one hundred and thirty years old. Lines of aspen adorn most streams; here and there where the soil is moist they expand into groves.

The wild-flower inhabitants of this great Park number more than a thousand species. Many of these are members of famous families, — famous for their antiquity upon the earth, for their delicate scent, for their intricate and artistic structure, and for their brilliant color.

The gentian family is represented by fifteen species, one of these being a fringed blue gentian, a Western relative of the fringed gentian celebrated by the poet Bryant. There are intricately-formed orchids. The silver and blue columbine is here at its best; it blossoms on the lower slopes in June, on the heights during September. The populous pea family, in yellow, white, and lavender, covers and colors extensive areas. Then there are asters, daisies, mariposa lilies, polemonium, wintergreen, forget-me-nots, black-

342

eyed Susans, and numerous other handsome flower people. These flowers are scattered all over the Park except in places destitute of soil. I have found primroses, phlox, and mertensia on the summit of Long's Peak. In the heights above the limits of tree-growth there are scores of other blossoms.

More than one hundred species of birds nest in these scenes. Among these are the robin, the bluebird, the wren, the hermit thrush, the hummingbird, the golden eagle, the white-crowned sparrow, and that marvelous singer the solitaire. Among the resident birds are the ouzel, the crested and the Rocky Mountain jays, the chickadee, the downy woodpecker, and the magpie. The ptarmigan and the rosy finch are prominent residents in the heights above the timber-line.

Once the big-game population was numerous. But the grizzly has been almost exterminated, and only a few black bear remain. There are a few mountain lions and elk. Deer are fairly common, and in localities mountain sheep are plentiful and on the increase. Specimen

343

# Rocky Mountain Wonderland

Mountain probably is one of the places most frequented by mountain sheep. A number of times flocks of more than a hundred have been seen on this mountain. A scattering of wolves, coyotes, and foxes remain. Conies are numerous in the slide rock of the heights, and snowshoe rabbits people the forests. The Frémont, or pine, squirrels are scattered throughout the woods. Lunch where you will, and the dear and confiding busy chipmunk is pretty certain to approach. The region appears to be above the snake line, and I have never seen a snake within the boundary. The streams and a number of the lakes have their population of rainbow and brook trout. Around the water's edge mink make their home.

The beaver has colonies large and small all over the park up to the limits of tree-growth. Houses, ponds, dams, tree-cuttings, canals, and other works of the beaver are here readily seen. Excellent opportunities are afforded to study beaver manners and customs and to comprehend the influence of his work in the conservation of soil and water.

THE FALL RIVER ROAD

ONTINENTAL DIVIDE

# Rocky Mountain National Park

Big game, and in fact all wild life, begin to increase in numbers and also to allow themselves to be seen from the instant they receive the complete protection which parks afford. This park will thus assure a multiplication of the various kinds of wild life which the region now contains. And this increased wild life, with no hunters to alarm, will allow itself to be readily seen.

There are only a few miles of road within the Park boundaries, but the Fall River Road, now under construction across the Continental Divide at Milner Pass, just south of Specimen Mountain, will be a wonderful scenic highway. Although there are a number of trails in the Park, so broken is the topography that most of the country a stone's throw away from them is unvisited and unknown.

A road skirts the western boundary of the Park and touches it at Grand Lake and Specimen Mountain. Another road closely parallels the eastern boundary-line, and from it a half-dozen roads touch the Park. This parallel road reaches the roads of Denver and of the plains

345

through the Boulder, Left Hand, Big Thompson, and two St. Vrain cañons.

The drainage of the western half of the Park concentrates in the Grand River on the western boundary and reaches the Pacific Ocean through the Grand Cañon of Arizona. A number of streams rise in the eastern side. These assemble their waters in the Platte River out on the plains. In their upper course, all these streams start from the snows and come rushing and bounding down the roughest, steepest slopes.

The climate of the eastern slope is comparatively dry and mild. The winters are sunny, but little snow falls, and the winds are occasionally warm and usually extremely dry. Though only a few miles from the eastern slope, the western rarely receives a wind, and its snow-fall is more than double that of the eastern.

Numerous authors and artists have made long visits in this region, and its scenery has received their highest praise. Bierstadt, the artist, came here in 1870. A few years later he was followed by the famous authors Isabella

# Rocky Mountain National Park

Bird, Anna Dickinson, and Helen Hunt. Frederick H. Chapin visited the region in 1888 and wrote a splendidly illustrated book about it, called "Mountaineering in Colorado." This was published by the Appalachian Club. In commenting upon the scenery of the region, Hayden, Father of the Yellowstone National Park, turned aside from scientific discussion in his geological report for 1875 to pay the following tribute to the scenic charm of this territory: —

"Not only has nature amply supplied this with features of rare beauty and surroundings of admirable grandeur, but it has thus distributed them that the eye of an artist may rest with perfect satisfaction on the complete picture presented. It may be said, perhaps, that the more minute details of the scenery are too decorative in their character, showing, as they do, the irregular picturesque groups of hills, buttes, products of erosion, and the finely moulded ridges — the effect is pleasing in the extreme."

Long's Peak is considered by mountain-climbers an excellent view-point. Standing aside one mile from the Continental Divide and rising above a large surrounding wonderland, its summit and upper slopes give splendid views and command a variety of scenes, near and far. While upon its slope, Mr. Chapin said: "I would not fail to impress on the mind of the tourist that the scenes are too grand for words to convey a true idea of their magnificence. Let him, then, not fail to visit them." It is an extremely rocky and rugged peak, but it is almost entirely free of snow and ice, so that climbing it is simply a day's work crowded with enjoyment and almost free from danger. Though it is two hundred and fifty feet lower than the highest peak in the Rocky Mountains and three hundred and fifty feet lower than Mt. Whitney, California, the highest peak in the United States, Long's Peak probably has a greater individuality than either. Alongside it stands Mt. Meeker, with an altitude of 14,000 feet. These sky towers are visible more than one hundred miles. The Indians of the Colorado and Wyoming plains used to call them the "Two Guides."

# Rocky Mountain National Park

It is possible, if not probable, that Long's Peak was originally one thousand or even two thousand feet higher. The mass of this peak stands apart from the main range and embraces three other peaks. These are Mt. Meeker, Mt. Washington, and Storm Peak. All are united below thirteen thousand feet. They may once have been united in one greatly higher mass. Much of the débris in the vast Boulderfield and Mills Moraines and a lesser amount from the enormous Bierstadt and St. Vrain Moraines must have come from the summit slope of the Long's Peak group. No small part of this may have come from above thirteen thousand feet. An exceedingly small percentage of the glacial débris which surrounds Long's Peak would, if atop the Long's Peak group, elevate it two thousand feet higher.

The Glacier Gorge region, which lies just to the northwest of Long's Peak, probably has the most magnificent scenery in the Park. Here are clustered enormous glaciated gorges, great glaciated walls, alpine lakes, waterfalls, moraines, alpine flora, and towering peaks.

349

# Rocky Mountain Wonderland

Wild Basin, a broken and glaciated region of twenty-five square miles, lies immediately south of the Peak. This basin is almost encircled by eight towering peaks, and the enormous St. Vrain Moraine thrusts out of its outlet and shows where the united ice-rivers formerly made their way from this basin. Within this wild area are lakes, forests, waterfalls, and a splendid variety of wild and lovely scenes.

The glacier lakes and wild tarns of this Park are one of its delights. Though most of these water fountains are small, they are singularly beautiful. They are in the middle-mountain zone, in a belt which lies between the altitudes of ten thousand and twelve thousand feet. There are more than a hundred of these, and their attractiveness equals that of any of the mountain lakes of the world.

The best known and most popular of these lakes are Fern and Odessa. These lie about twelve miles west of the village of Estes Park. Chasm Lake, on the east side of Long's Peak, is set in an utterly wild place. Its basin was gouged from solid granite by the old Long's

Peak Glacier. Mt. Washington, Mt. Meeker, and Long's Peak tower above it, and around it these peaks have flung their wreckage in chaotic confusion. A glacier almost crawls into it, and the east precipice of Long's Peak, the greatest precipice in the Park, looms above it.

Long, Black, Thunder, Ouzel, and Poudre Lakes have charms peculiar to each, and each is well worth a visit. Lake Mills, in the lower end of Glacier Gorge, is one of the largest lakes in the Park. The largest lake that I know of in the Rocky Mountain National Park is Lake Nanita. This is about one mile long and half as wide, and reposes in that wilderness of wild topography about midway between Grand Lake and Long's Peak. There are mountain people living within eight or ten miles of this lake who have never even heard of its existence. Although I have been to it a number of times, I have never found even a sign of another human visitor. A member of the United States Geological Survey is the only individual I have ever met who had seen it.

As originally planned, the Park was to have

more than twice its present area. I hope there
may be early added to this region Mt. Audubon,
Arapahoe Peak, and other territory to the south.
The summit of Twin Peaks on the east would
make another excellent addition. A part of the
Rabbit Ear Range to the northwest, and Medicine Bow Mountains and the headwaters of the
Poudre lying to the north, would make excellent park territory.

But even as it now stands, this splendidly
scenic region with its delightful climate appears
predestined to become one of the most visited
and one of the most enjoyed of all the scenic
reservations of the Government. In addition
to its scenery and climate, it is not far from the
geographical centre of the United States. A
number of transcontinental railroads are close
to it, and two railroads run within a few miles
of its border. The Lincoln Highway is within
twenty miles of it, and six excellent automobile
roads connect its edges with the outside world.

Each year visitors reach it in increasing numbers. During 1914 there were more than 56,000
of these, many of whom remained to enjoy it

# Rocky Mountain National Park

for weeks. It has a rare combination of those characteristics which almost every one wants and which all tired people need, — accessibility, rare scenery, and a friendly climate.

THE END

# Notes

Notes are keyed to page and line numbers. For example, 9:9 means page 9, line 9.

Frontispiece. The photographs and illustrations in this book, unless otherwise indicated, are those of Enos Mills.

Dedication: George Horace Lorimer (1867–1937) served as editor of the *Saturday Evening Post* from 1899 to 1937. During his long tenure, Lorimer changed the *Post's* format, attracted a stable of popular writers (such as Enos Mills), enlarged its circulation to over three million copies a week, and made his magazine a powerful influence on the nation's cultural life. As Mills notes in his Preface, seven of the eighteen chapters of *Rocky Mountain Wonderland* originally appeared in the *Post*. During his career Mills placed some fifty items with Lorimer's magazine, eleven before 1915.

Lorimer had a long-standing love affair with Estes Park and usually stayed at Longs Peak Inn. It was there in August 1908, in fact, that Lorimer first met Adelaide Neall, a recent Bryn Mawr graduate, who shortly thereafter joined the *Post,* where for some thirty-three years she served as one of his most trusted editorial lieutenants. John Tebbel, *George Horace Lorimer and the Saturday Evening Post* (Garden City, N.Y.: Doubleday and Company, Inc., 1948), pp. 254–55.

Preface

**viii:11**. In July 1914, acting on a suggestion made by Mills, the Nomenclature Committee of the Colorado Mountain Club made an attempt to restore to some of the yet unnamed physical features in Estes Park their original Indian names by bringing back from the Wind River Reservation in Wyoming two Arapaho patriarchs, ages 73 and 63, who had known the Estes Park region in their youth. Following a two-week trip by horseback through what would soon become Rocky Mountain National Park, the two elder Northern Arapahoes and their Indian interpreter were entertained by Mills at Longs Peak Inn.

**ix:18**. Longs Peak is now spelled without the apostrophe. For matters concerning mountain nomenclature, location, altitudes, and spelling, as well as the history of placenames in and around Estes Park, I have drawn on Louisa Ward Arps and Elinor Eppich Kingery's *High Country Names: Rocky Mountain National Park* (Estes Park, Co.: Rocky Mountain Nature Association, 1972).

## "Going to the Top"

**3:1–2**. Mills's initial reputation was as a Longs Peak guide, a career he carried on through the summer of 1906, when his busy career as writer, lecturer, and innkeeper caused him to turn that activity over to other, younger men whose training Mills personally supervised.

**6:4**. Mills's allusion is to the digestive ailment that brought him to Estes Park from Kansas in 1884.

**7:17–18**. Trampas is the villain of Owen Wister's 1902 novel, *The Virginian*, and the recipient of one of the most famous lines in all of western American literature: "When you call me that, *smile*." But the statement quoted—"In gatherings of more than six there will generally be at least one fool; and this company must have numbered twenty men"—belongs to the narrator, not to any of the novel's characters. Owen Wister, *The Virginian: A Horseman of the Plains* (New York: Grosset and Dunlap, 1902), p. 463.

**11:10–23**. Clarence King, *Mountaineering in the Sierra Nevada* (London: Adam and Charles Black, 1947), p. 99. The quotation is from the chapter titled "The Descent of Mount Tyndall." King's enormously popular *Mountaineering* was first published in 1872 and by 1886 had gone through eight American editions. Five more editions were published by Scribner's between 1902 and 1909. King (1842–1901) had been in charge of the Fortieth Parallel Survey, which scientifically explored a hundred-mile strip from eastern Colorado to the border of California from 1867 to 1872.

**13:15**. The Narrows, as the photograph opposite page 14 well illustrates, is a narrow ledge midway along a rock wall some 2,000 feet high on the south face of Longs Peak that climbers must traverse on their way to the top.

**14:11**. The practice of refusing tips extended to Longs Peak Inn, which Mills ran strictly as a "non-tip house."

**14:18–19**. The Keyhole is located at the head of the rock-strewn Boulder Field on the Longs Peak Trail. Frederick H. Chapin (1852–1900), in his classic *Mountaineering in Colorado: The Peaks about Estes Park* (Boston, 1889), accurately describes the Keyhole as "a cleft in the wall of the mountain, through which one must pass in order to climb the high peak from the west side, as the east face is inaccessible." For hikers bound for the top of Longs Peak, the Keyhole is where the hike ends and the climb begins.

**17:1**. As noted above (3:1–2), Mills's last season of guiding occurred in 1906.

**18:3–4**. See "Climbing Long's Peak," *Wild Life on the Rockies* (Boston: Houghton Mifflin Company, 1909), pp. 99–111. Mills identifies her home as "the 'big' end of the Arkansas River," presumably in the state of Arkansas where it joins the Mississippi. The Arkansas River, however, also flows through the states of Colorado, Kansas, and Oklahoma.

**18:13–15**. The source of Mills's allusion is found in John Tyndall's *Hours of Exercise in the Alps* (New York: D. Appleton and Company, 1899), p. 155: "I lingered for nearly three weeks among the Bernese and Valasian Alps. This time, however, was not wasted. It was employed in burning up the effete matter which nine months' work in London had lodged in my muscles—in rescuing the blood from that fatty degeneration which a sedentary life is calculated to induce." John Tyndall (1820–1893), the noted British scientist and mountaineer, was especially interested in glaciation. Tyndall Glacier in Rocky Mountain National Park now bears his name—a name, incidentally, that Enos Mills himself first suggested.

**19:11–12**: The source of the quotation is John Muir's *Our National Parks* (Boston: Houghton Mifflin and Company, 1901), p. 56.

### "Wild Mountain Sheep"

**23:1**. Glacier Gorge is an area of Rocky Mountain National Park lying northwest of Longs Peak. As Mills notes in the final chapter of this book (p. 349), it "probably has the most magnificent scenery in the Park."

**23:4**. Thatchtop Mountain (12,668 feet), located in the Glacier Gorge region of Rocky Mountain National Park, was so named because its appearance in the fall, when its green covering turns to brown, is not unlike the thatched roof of an English cottage.

**28:23–24**. John Charles Frémont (1813–1890) was an explorer and military officer whose experiences in exploring the Wind River range of the Rockies and whose expedition to the Oregon country with Kit Carson, (recounted in his *Report of the Exploration Expedition to the Rocky Mountains in 1842 and to Oregon and North California in 1843–44* (1845) earned him a national reputation and helped to trigger interest in the settlement of Oregon. Of his encounter with mountain sheep, Frémont wrote in his journal entry for July 30, 1843: "I have frequently seen the horns of this animal three feet long and seventeen inches in circumference at the base, weighing eleven pounds. . . . The use of these horns seems to be to protect the animal's head in pitching down precipices to avoid pursuing wolves. . . ." John Charles Frémont, *The Expeditions of John Charles Frémont,* Donald Jackson and Mary Lee Spence, eds. (Urbana: University of Illinois Press, 1970), I, 245.

**33:12**. The Elk Mountains, trending northwest and southeast, are located in central Colorado directly west of Leadville between the Gunnison River and the Roaring Fork of the Colorado in Pitkin and Gunnison counties. Its best known peak is Snowmass at 14,077 feet.

**38:8**. Specimen Mountain (12,489 feet) is located above Poudre Lake and Milner Pass. Though they once were believed to be an extinct volcano, geologists have now determined that Specimen Mountain and the adjacent Crater to the southwest are formed of ash and other volcanic material from an eruption that took place elsewhere. Early tourists noted the sheep trails leading over the Crater, and the area of Specimen Mountain still remains one of the best places within Rocky Mountain National Park to catch a glimpse of bighorn sheep.

**40:17**. Enos Mills built his homestead cabin in 1885–86 in Longs Peak Valley on the lower slopes of Twin Sisters Mountain across the road from the ranch that would become Longs Peak Inn.

**41:21**. Battle Mountain (12,044 feet), to the north of Mount Lady Washington and Longs Peak and overlooking Tahosa Valley, was so named by Enos Mills because its slopes seemed to bear the scars of the relentless "battling" forces of nature, including an early forest fire.

**42:2–3**. Mount Meeker (13,911 feet), which stands just to the southeast of Longs Peak, is the second highest mountain in Rocky Mountain National Park. It is named for Nathan Meeker (1817–1879), the agricultural editor of Horace Greeley's *New York Tribune* and a social reformer, who in 1869 came west to organize and run Union Colony, the agricultural cooperative that became the town of Greeley.

**42:21–22**. Chasm Lake lies in a glacial cirque beneath the East Face of Longs Peak at an elevation of 11,760 feet.

**43:20**. The Continental Divide (or "Great Divide") is the ridge of Rocky Mountain summits stretching from Canada to New Mexico, separating streams flowing into the Atlantic from those flowing into the Pacific.

**44:4**. Flattop Mountain (12,324 feet), originally called Table Mountain because of its appearance, is a broad, flat plateau or peneplain without a point one can call a summit located in the Glacier Gorge region of Rocky Mountain National Park. It is crossed by one of the oldest trails in the Park linking Estes Park and Grand Lake, a distance of some sixteen miles.

**44:7–8**. Marys Lake, a small alkaline body of water located in Estes Park to the southwest of Prospect Mountain at an elevation of 8,046 feet, was named by Lord Dunraven (1841–1926), the wealthy Irish earl who in the mid 1870s attempted, unsuccessfully, to turn the whole of Estes Park into his own private hunting preserve. Since the opening of the Rams Horn extension of the Alva Adams Tunnel in 1947, which brings water across Colorado's Continental Divide from the Western to the Eastern Slope and empties into Marys Lake, the lake itself has lost its original contours and much of its natural beauty.

**44:9**. The Crags, located some three miles south of Marys Lake at an altitude of 11,000 feet, is the name given to the rocky outcroppings on the northern slopes of Twin Sisters Mountain.

**46:13–17**. The allusion is to Mary Hunter Austin (1868–1934), a popular regional writer of the American Southwest and the author of such books as *The Land of Little Rain* (1903) and *The Flock* (1906). The exact source of the poem quoted, however, is unclear.

"The Forest Frontier"

**58:3–5**. The original lines from Muir, which Mills has rather freely adapted to his own purposes, read as follows: "Even bears take pains to go around the stoutest patches if possible, and when compelled to force a passage leave tufts of hair and broken branches to mark their way, while less skillful mountaineers under the circumstances sometimes lose most of their clothing and all their temper." John Muir, *Our National Parks*, p. 144.

**59:13–16**. Frank M. Chapman (1864–1945) was a noted ornithologist and the author of the first dependable modern guide to birds, *Handbook of the Birds of the Eastern United States* (1895). In 1899 he became founding editor of *Bird-Lore*, the official magazine of the Audubon Society. Chapman also served as curator of ornithology and mammalogy of the American Museum of Natural History between 1888 and 1908. The source of Mills's citation is Chapman's "A Naturalist's Journey around Vera Cruz and Tampico," *National Geographic* 25 (May 1914): 556.

**66:2**. After the pseudo-romantic style of French illustrator-engraver Gustav Dore (1832–1883), known for his dramatic and emotional effects. His illustrations include an edition of Milton's *Paradise Lost* (1865), which may provide the source of the allusion.

**66:5–6**. See 18:3–4.

"The Chinook Wind"

**69:3**. As the introduction notes, Mills first visited Montana in 1887, when he went to work as a tool boy at the Anaconda Copper Mine in Butte.

**70:15–16**. The "Cowboy Artist" is, of course, Charles Marion Russell (1864–1926), the self-taught American painter and sculptor who became famous for his renderings of cowboy and Indian life in the West. Until 1892, when he turned his full-time attention to art, Russell worked as a cowboy in Montana. Russell painted his two-inch-by-four-inch watercolor "The Last of Five Thousand, Waiting for a Chinook" at the O-H ranch during the winter of 1886–87, the most destructive ever recorded on the northern plains. It depicts, as Mills notes, a single starved-looking steer, the last remaining member of a large herd that Russell and his partner had been taking care of through a fierce Montana winter, hunched over in snow near death while two predators watch. According to Russell's own version of the story, it was his graphic way of informing the herd's owners what had happened to their investment.

**71:10**. The big copper refinery is undoubtedly the Boston and Montana Reduction Works (later purchased by the Anaconda Mining Company), a massive complex of some two dozen buildings to which significant structures and processing operations were added at various times between 1892 and 1896. The date of the episode referred to, however, is not clear.

**73:8**. "On December 1, 1896, the temperature observer at Kipp, Montana reported a temperature rise of 34 degrees in seven minutes. The observer further reported a total rise of 80 degrees in a few hours and that 30 inches of snow disappeared in one half day." Grayson Cordell, "Snow Eater: Montana's Chinook Winds," *Montana Weather,* Carolyn Cunningham, comp. (Helena, Mont.: Montana Magazine, Inc., 1982), pp. 114–15.

"Associating with Snow-Slides"

**79:2**. The reference to Bobtail Gulch here and Gregory Gulch below are unclear in the context of the San Juans. Yet these two names are among the most historic in Colorado's early gold mining history. The town of Central City, the largest and richest mining camp in Gilpin County and for a brief period the most important town in the Colorado Territory, was initially called Gregory Gulch because it was there, in the waters of North Clear Creek, that John H. Gregory made his famous strike in May 1859. Rich gold-bearing veins on Bobtail Hill, located to the south of Central City, were found on the surface a short time after the discovery of gold in the stream bed of Gregory Gulch, and shafts were soon sunk creating the Bobtail Mine, subsequently one of the area's richest mining properties.

**79:2**. As early Colorado journalist Ovando Hillister (1834–1892) noted in 1867, "Gulch is the distinctive appellation among miners of those tributaries of the creeks which convey into them the melting snows, but for the greater part of the year, are dry. Where they are washed for gold, the water has to be brought to them in canals for that purpose." Ovando J. Hollister, *The Mines of Colorado* (Springfield, Mass.: Samuel Bowles & Company, 1867), p. 141n.

**79:12**. The San Juan Mountains are located in southwestern Colorado and northern New Mexico. The discovery of gold and silver in the mid-1870s led to the establishment of supply centers like Ouray and Silverton and mining camps like Telluride.

**80:3**. The Sawtooth Mountains are a range of the Elk Mountains in west-central Colorado, located on the border between Pitkin and Gunnison counties.

**80:13**. The Alpine Pass over the Sawatch Range, southwest of Buena Vista, connects Chafee and Gunnison counties.

**84:16–17**. Mills visited the San Juans and many of the places described here in his role as State Snow Observer.

**84**: photograph opposite. Lizard Head Peak (13,113 feet), located in the San Juans southwest of Telluride, was first climbed in 1920. At the time it was believed to be the most difficult climb in America.

**90:6**. Grays Peak (14,270 feet), located in the Front Range near Georgetown west of Denver, was named for Asa Gray (1810–1898), the Harvard botanist.

**94:19**. The winter of 1904–1905.

"Wild Folk of the Mountain-Summits"

**104**: photograph opposite. Shown are the Poudre Lakes, located at Milner Pass on the Continental Divide.

**108:12**. Hallett Glacier (now Rowe Glacier) is a large crescent of ice partly surrounding a small tarn, which sits below Hagues Peak in the north-central part of Rocky Mountain National Park. It is one of the five "true" or living glaciers within the Park's present boundaries. Professor George H. Stone (1841–1917), a professor of geology at Colorado College, visited the glacier during the summer of 1887 and reported its discovery in an article, "A Living Glacier on Hague's Peak, Colorado," in the September 23, 1887, issue of *Science*: 153–54. Though Stone named the glacier after mountain explorer William H. Hallett (1851–1941), who had visited the glacier about 1883 and told Stone of its location, the name was changed by the U.S. Board of Geologic Names in June 1930 to honor Israel Rowe ( ? –1884), a guide and hunter, who made the original discovery in the late 1870s. Mills recorded his own first visit of 1895 in "A Canyon of Ice," published in *Outdoor Life* in 1898.

**108:13**. Glacial fissure.

"Some Forest History"

**127:1–2**. Mills is referring to the stairway of Longs Peak Inn. When he rebuilt the main building following the fire of 1906, he made extensive use throughout of fire-killed trees.

**135:2–3**. The Sangre de Cristo Mountains, the southernmost range of the Rockies and an extension of the Front Range, lie in south-central Colorado between the San Luis Valley and the Great Plains. Its dominant feature is Mount Blanca (14,338 feet), which for a time was considered the highest peak in the nation.

"Mountain Lakes"

**149:17–20**. The source of the allusion is the following lines from the opening chapter of John Muir's *The Mountains of California* (New York: The Century Company, 1913), p. 17: "And in the development of these [the features of the landscape] Nature chose for a tool not the earthquake or lightning to rend and split asunder, not the stormy torrent or eroding rain, but the tender snow-flowers noiselessly falling through unnumbered centuries, the offspring of the sun and sea."

**149:20–150:4**. John Muir, "The Glacier Lakes," *The Mountains of California*, p. 109.

**150**: photo opposite page. Crystal Lake and Little Crystal Lake lie above Lawn Lake on the northeastern slope of Fairchild Mountain within Rocky Mountain National Park.

**151:20**. The Snowy Range was the original name given to Colorado's Front Range.

**153:2**. Arapaho Glacier, located in the Indian Peaks Wilderness Area of the Roosevelt National Forest south of Longs Peak, some twenty miles west of Boulder, is the largest active glacier in Colorado.

**153:2–4**. Sprague, Hallett (Rowe), and Andrews glaciers are located within Rocky Mountain National Park. Sprague Glacier, located southwest of Stones Peak between Sprague Mountain and Sprague Pass and close to the Continental Divide, was named by Enos Mills in 1905 after Estes Park pioneer Abner E. Sprague (1850–1943). Andrews Glacier was named by Abner Sprague after one of his wife's relatives with whom he hiked and fished in the 1890s. The two other living glaciers within the Park are Tyndall and Taylor glaciers. Tyndall Glacier lies in the gorge between Flattop Mountain and Hallett Peak. The name, which honors British geologist and mountaineer John Tyndall (1820–1893), was apparently originally suggested by Enos Mills, though it was not officially adopted by the National Park Service until 1932. Taylor Glacier, which lies not far to the south under 13,153-foot Taylor Peak, was named after

Albert Reynolds Taylor (1846–1929), president of Kansas State Normal School in Emporia from 1882 to 1901, who vacationed in the area during the summer of 1895.

**153:3–4.** The unnamed glacier on Longs Peak, like its neighboring moraine, now bears the name Mills, after the author.

**157:15.** Grand Lake, the largest natural lake in Colorado, forms part of the western boundary of Rocky Mountain National Park.

**157:15.** Trappers Lake, located in the White River National Forest of northwest Colorado, has long been one of the best fishing lakes in the state. According to tradition, it owes its name to the trappers who once visited the area to hunt beaver and other furbearing animals.

**157:15.** Bierstadt Lake, located on top of Bierstadt Moraine above Bear Lake in Rocky Mountain National Park, was named after the German-born artist Albert Bierstadt (1830–1902), who had come to Estes Park in the autumn of 1876 to paint a large landscape for the Earl of Dunraven. The major legacy of Bierstadt's visit is the five-by-eight-foot painting, "Rocky Mountains, Longs Peak," which now hangs in the Western Room of the Denver Public Library.

**157:15.** Trout Lake lies twelve miles south of Telluride in the San Juan Mountains at an elevation of some 9,800 feet.

**157:16.** Mills is undoubtedly referring to Lake San Cristobal, located in Hinsdale County in the heart of the San Juans, four miles south of Lake City. The lake became famous in 1874 when the mutilated victims of the notorious Alfred Packer were discovered there.

**157:16.** The Chicago Lakes are located in Clear Creek County west of Denver, at an elevation of approximately 11,500 feet. They lie in a basin beneath the towering cliffs of Mount Evans (14,264 feet).

**157:16.** Thunder Lake is located at the upper end of Wild Basin region of Rocky Mountain National Park. Tradition has it that the lake was named by Harry Cole (who had a ranch south of Longs Peak Inn) after the booming sounds that came across the lake during mountain storms. Wild Basin, as Mills notes below (p. 350), is "a broken and glaciated region of twenty-five square miles" which forms the watershed of the North St. Vrain River.

**157:16.** Silver Lake is located in San Juan County, some five miles from Silverton.

**157:16–17.** Lake Moraine (or Mystic Lake as it was originally called) is located in a large natural amphitheater between Pikes Peak and Almagre (formerly Mount Baldy), at an elevation of 10,268 feet. Located some thirteen miles from Colorado Springs and five miles from the summit, Lake Moraine became a popular rest stop for those on their way to the peak. In 1890 the lake's natural dam was enlarged and together with

Seven Lakes became part of the water system for Colorado Springs. The lake is framed north and south by lateral moraines, hence its name.

**157:17**. The Twin Lakes (now Twin Lake Reservoir) in Mills's day were two natural lakes each about two miles wide and five miles in length produced by terminal moraines. They are located twelve miles south-southwest of Leadville in Lake County, at the foot of Independence Pass. Closeby are Mount Elbert (14,433 feet) and Mount La Plata (14,336 feet), two of the highest mountains in the state.

**158:2**. As Mills indicates, Ouzel and Thunder lakes are located in the wilderness area known as Wild Basin. Enos Mills named Ouzel Lake in honor of his favorite bird, the water ouzel, which he must have spotted in the vicinity.

**158:3**. Odessa Lake (10,020 feet), like its lower neighbor Fern Lake (9,520 feet), lies nestled in the bottom of Odessa Gorge, a scenic valley to the northwest of Flattop Mountain, framed by Notchtop Mountain at its head, the Little Matterhorn, and Joe Mills Mountain. The lake was named by Dr. William J. Workman, who pioneered the area, after his daughter, Dessa.

**158:4**. Loch Vale (10,180 feet), located in Glacier Gorge between Otis Peak and Thatchtop Mountain, is one of the most spectacular lakes in Rocky Mountain National Park. "Loch" is, of course, the Scottish word for lake.

**160:21**. Scotch was Enos Mills's famous dog, which he received as a puppy in 1902. He soon became Mills's constant companion and a fixture at Longs Peak Inn. Mills taught Scotch to extinguish fires, and his death in 1910 occurred because the dog tried to extinguish the fuse on a charge of dynamite being used by a local road crew. Mills wrote about Scotch and his adventures on a number of occasions, most completely in a small volume, *The Story of Scotch*, published by Houghton Mifflin in 1916.

**162.10–11**. Like Mount Richthofen (12,940 feet), Lake Agnes is located in the Never Summer Mountains to the west of Rocky Mountain National Park. According to tradition, it was named for a daughter of early pioneer John Zimmerman. Mount Richthofen was apparently named after Ferdinand Paul Wilhelm, Freiherr von Richthofen (1833–1905), who served as a volunteer with the Whitney Survey of California in the 1860s.

**163:13**. Mount Lady Washington (13,281 feet) lies directly north of Longs Peak overlooking the Tahosa Valley.

"A Mountain Pony"

**169:19**. Silverton, located in 9,288-foot-high Baker Park on the Animas River in southwestern Colorado forty-nine miles northeast of Durango, was a center of silver, gold, lead, and copper mining activity that began with a silver boom in the early 1870s. It was initially settled in 1860 by Charles Baker and a small party of whites, who trespassed on Ute land to mine placer gold and stayed on to lay out a townsite. The first townsite and mine diggings were abandoned, however, during the early days of the Civil War.

**170:4–5**. The mining town of Telluride (6,744 feet), northwest of Silverton, enjoyed a similar history. Following the discovery of gold in Marshall Basin in 1875, Telluride became a center of mining activity, which peaked about 1893, with a population that exceeded five thousand.

**171:4**. The town of Ouray, which lies in a mile-long mountain-fringed valley twenty-five miles north of Silverton at an elevation of 7,710 feet, developed as a mining center in the mid-1870s with the discovery of gold and silver in the immediate vicinity. Ouray takes its name from a famous chief of the Ute Indians, the tribe which once inhabited the area.

**172:8–9**. Presumably Mount Sneffels (14,150 feet).

**172:16**. The Camp Bird Mine in the Imogene Basin near Ouray was the site of a major gold discovery in 1895, which over time made it one of the three richest gold mines in Colorado. It operated until 1916, when it was closed briefly because of rising costs. By then it had taken some $27 million of gold out of the ground, and had made its discoverer, Thomas Walsh, so rich that he was able to purchase the fabled Hope Diamond for his wife.

**176:15**. Mt. Wilson (14,250 feet) lies in the San Miquel Mountains of southwestern Colorado some twelve miles southwest of Telluride. It was first ascended by members of the Hayden Survey on September 13, 1874.

**176:16–17**. The Ophir Loop is the name given to the spectacular section of the old Rio Grande and Southern Railroad line, lying northwest and down the valley from the town of Ophir, some six miles south of Telluride. It gained elevation through a series of bold curves and a 100-foot-high trestle.

"The Grizzly Bear"

**187:1**. "Park" in mountain parlance means valley. North Park is located in Jackson County northwest of Rocky Mountain National Park, framed by the Medicine Bow Mountains and the mountains of the Park Range.

**193:20**. Both Enos Mills and his younger brother Enoch "Joe" Mills (1880–1935) claimed credit for the 1903 capture and rearing of two bear cubs, Johnny and Jenny. Both bears were subsequently given to the Denver Zoo. Johnny died in 1925, Jenny in 1936. Enos told his version of their capture in *The Spell of the Rockies* (Boston: Houghton Mifflin, 1911), pp. 207–19, and in *The Grizzly: Our Greatest Wild Animal* (Boston: Houghton Mifflin, 1919), pp. 101–15.

**198:15.** The Selkirk Mountains of Canada lie mostly in southeastern British Columbia but extend into Idaho and Montana.

**203:16.** See 41:21.

**206:24–207:1.** The Bitterroot Mountains are a range of the Rockies extending along the Montana-Idaho line.

"Bringing Back the Forest"

**215:24.** Mills's second volume of collected essays, published by Houghton Mifflin in 1911.

"Mountain Parks"

**229:19.** As Mills notes, North, South, and Middle Parks, lying north to south across the northcentral part of the state, are among Colorado's largest mountain valleys. North Park lies in Jackson County, between the Medicine Bow Mountains and the Park Range. Middle Park, which is some sixty miles long, lies in Grand County, directly west of Rocky Mountain National Park. South Park lies in central Colorado in Park County. All three are rimmed by mountains. After gold was discovered in South Park in 1859, it became the site of a short-lived gold rush that attracted, among others, the parents of Enos Mills.

**230:11–231:11.** The description is taken from "The Middle Park," a chapter in Samuel L. Bowles's *A Summer Vacation in the Parks and Mountains of Colorado* (Springfield, Mass.: Samuel Bowles and Company, 1869), pp. 65–68. Bowles (1826–1878) for many years was editor of the *Springfield Republican,* in whose pages the chapters of his book first appeared as letters. Bowles visited Colorado in August and September of 1868, the year before the transcontinental railroad opened up Colorado and California to eastern tourists.

**231:14–24.** Frémont, *The Expeditions of John Charles Frémont,* I, 712–13. For the purposes of description, Mills has freely edited and combined two separate journal entries made by Frémont on June 14th and June 17th, 1844.

**232:1.** Hayden Valley is the name given to the broad, grassy valley of some fifty square miles extending along the Yellowstone River between Mud Geyser and the Falls. Its name honors Ferdinand Vandiveer Hayden (1829–1887), who served as a geologist with the Warren expedition which explored the area in 1856 and 1857, and then returned in 1871 and 1872 as head of the U.S. Geological and Geographic Survey of the

Territories (better known as the Hayden Survey).

**232:4**. Yellowstone Lake, located at an elevation of 7,735 feet in Yellowstone National Park, is the largest body of water in North America at that altitude.

**232:18–233–2**. F. V. Hayden, *Ninth Annual Report of the United States Geological and Geographical Survey of the Territories, Embracing Colorado and Parts of Adjacent Territories: Being a Report of Progress of the Exploration for the Year 1875* (Washington, D.C.: Government Printing Office), p. 437.

**242**: photograph opposite. Capitol Peak (14,100 feet), one of the highest peaks in the Elk Mountains, and Snowmass Peak (14,126 feet) are located in westcentral Colorado.

"Drought in Beaver World"

**249:7**. Mills had made these colonies, particularly the Moraine Park Colony located on the eastern flank of Longs Peak, the subject of his third book, *In Beaver World* (1913).

"In the Winter Snows"

**266:9**. Jackson Hole, east of the Tetons and south of Yellowstone in northwest Wyoming, is a fertile forty-eight-mile-long-by-sixty-eight-mile-wide valley, drained by Lake Jackson and headwater of the Snake River. Jackson Hole was the site of an annual trappers' rendezvous and was apparently named for David E. Jackson, who wintered there in 1829.

**268:16**. The Ute Indians, who originally occupied central and western Colorado as well as northwestern Utah, made the parks of Colorado their summer home.

"My Chipmunk Callers"

**278**: photograph opposite. This is the first photograph of himself that Mills chose to include in one of his books.

"A Peak by the Plains"

**295:1**. Pike's Peak (14,110 feet), the famous landmark of Colorado's Front Range, is located in El Paso County near Colorado Springs. It was discovered on November 15, 1806, by Lieutenant Zebulon M. Pike, the first official American explorer to enter the future state of Colorado, though his party failed in their attempt to make an ascent. That honor belonged to three members of the expedition commanded by Major Stephen H. Long (1784–1864), who successfully reached the summit on July 14, 1820.

**296**: photograph opposite. Cascade (elevation 7,421 feet), or Cascade Canon as it was known during the 1890s, was a railroad stop on the way to the top of Ute Pass. For some years after 1886, Cascade, which is located a few miles northwest of Manitou, was the site of a small summer resort community dotted with mountain cabins.

**296:7**. Mont Blanc (15,781 feet), the highest mountain in the Alps and one of the world's premier peaks, is located in southeastern France on the Italian border.

**296:14**. The famous Pikes Peak Cog Railroad, some eight and three-quarters miles long with an ascent of 8,100 feet, was completed in 1891, with a lower terminus at the entrance to Ruxton Canyon.

**296:15**. The automobile road to the top of Pikes Peak was finally completed in 1916.

**298:1**. The Royal Gorge, whose scenic granite walls rise in places more than a thousand feet, is a canyon on the Arkansas River in southcentral Colorado, eight miles west of Canyon City. It was known to early explorers as the Grand Canyon of the Arkansas.

**298:1**. Cripple Creek, in Teller County in central Colorado, ten miles southwest of Colorado Springs, became famous in the early 1890s with the discovery of large gold deposits. In its heyday, at the turn of the century, the Cripple Creek District, a six-mile-square area of mines and mining towns, could boast a population of between thirty and forty thousand.

**298:2**. As Mills notes, the region near Florissant in Teller County, some thirty-five miles northwest of Pikes Peak, famous for its fossil remains, was once the bed of an ancient lake. The shale fossil beds were formed by the intrusion of lava and mud.

**298:2–3**. The Garden of the Gods, consisting of a series of fantastically shaped eroded red-brick sandstone formations, lies a short distance north and west of Colorado Springs at the foot of Pikes Peak. It has long been a popular tourist attraction and resort site, and, since 1909, a 1,350-acre Registered National Landmark.

**298:3**. Manitou Mineral Springs, located in a valley in the foothills of the Rockies five miles west of Colorado Springs at an elevation of some 6,500 feet, was for many years regarded as the most romantic and best-known watering place in the Rockies ("the Saratoga of the West"). Its two dozen natural mineral springs were promoted for their restorative power, and provided the impetus for building a complex of hotels, bathhouses, bottling companies, and glass companies. Manitou is an Algonquin Indian word meaning "spirit" (taken from the reference in Longfellow's 1855 poem, "Hiawatha").

**298:3**. Glen Eyrie, north of the Garden of the Gods, is a large basin containing enormous pillars of tinted pink sandstone. It was here in 1904 that William Jackson Palmer (1836–1909), one of the founders of Colorado Springs and an important Colorado railroad man, built his handsome Tudor-style castle, the greatest manor house in the Rockies, which boasted a bowling alley and Turkish bath in addition to twenty bedrooms.

**298:4**. Crystal Park, a bowl-shaped valley located beneath Cameron's Cone, some two thousand feet above Manitou Springs, is noted for its view of the Garden of the Gods and the surrounding valley. As noted by the Colorado Springs Chamber of Commerce's 1911 guidebook, *Daily Doings in the Pikes Peak Region,* "A newly-built mountain roadway furnishes an exhilarating twenty-mile automobile ride affording a panoramic view of the entire Pike's Peak Region. Trails in the park lead to many delightful spots."

**298:4**. The Cave of the Winds, located in Williams Canyon, six miles west of Colorado Springs, was discovered in June 1880, and so named because of the sounds made by the wind blowing through its entrance.

**298:4–5**. Williams Canyon, near Manitou, is noted for Bridal Veil Falls and its geological formations.

**298:5**. Ruxton Canyon, named for the young British adventurer and author George Frederick Ruxton (1820–1848) who visited the area in 1847 and went home to write *Adventures in Mexico and the Rocky Mountains* (1847), is located to the southwest of Manitou Springs at the base of Pikes Peak. The trail along Ruxton Creek is the shortest and most-travelled path to the summit.

**298:5**. The natural wonders of South Cheyenne Canyon—an area long promoted for its scenic grandeur—are described below. It is the site of the famous Seven Falls.

**299:7**. Helen Hunt (1830–1885), or Helen Hunt Jackson as she became following her second marriage in 1875, the author of the popular novel *Ramona* (1884), moved to Colorado for reasons of health in 1873, and soon was writing enthusiastic essays about the scenic wonders of the American West and her new life in the Colorado Territory. They were collected in 1878 and published as *Bits of Travel at Home*. She also championed the displaced American Indian in her book A *Century of Dishonor* (1881). At her own request Helen Hunt Jackson was buried on the northern slope of Cheyenne Mountain (see below), though after the owner of the land began to charge visitors to see her grave, her remains were removed to Colorado Springs.

**299:13**. Cheyenne Mountain (9,500 feet) lies in the Front Range four miles southwest of Colorado Springs. The road up Cheyenne Mountain, leading to Seven Lakes and Pikes Peak, is noted for its magnificent scenic views.

**300:2**. The Pillars of Hercules refer to the solid granite cliffs that frame the entrance to South Cheyenne Canyon. According to an early guidebook (*In South Cheyenne Canon With Pen and Camera*: Colorado Springs, n.d.), "They seem to stand squarely across the canon, completely filling it and demanding a halt."

**300:6**. Prospect Dome, a symmetrical granite pinnacle more than three hundred feet high, is located in South Cheyenne Canyon, a short distance beyond the Pillars of Hercules. Beyond Prospect Dome is the foot of Seven Falls.

**300:12**. North and South Cheyenne Canyons sit about a mile apart on Cheyenne Mountain.

**301:6–7**. The Spanish expedition of 1598 was led by Juan de Onate, who traveled north from Mexico to explore an area stretching from Kansas to the Gulf of California. He did not, however, enter the future state of Colorado. Mills's allusion to the "separate" exploring expedition of 1601, however, remains unclear.

**301:13–21**. See *Zebulon Pike's Arkansaw [sic] Journal: In Search of the Southern Louisiana Purchase Boundary Line*, Stephen Harding Hart and Archer Butler Hulbert, eds. (Westport, Conn.: Greenwood Press Publishers, 1972), pp. 117–18. There is some question about which part of the Rockies Pike sighted first, Pikes Peak or the Spanish Peaks of the Sangre de Cristo range.

**302:4**. Dr. Edwin James (1797–1861) served Long as botanist, geologist and surgeon, and later compiled the official narrative *Account* of the expedition published in 1823.

**302:6–8**. Though the statement quoted by Mills is consistent with the ideas set forth in Montesquieu's great political treatise of 1748, *The Spirit of the Laws*, particularly those in Book XIV, its precise source is unclear.

**302:15**. Although the area around Pikes Peak attracted the attention of gold seekers in early summer of 1858, it was not there but some eighty miles to the north at Cherry Creek, in what would become downtown Denver, that the first major discovery of placer gold was made. The identification of Pikes Peak with the destination of gold seekers was no doubt caused by the fact that the mountain served as the most prominent landmark for those coming west along the Smoky Hill Road, often visible as far away as a hundred and fifty miles.

**303:5**. The Anglo-American Pikes Peak Expedition, which took place between July 12 and August 16, 1911, included such distinguished scientists as G. Gordon Douglas and J. B. S. Haldane, fellows of Oxford University; Yandell Henderson, professor of physiology at Yale University; and Edward C. Schneider, professor of biology at Colorado College (see below). As Mills indicates, their investigations of the physiological impact of high altitude—delivered in a 1913 report of 134 pages entitled *Physiological Observations Made on Pikes Peak, Colorado, With Special Reference to Adaptation to Low Barometric Pressure*—broke considerable new ground.

**303:22**: Dr. Edward C. Schneider (1874–1954), a graduate of Tabor College and Yale University, began his high-altitude studies on Pikes Peak in 1904. His work ultimately made him a pioneer in the establishment of modern aviation medicine.

**305:8**. The United States Army Signal Corps established a one-story stone weather station on the summit of Pikes Peak on October 11, 1873, which operated until 1889. In 1882 the building was replaced by a larger structure, the "Old Summit House." Briefly abandoned, the summit house, enlarged and transformed into a small tourist hotel, then became the upper terminus for the Pikes Peak Cog Railroad. In 1911 it served as headquarters for the Anglo-American Expedition. The new weather station that Mills refers to was opened in 1908. As the *Colorado Springs Gazette* of April 15, 1908, notes, the new station made possible "weather forecasts for periods from a week to fifteen days in advance."

**306:4**. Minnehaha Falls are located on Ruxton Creek which flows out of Lake Moraine to drain the east slope of Pikes Peak. By the side of the Falls lay Ruxton Trail, the shortest, most direct, route to the summit. The Pikes Peak Cog Railway substantially followed the route of the Ruxton Trail, and Minnehaha, at one time a small hamlet of rustic cottages, was the first stop out of Manitou.

**309:15**. Cameron's Cone (10,705 feet) is a knob located close to Pikes Peak. It is named for General Robert A. Cameron (1828–1894), who helped lay out Colorado Springs, as well as the towns of Fort Collins and Greeley.

**309:16**. The Crater is the hollow glacial depression between Cameron's Cone and the summit of Pikes Peak.

**309:18**. See 157:16–17.

**309:18**. Seven Lakes, a series of picturesque blue mountain lakes nestled in a basin at an elevation of nearly 11,000 feet, are accessible by way of South Cheyenne Canyon and the Cheyenne Mountain Road. From the Seven Lakes it is a five-mile hike to the summit of Pikes Peak.

"The Conservation of Scenery"

**314:6**. Colorado achieved statehood in 1876.

**314:9**. William Tell, of course, refers to the legendary hero of Switzerland's fourteenth century struggle for freedom against Austria.

**314:11**. The chamois is an extremely shy, goatlike antelope that is native to the high mountain regions of Europe and the Caucases. Chamois are difficult to hunt, or capture in photographs, because of their alertness and quickness.

**315:n**. The final passage of the bill establishing Rocky Mountain National Park took place on January 18, 1915.

**325:18**. Robert E. Lewis (1857–1941), a native of Missouri, served as judge of Colorado's fourth circuit from 1903 to 1906 and, as a Theodore Roosevelt appointee, as judge of the U.S. District Court of Colorado from 1906 to 1921. He later served as the first senior judge (now called chief judge) of the newly created Court of Appeals for the Tenth Circuit. The precise judgment Mills cites, however, is unclear. Ironically, on September 4, 1919, it was Judge Lewis who peremptorily turned down Mills's attempt to obtain a court order forcing the National Park Service to permit cars for hire, including his own, from traveling over the roads in Rocky Mountain National Park.

**326:24–327:6**. The decision of the National Academy of Sciences to send a special forestry commission to the West in 1896 to survey the nation's forest resources and recommend specific legislation is credited as heralding the beginning of a new federal policy towards conservation. A year later, in 1897, two weeks before the end of his second term, President Grover Cleveland (1837–1908) used the Academy's recommendations as justification to withdraw by proclamation some twenty-one million acres from the public domain and create thirteen new forest preserves over the opposition of many westerners.

**327:21–24**. The Dominion Forest Reserves and Parks Act of 1911 established a Canadian Park Service similar to the National Park Service established by the United States in 1916.

**328:4–5**. "Woodman, Spare that Tree!" is the first line from the well-known poem appealing for the presentation of an oak tree by George Pope Morris (1802–1864), first published in 1830 in the *New York Mirror*.

**329:15**. William Penn (1644–1718), the English Quaker who became the founding proprietor of Pennsylvania where he sought to establish an ideal commonwealth, wrote a number of enticing accounts of his province, including the pamphlets *Some Account of the Province of Pennsylvania* (1681) and *A Further Account of the Province of Pennsylvania and Its Improvements, for the Satisfaction of Those That Are Adventurers and Inclined to Be So* (1685).

**329:16**. William Cullen Bryant (1794–1878) wrote a number of nature poems celebrating the American landscape, the most famous of which is "The Prairies" (1833).

**329:18–19**. Mills's source of information about Yellowstone, its enabling legislation, and Hayden's role in its creation was undoubtedly Hiram Martin Chittenden's enormously popular *The Yellowstone National Park,*

*Historical and Descriptive,* first published at Cincinnati in 1895. By 1914, Chittenden's book was in its eighth ("Revised and Enlarged") edition. Mills apparently met Chittenden in Yellowstone in the spring of 1891.

**330:6–8.** In May 1908, President Theodore Roosevelt (1858–1919) convened a White House Conference of Governors on Natural Resources as a means of publicizing and promoting the Pinchot-Roosevelt conservation agenda.

"The Rocky Mountain National Park"

**335:7.** See 232:1.

**335:18–336:1.** When William S. Cooper (1884–1978) surveyed and mapped Wild Basin in 1908, he initiated an unsuccessful campaign to change the name of Copeland Mountain (13,176 feet) to Mt. Clarence King in honor of Clarence King (1842–1901), who directed the 40th Parallel Survey and later became the first head of the U.S. Geological Survey. The original—and current name—of the mountain honors John C. Copeland, who homesteaded near what became Copeland Lake at the entrance to Wild Basin.

**337:14–15.** See 38.8.

**337:22–23.** See 108:12.

**337:24–25.** Hagues Peak (13,560 feet), located in the Mummy Range northwest of Estes Park, is named after Lieutenant Arnold Hague (1840–1917), a geologist, who, as a member of Clarence King's Geological Survey of the Fortieth Parallel, apparently used the mountain as a triangulation point in 1871.

**337:25.** See 108:12.

**338:1.** Stones Peak was named after Professor George H. Stone (1841–1917), a professor of geology at Colorado College who explored the area during the 1880s.

**338:1.** See 108:12.

**338:1–2.** See 44:4.

**338:2.** Hallett Peak (12,713 feet), one of the most photographed mountains in Rocky Mountain National Park, is named for William S. Hallett (1851–1941). Hallett, a native of Massachusetts and an engineer by training, came to Estes Park in 1878 and a year later returned with his bride. In 1881 the Halletts took up ranching in the Park and built a summer home, Edgemont, just northwest of Marys Lake above Beaver Point. When not ranching, Hallett climbed and explored the mountains surrounding Estes Park and guided summer visitors like Frederick Chapin of the Appalachian Club, who later wrote about his experiences (see 14:19).

**338:2**. See 108:12.

**338:3**. See 158:4.

**338:13–15**. David Starr Jordan (1851–1931) and Vernon L. Kellogg (1867–1937) were among those who enjoyed the hospitality of Longs Peak Inn. Jordan, a distinguished natural scientist, served as president of Indiana University (1885–1891) and Stanford University (1891–1913). Kellogg, a zoologist, served as professor of entomology at Kansas (1890–1894) and Stanford (1894–1920). The two men co-authored a number of books, including *Animal Life* (1900), *Animals* (1902), *Animal Studies* (1903), *Evolution and Animal Life* (1907), and *The Scientific Aspects of Luther Burbank's Work* (1909). Kellogg contributed an illustrated article titled "Parks and Peaks in Colorado," focusing on the Estes Park region, to the February 1901 issue of the *Sierra Club Bulletin*.

**338:16**. Edward L. Orton, Jr. (1865–1932), as a member of the Ohio State University Department of Chemistry, carried out a geological survey of Mills Moraine and the Longs Peak region during the summer of 1908. Mt. Orton (11,724 feet) in Wild Basin, the wilderness area south of Longs Peak, is named after Professor Orton's father, Edward Orton, Sr. (1829–1899), the president of both Antioch College and the Ohio State University between 1882 and 1899.

**338:23**. Moraine Park, located near the eastern boundary of Rocky Mountain National Park, takes its name from the two lateral glacial moraines to the north and south responsible for its creation. Between these moraines flows the Big Thompson River.

**338:24**. See 23:1.

**339:4**. Bierstadt Moraine, like Bierstadt Lake, was named for the romantic landscape painter Albert Bierstadt (see 157:15).

**339:4**. St. Vrain Moraine forms the southern boundary of Wild Basin, the wilderness area south of Longs Peak.

**339:4**. Mills Moraine, named for the author, lies on the eastern flank of Longs Peak above the Tahosa Valley and the site of Mills's Longs Peak Inn.

**339:10**. See 42:21–22.

**339:21**. Shoshone Peak was the name briefly given to Mt. Alice (13,310 feet) in Wild Basin. For a short period, which began in May 1914 and included the date that Mills's book was published, Ellsworth Bethel (1863–1925), a retired Denver high school botany teacher, led a campaign to have many of the mountains in what would become Rocky Mountain National Park named or renamed after Indian tribes of the Great Plains. The U.S. Board on Geographic Names, to whom Bethel had applied, ultimately rejected five of his names, including Shoshone. Mt. Alice was thus destined to remain Mt. Alice.

**339:22**. McHenrys Peak (13,327 feet), located in Glacier Gorge, is named after Benjamin F. McHenry (1837–1915), an 1869 graduate of Oberlin College who for many years served as a professor of mathematics and natural science at Union Christian College, Merom, Indiana. McHenry, whose hobby was geology, spent many of his summer vacations exploring in the Rocky Mountains with his students, much of the time in the Estes Park area.

**340**: photograph opposite. The photograph is of the western end of Horseshoe Park looking up into Endovalley. Old Fall River Road generally follows the dirt road visible at the far right of the photograph. It was just to the west of where this photograph was taken that the ceremonies dedicating Rocky Mountain National Park were held on the afternoon of September 4, 1915.

**340:3**. Otis Peak (12,586 feet) lies along the Continental Divide northwest of McHenrys Peak. It is named after Dr. Edward Osgood Otis (1848–1933), a Boston physician with an interest in climatology and long-time faculty member of Tufts College, who climbed in Estes Park with fellow New Englander Frederick Chapin and his party during the summer of 1887 (see 14:19).

**340:12**. Green Mountain (10,313 feet) is situated north of Grand Lake along the western boundary of Rocky Mountain National Park.

**340:14–15**. See 338:23.

**341:18**. Fall River originates below Fall River Pass (which sits at 11,796 feet) in the Mummy Range, flows eastward through Horseshoe Park and into the town of Estes Park where it joins the Big Thompson River on its way to the South Platte.

**341:18**. According to tradition, the Cache la Poudre River, which flows northeast out of Poudre Lake to the east of the Continental Divide at Milner Pass, was so named in 1836 by a party of French trappers from St. Louis who over the course of one winter safely deposited some of their supplies, including a quantity of black gunpowder, close by its banks.

**341:19**. Forest Canyon, known as Willow Canyon in the late 1880s when Frederick Chapin and his companions explored there, lies between the Continental Divide and Trail Ridge in the central area of Rocky Mountain National Park. The Big Thompson River flows through the Canyon, which remains remote and inaccessible to all but the most experienced of backcountry hikers.

**342:16–17**. The allusion is to William Cullen Bryant's poem "To the Fringed Gentian," written in 1829.

**343:22**. Though once plentiful in the Estes Park region, the elk did not survive the greediness of early hunters and by the 1880s had become rare. In 1913 local residents raised enough funds to purchase a herd of twenty-nine elk from Montana. An additional herd of twenty-four was added in 1915. As a result, elk are once again a familiar sight throughout the area.

**343:24–344–1.** See 38:8.

**345:11–12.** Fall River Road, built by convict laborers from the Colorado Penitentiary beginning in 1913, was officially opened on September 14, 1920, after nearly eight years of work. The road follows the course of Fall River, ascends the top of Fall River Pass, then descends a thousand feet to cross the Continental Divide at Milner Pass, and proceeds on to Grand Lake. The impetus to build the road was part of the campaign to persuade Congress to create Rocky Mountain National Park. When Trail Ridge Road opened in 1932, Fall River Road, still unpaved, was restricted to one-way up traffic as it is today.

**346:1.** Boulder Canyon is situated west and south of the city of Boulder. It is bisected by Colorado Highway 119 linking Boulder and Nederland.

**346:1.** Left Hand Canyon, northwest of Boulder, contains the road to Ward and Jamestown. Through it flows Lefthand Creek, a right-hand branch of St. Vrain Creek that eventually leads to the South Platte River. It was named for Ni-Wot (Left Hand), an Arapaho Indian chief who befriended early settlers and prospectors. The canyon was the site of considerable early mining activity.

**346:1–2.** Big Thompson Canyon is named after the river that flows through it. In 1903 a road was completed through the canyon linking Loveland and Estes Park. It replaced the older Bald Mountain Road that made its way through Rattlesnake Park, over Pole Hill, and emerged in Estes Park where the Crocker Ranch now stands.

**346:2.** St. Vrain Creek rises in two branches near Mount Audubon (13,223 feet) in the Indian Peaks, and flows east and northeast through canyons for some sixty-eight miles past Lyons and Longmont respectively before entering the South Platte.

**346:22–23.** See 157:15. Bierstadt did not visit Estes Park until 1876.

**346:24–347:1.** Isabella Bird (1831–1904) was the Englishwoman who recorded her adventures in Estes Park, climaxing in the October 1873 ascent of Longs Peak, in her book *A Lady's Life in the Rocky Mountains* (London: John Murray, 1879).

**347:1.** Anna Dickinson (1842–1932), a well-known author and lecturer, on September 13, 1873, became the first woman to climb to the top of Longs Peak when she made the ascent with members of the Hayden Survey. Dickinson recalled her experiences in *A Ragged Register (of People, Places and Opinions)* (New York: Harper and Brothers, 1879).

**347:1.** See 299:7.

**347:1–5**. Frederick H. Chapin (1852–1900), was the Hartford, Connecticut druggist, who spent the summers of 1886, 1887, and 1888 climbing in Estes Park with several other New Englanders under the guidance of Carlyle Lamb and William Hallett. In 1889 he published an account of his adventures entitled *Mountaineering in Colorado: The Peaks about Estes Park* under the auspices of the Appalachian Mountain Club of Boston. Chapin's book, with an introduction and notes by the present author, was reprinted by the University of Nebraska Press in 1987.

**347:12–23**. Hayden, *Ninth Annual Report of the United States Geological and Geographical Survey*, p. 437.

**348:6–10**. *Mountaineering in Colorado*, p. 60.

**349:6**. Storm Peak (13,326 feet) is located just north of the Keyhole on Longs Peak and west of Mount Lady Washington.

**350:20**. Scenic Fern Lake lies below Odessa Lake at the foot of Odessa Gorge at an altitude of 9,530 feet.

**351:7**. Long Lake, covering an area of nearly forty acres, is located in the Indian Peaks Wilderness Area to the south of Rocky Mountain National Park.

**351:7**. Black Lake, located at 10,620 feet, is one of the Glacier Gorge Lakes to the west of Longs Peak.

**351:9**. Lake Mills (9,940 feet), at the head of Glacier Gorge, was named by Estes Park pioneer Abner Sprague (1850–1943), its original owner, after the author.

**351:12–13**. Mills is nearly correct. Of the lakes in Rocky Mountain National Park, only Arrowhead Lake (11,130 feet), lying among the remote and difficult-to-reach Gore Lakes above Forest Canyon, is larger.

**351:24–352:1**. The original recommendation made in January 1913 by Robert B. Marshall of the U.S. Geological Survey, who had come to the Estes Park area the previous fall to study the feasibility of a national park, called for setting aside an area of some 700 square miles. By the time the Park bill worked its way through Congress, the area had been reduced to 358.5 square miles.

**352:3**. North Arapaho Peak (13,502 feet) and South Arapaho Peak (13,397 feet) surround Arapaho Glacier. See 153:2.

**352:4**. Mills is referring to Twin Sisters Mountain (11,428 feet), located in the Tahosa Valley across from Longs Peak Inn. In 1917 Mills got his wish, when Rocky Mountain National Park was enlarged to include the top of the Twin Sisters as well as Deer Mountain and Gem Lake, an area totalling some 25,000 acres.

**352:6**. The Rabbit Ear Range, part of the Park Range of the Rockies, is located along the Continental Divide in northcentral Colorado just east of

Steamboat Springs. It takes its name from the peculiar rock formation on
top of Rabbit Ears Peak (10,719 feet).

**352:6–7.** The Medicine Bow Mountains are an extension of the Front
Range located in northern Colorado and southeastern Wyoming. They
extend for some one hundred miles, from Cameron Pass, just west of
Rocky Mountain National Park, to the town of Medicine Bow in Wyoming.

# Index

# Index

Alpine Pass, 80.
Alps, the, compared with the Rocky Mountains, 313, 314; conservation of scenery in, 315, 323.
Altitude, effects of, 10–12, 302–305.
Andrews Glacier, 153, 338.
Arapahoe Glacier, 153.
Arapahoe Peak, 352.
Aspen, 61, 214, 215, 218, 219.
Austin, Mary, quoted, 46.

Battle Mountain, the mountain sheep of, 41–46.
Bear, black, 63; above timber-line, 107; eating dead trout, 136.
Bear, grizzly, and mountain sheep, 43; tearing up dwarfed trees, 61; hibernation, 63, 201–203; above timber-line, 107; eating dead trout, 136; watching a forest fire, 142; a grizzly observed at close quarters, 187–189; caution, 188; alertness and brain-power, 189; following a grizzly, 190, 191; a cattle-killing grizzly, 191, 192; curiosity, 192, 193; attitude towards man, 194–196; stories of, 196, 197; food, 197–200; fishing, 198, 199; a mother and two cubs, 200, 201; hibernating habits, 201–203; emerging from hibernation, 203–205; young, 205; cubs as pets, 205, 206; color and races, 206, 207; size and agility, 207, 208; age, 208; verging on extermination, 208; shortening the life of a mountain park, 235.
Bears, emerging from snow, 63; an encounter on the Hallett Glacier, 108, 109; benefited by deep snow, 269.
Beaver, 136; the Cascade Colony annihilated by drought, 249–256; benefited by deep snow, 269, 270; in the Rocky Mountain National Park, 344.
Beetle, battle with a wasp, 111.
Bellflower, 120.
Bierstadt, Albert, 346.
Bierstadt Lake, 157, 158.
Bierstadt Moraine, 339, 340.
Bighorn. *See* Sheep, Mountain.
Birch, black, 61, 62.
Bird, Isabella, 346, 347.
Birds, visiting the summit of Long's Peak, 102; of the mountain-summits, 112–115; in winter, 271–274; on Pike's Peak, 306, 307; of the Rocky Mountain National Park, 343.
Bobtail Gulch, 79.
Boulderfield, 15, 349.
Bowles, Samuel, quoted, 230, 231.

# Index

# Index

137, 142; up and down slopes, 140, 141; heat at a distance, 141; varying speed, 141, 142; brilliant displays, 142–145; cause of some mountain parks, 233, 234.

Forest Reserves, should be kept separate from National Parks, 326–329.

Forester, and scenery, 328, 329.

Fossil-beds, 298, 299.

Fox, silver, 109.

Frémont, John C., 28; quoted, 231.

Game, big, in deep snow, 259–268; yarding, 262–265; winter food, 265, 266; bunching habit, 267, 268.

Gentians, 342.

Glacier Creek, 340.

Glacier Gorge, 23, 43, 158, 338–340; scenery, 349.

Glacier meadows. *See* Meadows.

Glaciers, as makers of lake-basins, 150–153; in Colorado, 153; in the Rocky Mountain National Park, 337, 338; glacial records in the Rocky Mountain National Park, 338–340.

Goat, mountain, 36.

Grand Lake, 157, 158.

Gray's Peak, 90.

Greagory Gulch, 79.

Great Falls, Mont., 71.

Green Mountain, 340.

Grosbeak, Western evening, 307.

Hague's Peak, 337.

Hallett Glacier, 108, 153, 337.

Hayden, Dr. F. V., 330, 335, 338; quoted, 232, 347.

Hayden Valley, 232.

Hesperus, a return horse, 173, 174.

Horses, the story of Cricket, 169–183; return horses, 170–176.

Hunt, Helen, 299, 347.

Insects, on the heights, 108, 111.

Jay, Rocky Mountain, 64, 265.

Jordan, Dr. David Starr, 338.

Junco, gray-headed, 115.

Kellogg, Vernon L., 338.

King, Clarence, his "Mountaineering in the Sierra Nevada" quoted, 11.

Lake Agnes, 162.

Lake Mills, 351.

Lake Moraine, 309.

Lake Nanita, 351.

Lake Odessa, 158, 350.

Lakes, made by glaciers, 149–153; beauties of, 154–160; names, 157, 158; ice on, 160; filled by débris and landslides, 161–165; in Rocky Mountain National Park, 350, 351.

Landslides, destruction of lakes by, 162–165.

Leucosticte, brown-capped. *See* Finch, rosy.

Lewis, Judge Robert E., decision as to scenery, 324–326.

Lion, mountain, a game-hog, 42; pursuing mountain sheep on the heights, 106, 107; killing a herd of deer, 265.

383

# Index

# Index

landing on horns, 28, 29; shape and size of horns, 29, 30; a wild leap, 30–32; accidents, 32, 33; an agile ram, 33–35; hoofs, 35; size, color, and other characteristics, 35, 36; species and range, 36, 37; in winter, 37; excursions to the lowlands, 37, 38; composition of flocks, 38; craving for salt, 38; lambs, 38, 39; near approach to, 40; a ram killed by a barbed-wire fence, 40, 41; the flock on Battle Mountain, 41–46; fights, 44–46; threatened extermination, 46; at high altitudes, 105–107; watching a forest fire, 142; clings to the heights in snowy times, 266, 267.

Shoshone Peak, 339.

Silver Lake, 157.

Silverton, 171.

Snow, on summits of the Rocky Mountains, 103; and animal life, 259–275; a great snow, 268; and the Chinook wind, 269.

Snow-slides, started by dynamite, 79; a prospector outwitted, 79–84; habits, 81; observation of, 84–86; classification, 87–90; coasting on a slide, 91–94; a large slide, 94–97.

Solitaire, Townsend's, 64, 154, 241.

South Cheyenne Cañon, 298–300.

South Park, 229.

Sparrow, white-crowned, 64, 102, 115, 154.

Specimen Mountain, 38, 335, 337, 343, 344.

Sprague Glacier, 153, 337.

"Springfield Republican," quoted, 230, 231.

Spruce, Douglas, 140.

Spruce, Engelmann, 61.

Squirrel, Frémont, or pine, 64, 344.

Squirrels, and deep snow, 270, 271; hibernation, 271.

Stone's Peak, 338, 341.

Storm Peak, 349.

Switzerland, conservation of scenery in, 313–315, 323, 327.

Telluride, 171, 172, 174–176, 183.

Thatch-Top Mountain, mountain sheep on, 23–28.

Thunder Lake, 157, 158.

Timber-line, characteristics of, 49–58; altitude, 50, 59, 60, 101; determining factors, 58, 59; temperature, 60; species of trees at, 60, 61; age of trees at, 61, 62; animal life at, 63, 64; flowers at, 65; impressions at, 65, 66; animal life above, 101, 102, 105–115; flowers above, 116–120.

Trapper's Lake, 157.

Trees, species at timber-line, 60; age at timber-line, 61, 62; resistance to fire, 128–130; methods of reproduction, 214–216; tolerance and intolerance, 216–218; of Pike's Peak, 308. *See* also Timber-line.

Trout Lake, 157, 176.

Twin Lakes, 157.

386

# Index

Other Books by Enos A. Mills Available in Bison Book Editions
with introductions by James H. Pickering

In Beaver World
The Spell of the Rockies
Wild Life on the Rockies